CHRISTMAS ALCHEMY

Harnessing Cosmic Energy

KELLY-MARIE KERR

Copyright © 2024 by Kelly-Marie Kerr SEEK VISION

All Rights Reserved. No part of this publication may be reproduced in any form or by any means, including scanning, photocopying, or otherwise without prior written permission of the copyright holder.

UKCS Registration Number: 284827422

www.seekvision.co.uk

ISBN 978-1-0685819-9-1
First Printing, 2024

Printed in the United Kingdom

DISCLAIMER:
This book contains general medical information only. Nothing in this book is intended to be a substitute for qualified, certified professional medical or psychological advice, diagnosis or treatment. You must NOT rely on the information in this book as an alternative to medical advice given by a professional healthcare provider or doctor. Consult a qualified professional healthcare provider or Medical Doctor (MD) with questions or concerns regarding practices or substances mentioned in this book that may affect your health or general wellbeing. You should always seek immediate professional medical attention if you think you are suffering from any medical condition. The medical information within this book is provided without any representations or warranties, express or implied. The medical information contained within this book is not professional medical advice and should not be treated as such. The medical information contained within this book is ONLY provided to highlight comparisons within the topics presented here, further personal research and professional guidance is always recommended.

CHRISTMAS ALCHEMY

Harnessing Cosmic Energy

Acknowledgements

To be in love with God, is to be in love with life and all that it encompasses. The simple prayer, *"Divine Love, manifest thyself in me always and in all ways"* has been central to all aspects of my daily life, including my work. Divine Love -- God, never fails to show itself in all my challenges and celebrations alike and for this I am deeply thankful.

God is my anchor point, origin, friend, and guide. My first and foremost acknowledgement is, and always will be for the grace, love, and presence of the Perfect Light -- God.

Secondly, I would like to thank all of you! You truth-seekers, with your curious minds that won't settle for illusions, thank you! Journeying with you and reading your questions and comments makes this experience all the more ONE-derful. To everyone that has supported me via Patreon and other platforms, thank you! Your support and kind encouragement really does make a huge difference.

Next, I'd like to say a big thank you to all the pioneering teachers and spiritual leader's past, present and future. On behalf of myself and others, we are so grateful that these truths were preserved throughout the generations thus enabling us to have access to them. Without you it would be so much harder to recognise and or access our true potential. I really can't imagine what state humanity would be in were it not for your beautiful hearts, light-filled minds, and undefeatable approach to sharing sacred knowledge, forbidden truths, and keeping the light of truth blazing brightly.

Last, but by no means least, I thank my cherished family and friends for all the funny and unpredictable adventures you bring to my life. When my mind wanders off into unknown territories, you bring me back to my simple and loveable existence. I thank you for all the love, lessons, and smiles that warm my heart and remind me to savour every moment of this short, sweet incarnation as "Kelly-Marie."

True Source Love,

For every blessing, big and small.

For the ones that I know about,

And for the ones I have no idea of,

Thank you.

Contents

FOREWORD 11
ACKNOWLEDGEMENTS 5
PREFACE 13
INTRODUCTION 17
SOLSTICE 21
ANALYSING THE WORD CHRISTMAS 24
INNER SOLSTICE (REBIRTH) 29
DICTIONARY OF CHRISTMAS SYMBOLS 51
    Angelo Morphism 53
    Bethlehem 57
    Boots and Stockings 59
    Candle 64
    Candy Canes and Shepherds Staffs 66
    Christmas Tree, the Tree of Life 70
    Chimney 75
    Circumcision 77
    Claustrum 81
    Coal, Lead and Carbon 84
    Cracker 98
    Dual Life Force 100
    Egypt 104
    Faunalia 111
    Gabriel, the Angel of the Lord 115
    Giving and Generosity 117
    Grottos and Caves 120
    Jesus Christ 124

Joseph – Jesus's Father 141
Julbastu (Sauna) 143
King Herod 147
Lucy's Day 150
Manger 153
Mary – The Virgin Mother 155
Mistletoe 158
Nasarean (Nazarian) 162
Naughty and Nice 165
North Pole 169
Oil and Cerebrospinal Fluid 172
Presents, Presence and Gifts 179
Reindeer 184
Rice Porridge (Risgrynsgröt) 193
Santa's Sack 195
Saint Nicholas 198
Santa Claus 207
Saturn and Saturnalia 212
Saturn, Santa and Satan 215
Saturn Eats the Children and Herod Kills the Children 226
Sea of Galilee 231
Shepherds and Fields 235
Sleigh 237
Sleigh Bells and Christmas Bells 241
Stable 248
Star of David, 6-Pointed Star 250
Stars in General 253
Swaddling Clothes, Wrapping Paper, Veil 257

Three Wise Men 263
Three Wise Men (Part 2) 265
Wreath... 278
ASSEMBLING LIGHT AT SOLSTICE................................. 283
Bibliography 295

FOREWORD

By Derek William Grosskurth aka "Truthseekah"

In a world where ancient wisdom is often buried under layers of misunderstanding, and destructive regurgitation, rediscovering the true essence of sacred mysteries is both urgent and transformative. When it comes to understanding the sacred mysteries hidden within The Holy Bible and other sacred texts, we must be willing to view those ancient truths in a renewed light – a dazzling light that has the power to ignite the spirit and elevate the soul. Over the years, I have met numerous mystics, theologians, and scholars who hold a deep reverence for the sacred mysteries, devoting their lives to uncovering their intrinsic value. Some of these theologians spend countless hours in solitude, studying the texts and rediscovering the previously long forgotten truths within them. Kelly-Marie stands among these revelators.

Many people approach religion with a literal interpretation of scripture. Others come to see the parables through a transformative lens, understanding its ancient words as metaphor and allegory for the sacred sciences and other rich interpretations. Some see the scriptures as a beautiful dance between soul and spirit, a journey of ascending human consciousness. What I admire about Kelly-Marie's work is her ability to embody all the realities of scripture and hold them in equally high regard. She brings scripture to life, recognizing that the real magic happens only when its supernatural qualities are practiced and awakened within ourselves. For her, understanding these texts is not merely an intellectual pursuit but an act of transformation, a call to ascend to our highest selves.

Kelly-Marie's pursuit to know God led her into intimate communion within her own prayer chamber. In this sacred space, she experienced profound unity with her Savior, unlocking something ancient and transformative within her. As her relationship with her Creator deepened, Kelly-Marie's sense of unity and compassion grew, caring and feeling even more deeply for those who were in a state of disillusion, pain or need. Her burdens became lighter as she placed the needs of others above her own and her life was transformed from the inside out.

Christmas Alchemy: Harnessing Cosmic Energy sheds necessary light on the unequivocal value of *living* the Word, rather than just reading or studying it. **An inspiration to not only understand the sacred mysteries but to live them and feel them working within every cell of the body.** The practical application of the sacred sciences is what really catalyses the inner transformation, revitalizing every part of the body, and bestowing a visceral glow upon the faces of those who experience it. The alchemy of ascension detailed within the pages of this book cultivates an "aroma," pleasing not only to God but to everyone around them. This is your invitation to harness a powerful cosmic energy that has the potential to reshape your life, a way to activate the sacred forces within, to set yourself on a path of spiritual regeneration, and to feel the lightness of truth streaming through you.

Preface

Isn't it beautiful how regardless of our conflicts and differences, families still come together at Christmas? Isn't it exciting to see a child's face light up on Christmas morning? Isn't it nice to have an extra day off work, to unplug from your normal obligations and prepare a dinner that all your guests will love? Isn't it great to switch from self-centred thought, into the generous mind when deciding what gifts to give your loved ones? I think it is. I think it's lovely how the appreciation that wells up within us at Christmas inadvertently helps us to recognise how truly blessed we are, which in turn makes us more generous to those who may be less privileged. I love how Christmas has a certain kind of loving cheer deeply embedded in its traditions and customs. Looking at old cards, with sweet notes scrawled inside them, or reminiscing about where old tree decorations were brought stokes the fire of reflection and joy within as we take stock and appreciate the sweet memories of life's journey. At the heart of Christmas there's a love of life and all its blessings.

> *"The same germinative force which leavens the seed in the Earth and prepares it to reproduce its kind in multiple, stirs also the human mind and fosters altruistic activities which make the world better. Did not this great wave of selfless Cosmic Love culminate at Christmas, did it not vibrate peace and good will, without it there would be no holiday feeling in our breasts to engender a desire to make others equally happy; the*

> *universal giving of Christmas gifts would be impossible, and we should all suffer loss."*
> Page 16, Ancient and Modern Initiation by Max Heindel 1929

But beneath all this, there's an underlying tone of greed, and desire. A certain type of commercialism or, "death culture" that has people binge eating and getting excessively drunk. Whether deliberately orchestrated or not, "death culture" has the majority of peoples energies locked in their lower chakras, disallowing them to see certain universal truths that "hide" in plain sight. The adverts that drive children and adults alike to feel like they need a million toys or gadgets, leave us in a state of "want" rather than a state of contentment. This "death culture" hacks the biochemistry (alchemy) of our bodies, leaving us susceptible to all sorts of insecurities and illusions which ultimately promote discomfort, disease and eventually death.

Degenerative customs take away from the true light of Christmas and blinker our eyes into a narrow vision that can't perceive the truth about this sacred time of year. "Death culture" obscures our sight and has us blindly following the proverbial carrot of deception.

Through the extraordinarily fast growth of commercialism, humanity has lost touch with a lot of its natural rhythms and mechanisms. For example, the diabolical historical act known as the "destruction of bells" largely masked and partially erased knowledge regarding the miraculous scientific art of sound healing, and the thrust of pharmaceutical medicines upon society has cast shadows that leave traditional plant medicines like mistletoe forgotten and in the dark. All these ideas and many more are explored in the pages of this book.

This book serves as a modality for unveiling and reintroducing the true sacred science of Christmas, written to **shed light on the wonderful process of regeneration that happens on all the miraculous levels of creation from the infinitesimal subatomic particles of light to the cells of the body, and to huge solar bodies, such as the Sun.** The date assigned for Christmas is very specifically aligned with the body's ability to renew or "rebirth" itself. The motions of celestial objects occurring at this time of year influence both the cosmos and our temple-bodies. The regenerative power of the Winter Solstice lies in its symbolic death and rebirth cycle. This celestial event marks not just a solar shift but an opportunity for the soul to regenerate and renew its divine connection to the cosmos. In order to preserve these truths from the threat of the commercial world and its detrimental influence against our own innate healing and transformative abilities we must endeavour to follow spiritual promptings and help keep the candle of wisdom glowing. Christmas is a time for resetting and regenerating: body, mind, soul, and spirit! **When we peel through the layers of commercial distractions, and distorted histories, what's left is the magical potential for Christmas alchemy and the harnessing of cosmic energy.**

INTRODUCTION

Christmas is the most widely celebrated of all the yearly customs, festivals, and holidays. Every year people decorate their homes, bake delicious treats, and visit the customary pantomimes where they eagerly shout, *"Boo hiss,"* or *"she's behind you"* about the bad-guy archetype -- one of the many emblems explored in this book! But Christmas is far more significant than we may realise. More than a story about Santa and the elves, or baby Jesus in a manger, the magic of Christmas is all encompassing. It happens in the dance of macrocosmic objects, like the sun and the moon in the sky (solstice), in nature, and it happens inside us.

> *"Christmas is a cosmic event that must be performed in each one of us. The nativity is absolutely individual. It is necessary for the Christ to be born in each one of us."*
> **Page 55, The Path of Initiation in the Sacred Arcana by S. A. Weor 1978**

In understanding the dynamics of the sun, moon, and other influential stellar "objects" and how they initiate the rebirth of nature, we can begin to appreciate and experience the opportunity for renewal in ourselves (our cells). Therefore, we start our magical Christmas journey with a brief synopsis of the winter solstice.

> *"As Angelus Silesius said, 'Though Christ a thousand times in Bethlehem be born yet not within thyself, thy soul will be forlorn!'"*
> **Page 23, Ancient and Modern Initiation by Max Heindel 1929**

The first section of this book, including "Solstice," and "Inner Solstice" share insights and perspectives on the transformation opportunity that is available to each of us at this holy time of year, and the second section has been formatted as a "Dictionary of Christmas Symbols."

There are dozens of significant Christmas and Solstice traditions and signs that felt necessary to address. When considering the alchemy of inner solstice, each entry has its own significance and importance. I thought it would be easier for the reader to digest if I simply put the entries in alphabetical order rather than recontextualising each point on the way through. Jumping between cultures, belief systems, and conflicting renditions appeared confusing and repetitive, so hopefully this point-by-point structure sews the subjects together in a smooth and cohesive way.

Rest assured, I have strived to shed light on all the most compelling subjects from the **"Santa is Satan"** argument, and how **Saturn plays a role in the "Christmas Drama,"** to the **"Saint Nicholas"** legend and the importance of **"stockings."** Throughout the book, we'll be focusing on the relation of these concepts and traditions to the **alchemy of ascension,** or **biochemistry of Super Consciousness Awakening**, and the helpful application of these deeper meanings to every individual.

SOLSTICE

**In short, "Solstice" means "sun-pause"
-- "Sol" means sun, and "stice" means stand still or pause.**

Due to the position of the sun during the winter months, the days gradually get shorter and shorter, i.e., the hours of daylight slowly reduce, and the hours of moonlight or "darkness" gradually increase. The reduction of sunlight comes to its climax on the shortest day of the year, which is on or around the 21st of December. On this day, the sun appears to pause or "go dark" for approximately 3.5 days and can finally be seen to begin its upward path on the 25th of December. Upon seeing the sun "restart" its ascending trajectory, the ancients celebrated because they knew spring was on its way! They saw the 25th as a holy day (holiday), as a day to be thankful for new life and new hope, as a day when the sun is reborn or "resurrected." They knew it was the day when the hours of warmth and daylight gradually began to lengthen.

Another guise that the solstice celebration appears under is the "wheel festival." Wheel celebrations give recognition to the great cosmic wheel (rota, tora(h), taro) that compels universal cycles. In line with solstice, **the mystical wheel is said to stop and pause, before turning back in order to redeem people from the miseries of winter.**

This cosmic cycle finds its reflection in both nature and the biology of our bodies. The same elements that assimilate to create everything we see, use, and enjoy in the "outer world" also coagulate to produce our astral (atomic) make up and consequently the cells of the body. These elements, such as hydrogen, nitrogen, oxygen, and carbon etc. are born in the stars (like our local sun) and filtered or directed to earth by the majestic white light filtered and reflected by the moon -- without the moon all of life would be extinguished by the intensity of the sun. The sun and moon are both essential forces for the manifestation of life on earth and the human experience of reality.

> *"The universe is filled with a magnetic force, which is also found in the human body in consequence of transference from the stars (as a siderial entity). The human being is nourished not only in the obvious sense through food but by the magnetic power distributed throughout nature. A mutual attraction exists between the stars and the human body."*
> **Page 5, Der Hypnotismus by Doctor L Loewenfeld 1901**

The natural law of correspondence (also known in science as the **Implicate Order**) says that everything in the macrocosm has its reflection in the microcosm, and that everything in the unseen, energetic realm has its reflection in the seen, material realm. Due to this law, all of nature and indeed our individual bodies are susceptible to the influence of cosmic cycles. For example, reduced hours of daylight cause some plants to decay and die, but others, like Holly and Mistletoe, revel in the increased hours of moonlight which causes them grow and flourish. This highlights the fact that the extended hours of "darkness" around the time of solstice have their benefit as well as their seemingly detrimental cold, dark, effect.

"Winter Solstice is a time for sanctuary and hibernation, like a child in a womb preparing to be born and rebirthed into the next phase of life and light." Page 141, The Soul Searcher's Handbook by E. Milton 2015

Further context into the origin of Christmas will build a strong foundation for understanding how longer hours of moonlight affects the human body, and how the suns yearly "rebirth" acts as a catalyst for enlightenment and the expansion of consciousness.

ANALYSING THE WORD CHRISTMAS

The name Christmas comes from the roots "Christ" and "Mas," investigating these words helps to clear the dusty waters of misconception and easily see the picture of Christmas for what it truly is.

Christ:

- From the Sanskrit "Krsna" meaning "appearing from 'nowhere'," "source," "creating from 'nothing'."
- From the Hebrew "Meshach" meaning "oil." Strongs Concordance 4887.
- From the Greek "Kristos" and the Latin "Christus" also meaning "oil" or "anointing."

Macrocosmic Interpretation:

In the macrocosm, "Christ" is Creative Light, scientifically known as electromagnetic energy. Other corresponding terms include,

General: solar-light, sunlight, daylight

Mystic: life force energy, the son/sun, solar seed -- *"to thy seed, which is Christ"* Gal 3:16-18

Scientific: electromagnetic energy, photon light, solar wind, quanta, electrons (photons coalesce to create electrons).

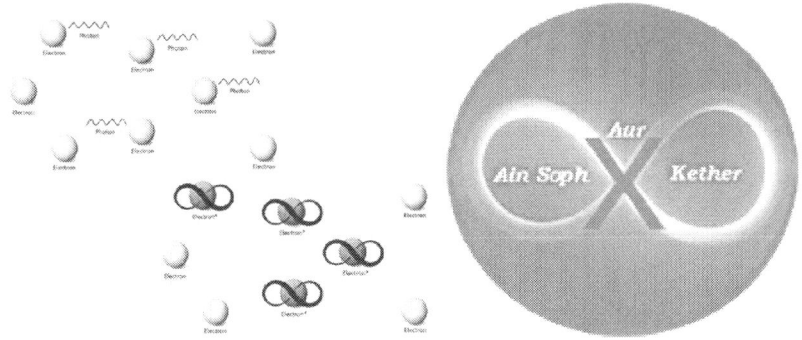

In ancient Greek, "X" is the symbol used for the sound "Ch" or "Chi." This "X" symbol, as seen in the words "Christmas" and "Christ" is shown in the centre of the gnostic symbol for infinite Creative Light or "Solar Force" highlighting its association with the origin of all that's created. The "Christ" or "Solar Force" is also known as "sexual energy" or "procreative energy" because of its dual poles and the way in which it operates. The duality of light can be heard in its scientific name "electro-magnetic" energy, i.e., electricity and magnetism in one unified force. The Indians call this vital energy Surya-Prana (Solar Od). The yogi Swami Sivananda Sarasvati, also known as Doctor P. V. Kuppuswamy Lyer M.D. said, *"The rays of the rising sun are a veritable gift from God for the preservation of life, health and the healing of diseases."*

Microcosmic Interpretation:

In the microcosmic body "Christ" relates to the secret "Christ Oil," scientifically known as Cerebrospinal Fluid (CSF).

Creative Light (electromagnetic energy) precipitates or emerges as CSF in the body. Thus "Light" and "Christ Oil" are synergistic.

> *"CSF acts as a conveyer and storage field for light energies."*
> **Doctor Zappaterra in the Science and Nonduality Lecture.**

Mas:

Then we have the second syllable in Christmas, -- "mas."

- From the Sanskrit "Masa" meaning "moon," which is also where we get the words "month" and "cycle" from.

- From the Hebrew roots "ma" and "mas-ah". "Ma" means "substance," and "form" or "energy and substances forming" as in "**ma**tter," "**ma**ss," "**ma**de" and "i**ma**ge." "Mas-ah" means "causing to flow," "blending or fusing" i.e., particles gathering in a "mass."

- In ancient Somali, the word "mas" means "snake."

- In Latin, "mas" is said to be derived from the word "rite" as in "rite of passage" or "process of natural law" (universal principle).

From these origin studies, it can be seen that the "mas" of Christmas coincides with the moon and its role in creation i.e., matter "rising from" or "emerging from" electromagnetic energy (light).

In simple terms, Christmas is a luni-solar festival -- Mas (lunar) and Christ (solar).

Ancient mystics observed how the moons (masa's) cycles from new and crescent to full could be likened to a serpent or snake periodically shedding its skin and regenerating, thus serpents and snakes became symbols for the moon and its energy and characteristics.

> *"What clearly emerges from the varied symbolism of snakes is their lunar character... their powers of fertility, of regeneration, of immortality through metamorphosis."*
> **Page 169, Patterns in Comparative Religions by Mircea Eliade.**

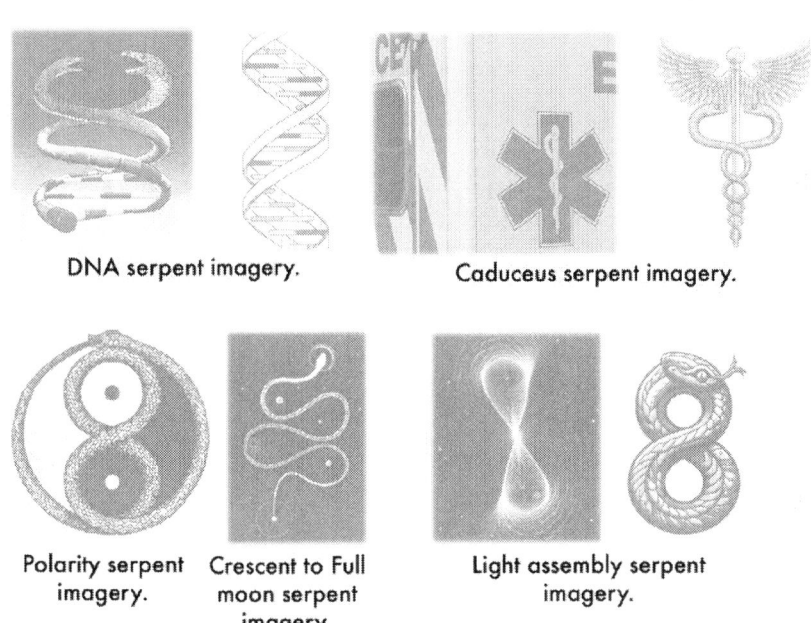

DNA serpent imagery.

Caduceus serpent imagery.

Polarity serpent imagery.

Crescent to Full moon serpent imagery.

Light assembly serpent imagery.

Further research shows that serpents and snakes have long been used to illustrate not only lunar energy and cycles, but also the dual energies of positive and negative, yin and yang, masculine and feminine, electricity and magnetism (the duality of light, electromagnetism), solar and lunar etc. and Winter Solstice or Christmas time is indeed a dance of energies creating/preserving, dissolving/destroying, and regenerating all life on earth.

With the analysis of the word Christmas in place, it's fair to say that the forgotten or widely unrecognised **origin of Christmas is the relation between cosmic influences and the magic of nature, such as the effects of solar-Christ energy and lunar-Mas energy with earth.**

The cosmic process of Winter Solstice repeats every single year. Everyone receives the luni-solar blessing regardless of their religion or beliefs. As explained earlier, by divine law or the natural law of correspondence, the cosmic processes are also reflected within our bodies.

INNER SOLSTICE (REBIRTH)

> *"When we apply Christmas to the microcosm, to our own consciousness and being and interpret it in terms of the lesser mysteries, the first thing we notice is that this event is not something that applies to the members of one religion only, but to all human beings regardless of their faith and religion or lack thereof! As such, it is truly a human and even cosmic event that applies to humanity and to the world."*
> **Page 135, Religion, Spirituality and Healthcare by P. Roche de Coppens**

The sun is not just a 'stellar object' as science puts it, but an intelligent, divine, creative force or consciousness. Similar to the human heart, the sun has a rhythm that can be described as a "pulse." This "pulse" relates to its magnetic field and solar activity. Scientifically, the sun exhibits a rhythmic behaviour through its solar cycle, which occurs approximately every 11 years. This cycle is characterized by varying levels of solar activity, including sunspots, solar flares, and coronal mass ejections.

The Sun's vibrations are known as "helioseismology," they create sound waves, *"in the beginning was the word,"* **John 1:1 (KJV)** that resonate throughout the Sun, much like the vibrations of a heart pumping blood. Scientists study these vibrations to learn about the Sun's internal structure.

The Sun's pulsing energy affects the entire solar system, with solar winds, mystically known as "solar seeds" influencing planetary magnetospheres, and cosmic energy cycles echoing the patterns of the

Sun's activity. This is sometimes compared to the way the heart's pulse sends waves of energy throughout the body, energizing and maintaining life.

In esoteric terms, the Sun's pulsing has been connected to cosmic rhythms, symbolizing the heartbeat of the universe and its role in the cyclical regeneration of life and consciousness. This cosmic "heartbeat" resonates with many ancient spiritual traditions that see the Sun as a life-giver, echoing the rhythmic, vital pulse of the human heart, which sustains life in the body. The Sun mysteriously forges the atoms that construct all life. Its radiant energy nourishes and sustains us, animates us and allows or facilitates consciousness within us. As my Mum always used to say, *"God wasn't messing around when he created the sun Kelly-Marie!"*

Every nucleus (or nucleoli specifically) of every cell is a microscopic sun, operating in its own miniscule universe. In this way, the intelligence of Creative Light (and sound) abides in us, in every cell and atom of our being --"Christ" is everywhere! And all the ancient religions, teachings, and secret societies emphasise the importance and incomparable benefits of learning and practising how to retain and transform this miraculous energy. Christian mystics refer to the practice of light assembly in the body as "permuting themselves into solar beings," i.e., "Angelo morphism" meaning, "becoming angels." "Angelo morphism" or "Angelo morphosis" refers to the transformation of a human into an angelic, spiritual, or solar being, especially within esoteric Christian mysticism. This concept is deeply connected to the notion of the human soul's ascension and spiritual purification, where one becomes illuminated with divine light, often associated with the sun. This mystical practice is described as a state of heightened spiritual awareness and unity with God, akin to becoming angelic in form and essence.

> *"And so, the soul becomes heir of the heavenly estate and receives the immortal, vital principle of spiritual union, and awakes from the son of Earth a God-like being, free from the shackles of time -- a dweller in eternity."*
> **Page 149, The Light of Egypt by Thomas H. Burgoyne**

In the past, the knowledge of angelo morphism, parallel to the notion of "Christifying" oneself was kept for those who had passed various tests in their initiate schools. The only clues to the teaching were hidden in coded Scriptures such as the Bible, where for example -- Christs 33 years of life are parallel to the 33 vertebrae of the spine and to the way in which light assembles in the body via this channel or pillar within. Those who received the knowledge were sworn to secrecy, with death as the penalty for breaking their oath of silence.

For this reason, the majority of people weren't and aren't aware of this "magic" or how to take advantage of the Christ-Mas force for themselves, through no fault of their own, people think of Jesus Christ only as a person and Santa Claus as a mortal being or made-up story. Sadly, the truth has been diluted and convoluted to the point where people believe Jesus was the only one who could be Christed or Christified. The same mistake is made when people think there is only one Buddha, when in reality Gautama Sakyamuni Buddha demonstrated the path for any one of us to become a Buddha because the light of God is, *"in all and through all."* **Ephesians 4:6 (KJV)**. Through "right living" and truthful knowing, the birth and nativity of Christ occurs within the human being by degree, and his life and teachings show us how to embody Christ energy and transform into "solar beings."

Fortunately, at this time in history, the Great Law is offering us a chance to learn the secrets and understand that the Creative Light, Christ is a universal energy, a natural principle. If you know how to take advantage of it, the benefits of Creative Light alter and enhance your body, mind, soul, and spirit. Nowadays, many enlightened souls are aware that many other figures, or "Gods" born on the 25th of December signify and teach the embodiment of Creative Light too! This is shown by their characteristics and the parallels between each of them. For example:

- Mithra

The Persian God Mithra was known as the "orderer of the universe" who led the chosen ones through a **river** of **fire** ("water and spirit," John 3:5 KJV) to a blessed immortality.

- Horus

The Egyptian God Horus is a sun God born to a virgin mother, who was known for his battles against Set, the God of Darkness.

Then there's Krishna of India, Quetzalcoatl of Mexico, Zeus of Greece, Avalokitesvara of China, and Amida of Japan just to name a few!

They all represent the true magic of Christmas and Winter Solstice -- REGENERATION, REBIRTH and INVIGORATION! **The potential for all mankind to be anointed (Christed).**

We'll investigate these themes thoroughly as we journey through the deeper meanings of many Christmas symbols, but for now it's important to bear in mind that, the way to take advantage of this formerly forbidden knowledge is by understanding that true rebirth occurs by "water and fire/spirit" (as stated in the Bible). Water coincides with the moons (masa's) cooling, filtering, forming, and ever renewing influence and fire or spirit coincides with the suns (Christs) empowering, continuous life force.

In the body, "water" coincides with vital fluids, and "fire/spirit" pertains to nervous pulses -- the "electricity" of life.

To be "reborn of water" is to be cleansed of all impurities (physical, mental, emotional, and energetic). Thus, cleansing and detoxification of the body, mind, soul, and spirit is required to prime the body for receiving light.

To be "reborn of fire" is to "come into the realisation of" or "raise your vibration to" the consciousness of divine law, which consequently adjusts the solar aspect of every cell of your body via DNA alterations (epigenetics). Thus, aligning your thoughts, feelings, and deeds with the higher self, and recognising your abundant essence is also required to prime the body for receiving light.

> *"Finally, brethren, whatsoever things are true, whatsoever things are honest, whatsoever things are just, whatsoever things are pure, whatsoever things are lovely, whatsoever things are of good report; if there be any virtue, and if there be any praise, think on these things."*
> **Philippians 4:8 KJV**

The combined baptism essentially raises your vibration and bio hacks your entire temple -- body, mind, soul, and spirit, which culminates in total personal renewal and transcendence (resurrection).

As stated in the introduction, during the latter months of the year the hours of daylight gradually shorten in the Northern Hemisphere, the consequence of this is what we call "Winter." Winter is the coldest and darkest time of year, and the absolute shortest day is on or around the 21st of December, marking the beginning of winter solstice (sun-pause). On the "darkest day," some locations in the far North experience as much as 19 hours of night!

Before the developments of electricity, insulated housing, and long-life foods, humans would have been forced to hibernate in a similar way to animals at this time of year. Rationing all the supplies they'd managed to gather in the summer and autumn months, humans would have naturally eaten less and been in a state of detoxification, rest and digest and even autophagy (cell clearance and renewal) during the peak winter days. This natural or "God designed" yearly fast would have caused people to be highly sensitive to the marvellous, transformational rays that fill the atmosphere at this holy time of year allowing them to assemble more light within and reap the benefits of doing so. By readopting these natural practises, we too can harness Creative Light toward rebirth and renewal.

"At this time of year, a new life, an augmented energy, sweeps with an irresistible force through the veins and arteries of all living beings, inspiring them, instilling new hope, new ambition, and new life, impelling them to new activities whereby they learn new lessons in the school of experience. Consciously or unconsciously to the beneficiaries,

> *this outwelling energy invigorates everything that has life. Even the plant responds by an increased circulation of sap, which results in additional growth of the leaves, flowers, and fruits whereby this class of life is at present expressing itself and evolving to a higher state of consciousness."*
> **Page 81, Rays from the Rose Cross Magazine, Cosmic Christmas Article by M. Heindel, 1992**

In winter, as the hours of daylight shorten, the hours of night-light (moonlight) simultaneously lengthen. This has a beneficial effect on the human body because the moon influences our vital fluids in the same way that it does the earth's oceans and tides. This effect is mirrored in tree sap which also increases in flow during winter. This is why Christmas pine trees last so well even after they've been chopped down. In fact, wood is often harvested from other types of trees during winter too, because the conditions cause sap levels to rise, which helps preserve the wood more effectively, making it more durable for long-term use. The invigoration of tree sap in the trunks or "spines" of trees by lunar light reflects the enhanced flow of blood and lymph (including CSF) in the human body at this time of year. Pine rods from "Christmas" trees were used as candles and torches due to their long burning resin, sap or "oil". As a fuel for the human body derived from solar light, CSF (Christ oil) was seen as similar to pine oil or sap, and so the "solar gland" was dubbed the "conarium" and "pineal" after the pinecone.

The comparison between the pineal gland's function and the opening and closing of pinecones during the solstice is an esoteric metaphor. Pinecones open and close in response to environmental changes, particularly light and temperature, which can be linked to how the pineal gland responds to light, especially during periods of increased darkness, such as the winter solstice. In the absence of light, the pineal gland produces more melatonin which is the basis for endogenous DMT secretions and the production of the other biochemicals of enlightenment. Melatonin and its chemical "upgrades" foster deep rest, spiritual vision, meditation, healing, inner awareness, and other enlightening or "supernatural" effects which parallel the spiritual transformations that are often associated with winter solstice traditions.

Pinecones have been long revered in spiritual traditions as symbols of immortality and enlightenment, often found in depictions of gods or spiritual leaders (such as the staff of Osiris or the Vatican's Pinecone Court). Esoterically, the pineal gland is believed to contract and expand in response to inner spiritual forces, mirroring how pinecones respond to moisture and temperature.

Pinecone Imagery in association with the Pineal Gland.

Just as pinecones open to release seeds, which represent the potential for new life, the opening of the pineal gland during the solstice can be seen as the release of spiritual seeds -- new insights, higher consciousness, and awakening. So, even though it's a "dark" time of year, with the invigoration of CSF and the promotion of melatonin upgrades, we can celebrate the purification and renewal that's occurring both in nature and our bodies.

Even though Jesus's crucifixion and subsequent resurrection is usually celebrated at Easter time, the approximate 3.5 days of sun-pause after the shortest day in December can be seen to coincide with Jesus's few days of darkness in the tomb. Many scholars and researchers have discussed and highlighted what's commonly referred to as 'the great Christmas/Easter mix-up.' Those few days in the tomb, just prior to the resurrection are viewed by Christian mystics, Gnostics, and the Essenes as days of regeneration, days to withdraw from outer influences, days of reflection and meditation. They view the rebirth of the sun on the 25th of December as a direct macrocosmic parallel to the inner alchemy or inner biochemical processes of the body. In "Thinking and Destiny," Harold Percival corroborates that the body is in a favourable condition for *"getting light"* during the peak of winter. He describes in detail how due to the microcosmic orbit; "lunar and solar germs (cells)" are performing a rebirth or regenerative effect inside the body in the exact same way that the sun and moon are performing a rebirth in the sky.

The case for the 'great Christmas/Easter mix-up' is further strengthened by the fact that, not long before the sun "pauses," "goes dark," or "enters the tomb" around the 21st of December, the Sun passes a constellation called the "Southern Cross" (Crux) which is seen as parallel to the crucifixion cross on which Jesus was hung. And, when resurrecting from the "tomb," the sun then passes the constellation of Virgo (related to the Virgin Mother Mary) as it's "reborn." Biblically speaking, "Mary" is present at both the moment of baby Jesus's birth and his resurrection as a man, but there seems to be a discrepancy between the celestial rebirth and the time that the celebrations are assigned to. As highlighted here, the astrological movements occurring in December contradict the fact that the "tomb" and "cross" are usually associated with

Easter. Therefore, it seems that the crucifixion parable is indeed a "Christmas" or solstice story. Throughout the book, you'll recognise how other Christmas traditions and symbols reinforce the notion of the 'great Christmas/Easter mix-up.'

In this interpretation, where Christ's death *and* resurrection are aligned with the winter solstice, the story seems to reach its symbolic conclusion by December 25th with the "rebirth" of the sun or son. This begs the question: What does the spring equinox (in association with Easter) symbolize if the winter solstice has already encapsulated the death and resurrection allegory?

It's put forth that winter solstice represents the "inner resurrection" and spring equinox, the "external manifestation." In many esoteric traditions, such as the Rosicrucian Manifestos "Fama Fraternitatis," winter solstice represents the "inner birth" of the Christ consciousness, an alchemical (biochemical) process where "light" is rekindled in the darkness, and the spring equinox is the outer manifestation (ascension) of this light -- the time when new spiritual energy fully blossoms and expresses itself outwardly in the physical world. This is why Easter, and the equinox are celebrated with symbols of fertility, growth, and abundance, reflecting the springing forth of life after the "rebirth" or inner work completed during winter. In this way, the Christmas and Easter parables are part of a cyclical spiritual journey:

- Winter Solstice (Christmas): The **inner rebirth**, or the "birth of the light" (Christ consciousness) in the darkest time.

- Spring Equinox (Easter): The **outer victory and ascension** of that inner light into full expression, symbolizing enlightenment and the triumph of spiritual life over death.

Biblically, it's stated that Jesus remained on Earth for "40 days" between His "resurrection" and final "ascension." This period is explicitly mentioned in the New Testament book of Acts. During those 40 days, Jesus continued to teach His disciples and appeared to many followers, solidifying the message of His resurrection before His ascension into heaven.

Forty is a significant number in both the Bible and mystical traditions. It often represents a period of preparation or transformation, which aligns with the 40 weeks of foetal gestation in the womb. The Israelites wandered in the desert for 40 years, and Jesus fasted for 40 days in the wilderness. This time frame is seen as a preparation cycle before the climax of spiritual ascension. Jesus' resurrection symbolizes the awakening of spiritual consciousness (Christ consciousness), while the ascension represents the soul's ultimate union with the divine. The 40-day period between these events symbolizes the time of integration, where the higher spiritual truths are made real (gestated) within the physical and mental body before the soul transcends fully. In this context, the 40 days can be seen as the time in which one must continue to live, learn, and grow in their "newly awakened state," preparing to "transcend the material world."

Circling back to the focal point of this book, the inner regeneration and cosmic "rebirth" occurs both in the sky and in our bodies during winter solstice. The interplay of Christ (solar) and Mas (lunar) energies during December are extremely significant to all of nature and the DNA antennae in every cell of our bodies are continuously picking up fresh astral substances from all around us.

With the conditions of nature supporting and assisting your endeavours, it's easy to understand why winter solstice is a favourable time to fast. Whether you do the Daniel Fast (a natural plant-based diet), a juice fast, or something more extreme is up to you to discern. Of course, it goes without saying that you should choose a fast that's at the right level for you personally, and always consult a medical professional if necessary.

With all of this in mind, the potential for deep spiritual purification and awakening during winter is absolutely apparent. It's no wonder then, that society and the media surround us with more temptations than ever, mostly in the form of sugar and alcohol, at this holy time of year.

TIMING

> *"Man, the microcosm, is, in himself, a miniature universe; composed of infinite atoms; which are in a constant state of action and re-action; not only among themselves; but also, with the infinite atoms of the larger universe, the macrocosm."*
> **Page 282, The Light of Egypt by Thomas H. Burgoyne**

As smaller reflections of the universe at large, certain "in-tandem" processes take place within us as they occur in nature. Winter solstice is one example of this simultaneous mechanism. As mentioned earlier, the micro/macro phenomenon is known in science as **Implicate Order**. Implicate Order proposes that the physical, psychic, and spiritual (invisible or energetic) realms are ultimately connected. It is this connection that leaves us susceptible to various combinations of energetic stellar, planetary, and lunar influences. Implicate Order, a concept introduced by physicist David Bohm offers a holistic account of the human being and his environment. This idea underscores the concept that stellar, planetary, and lunar energies influence human physiology, spirituality, and even consciousness.

As part of our mirrored relationship with the universe, the sun is seen as parallel with the pineal gland, mineral body, electric nervous system, thought, and the "spirit" of the body. While the moon is seen as parallel with the pituitary gland, fluidic body, magnetic lymph and endocrine systems, emotion, and the "soul" of the body.

As stated in previous offerings, such as my yearly **"ReGENEration Calendar:"**

- The regeneration of the **mineral (solar) body happens yearly,** coinciding with the sun.

- The regeneration of the **fluidic (lunar) body happens monthly,** coinciding with the moon.

The monthly regeneration, known as the **sacred secretion time-phase,** or **super consciousness awakening practise time** is when the moon traverses through the individual's zodiac sign each lunar cycle. There are 13 lunar cycles in every solar year. Therefore, there are 13 opportunities to experience the **fluidic lunar regeneration** each year.

> *"When the Moon, in the course of her motion, arrives at the same point during each month, she impregnates these "seeds" and endows them with magnetic life; therefore, in an occult sense, she confers upon humanity the powers and possibilities of magical forces. It is this Luni-Solar influx of Naronia within the human constitution, then, that controls the real foundation and basis of spiritual development and occult power."*
> **Page 126 Light of Egypt" by Thomas H. Burgoyne**

The concept of the Moon influencing regeneration is echoed in the "Book of the Moon" by Rick Stroud, where it is suggested that lunar cycles influence genetic and cellular patterns within the human body, contributing to its capacity to heal and regenerate. This links to the understanding that the Moon governs psychic and emotional aspects, while the Sun governs physical and material regeneration, especially around the solstice.

The "monthly" regeneration is explored, and explained from various perspectives in *The God Design: Secrets of the Mind, Body, and Soul* (a contextual study with practical guidelines), *The Cell of Life: Awakening and Regenerating* (focusing on the journey of the "Christ Seed" born every 29.5 days), and *The Sacred Secretion: Your Guide to Kundalini Energy, Christ Oil, Alchemy and the Monthly Seed* (a compendium of information from the first two books with further insights and practical guidance). I am not explaining the contents of these previous books in order to "plug them" or unashamedly promote sales. I am simply highlighting the difference between what's already been said about the sacred secretion time-phase in association with the moon and stars, and the yearly mineral-solar regeneration that's being addressed in this Christmas offering.

In contrast to the monthly lunar regeneration, the mineral (solar) body is said to regenerate annually during key solar cycles, such as winter solstice. The term mineral body refers to the more physical, grounded aspects of human existence. Winter solstice, often seen as a time of renewal, is when the body, mind, and spirit can reset in alignment with the longer solar cycles. During this period, the Sun's "return" mirrors the rebirth of energy and light within us, just as the Moon continues to affect us more subtly on a monthly basis. These cycles resonate with traditions like the Rosicrucian and Hermetic approach to the winter solstice, where the emphasis is on regeneration and transformation, drawing from the spiritual forces of both the solar (Christ) and lunar (Mas) cycles to balance emotional and material aspects of life. The inner solstice enables deep spiritual development as the "luni-solar" influx influences the genetic and cellular make-up of the body. As solar energy "re-enters" the world and impregnates nature with its procreative "solar seeds" that materialise or manifest as new tree buds, and flower sprouts it also endows our body with a resurgence of life force energy.

> *"For the etheric vibrations impinge on the human ether and can so change the in-harmonic human vibrations into harmonic ones."*
> Page 5, Der Hypnotismus by Doctor L Loewenfeld 1901

The "inner solstice" is a microcosmic reflection of the macrocosmic solar events:

As Winter Solstice approaches, nature undergoes a profound shift. Tree sap rises in trees during December, especially near the solstice, a process mirrored in the human body through the movement of cerebrospinal fluid (CSF), which allows for a deep cellular cleansing of body fluids, and brain fluids (glymphatics).

The inner "rise" or amplification of CSF is linked to the "Christ Seed" or solar energy within the body. This "seed," a microcosmic version of the outer sun, ascends through the temple-body toward higher centres of consciousness, as the sun simultaneously "returns" in the sky. As the outer sun confers new life to nature, the Christ seed confers new life to the body.

During the approximate three-and-a-half days of darkness during the solstice, the body's lack of exposure to sunlight stimulates the heightened production of melatonin. Melatonin not only governs sleep and circadian rhythms but also plays a role in triggering the biochemicals associated with enlightenment and spiritual awakening. This period of darkness, therefore, serves as a time of deep inner transformation, where the "darkness" outside and inside prepares the individual for the return of the light. It's a time when the initiate withdraws, fasts, and optimises his alchemical state for the reception of light.

Ultimately, the Winter Solstice is not only an external event but also a profound movement of inner alchemy, where both the cosmic sun and the "solar energy" within the individual are reborn.

In "Xxenogenesis Nuclear Fusion," the writer "Xxey" explains that **there are both monthly and bi-yearly opportunities** to *"fuse the lunar and solar germs within,"* although "he" doesn't elaborate on this point, it makes sense that, as well as our usual "monthly" sacred-secretion time phases, the winter solstice (December for the Northern hemisphere and June for the Southern) are the other two time-phases optimised by cosmic alignments.

According to Harold Percival in *"Thinking and Destiny"* the "sacred secretion" or "Christ seed" is travelling through the lower chakras when the moon is in the individuals sun sign, meaning that cosmic influences endow the lower centres during these times, making them a prime-time to "save-seed." Due to the proximity of the sun and moon in December (particularly in the Northern Hemisphere), it's logical that astral influxes are extremely potent then too.

Of course, these are the minimum windows to practice retention, and other spiritual practises because any increased duration will add to the concentration of life force in your temple-body and have positive effects throughout the body and experience of life too.

Another element of the yearly solar regeneration occurs on each individual's birthday. In astrology, a person's "solar return" is when the

Sun returns to the exact position it occupied at the time of birth. This return marks a moment of **personal renewal** and empowerment, offering a chance to set new intentions and harness cosmic energy for personal growth and transformation. The concept of solar returns is central in astrological traditions, such as those explored by Dane Rudhyar and others in modern astrology.

> *"Man, also makes the annual journey around the solar centre, when, at the beginning of each new year to him, the life forces of his soul are renewed, regalvanised, so to say, according to the magnetic polarity of his constitution."*
>
> **Page 10, The Light of Egypt by Thomas H. Burgoyne**

The solstice regeneration and the birthday regeneration serve different functions:

- The **Winter Solstice** represents a <u>**universal** moment of solar regeneration,</u> tied to the <u>collective consciousness</u> and life force on Earth. This is when the Sun's energy begins to increase, **affecting all living beings in terms of vitality and spiritual growth.**

- The **Birthday (Solar Return)** is a <u>**personal** moment of renewal,</u> specific to the <u>individual's consciousness</u> and cosmic alignment with the Sun.

By considering both the universal (winter solstice) and personal (birthday/solar return) aspects, we get a holistic understanding of how solar regeneration operates within esoteric and occult frameworks.

"But when she (the moon) is configurated with other orbs; her influx becomes exceedingly potent as she receives and transmits to us the intensified influence of those stars aspecting her. The moon, therefore, may be called – the great astrological medium of the skies." Page 20, The Light of Egypt by Thomas H. Burgoyne

In previous offerings, I have spoken at length about the benefits of fasting for a 3.5-day time period. But just to reiterate, ancient beliefs and the latest scientific research agree that 3.5 days is a significant duration to fast for. Whether in plight of physiological health and regeneration, or for divine connectivity -- 84 hours is an efficacious time frame.

> *"And after three days and an half, the Spirit of life from God entered into them, and they stood upon their feet"*
> Rev 11:11 (KJV)

Here are some insights that relate this specific duration to significant positive changes in the body, mind, soul, and spirit:

- It takes roughly 3 days for the body to form new neurite pathways, if the conditions are favourable. **Growth factors like BDNF (Brain-Derived Neurotrophic Factor)** play a crucial role in the formation of neurite pathways. They encourage the growth of neurites, forming pathways that **enhance cognition, emotional stability, and even facilitate the detoxification of stress hormones (such as cortisol).**

- During cleansing, particularly, omega-3 fatty acids, B-vitamins, and antioxidants can promote neurite outgrowth and neurogenesis (the formation of new neurons -- **new brain cells),** linking a detoxified, rejuvenated body to improved brain function.

- 3-4 days is hailed for being an effective amount of time for deep cellular cleansing in the state of autophagy. **Fasting or detox diets** can induce autophagy (a process where the body clears out damaged cells). This is important in renewing cells and tissues and fostering cognitive health.

- **Neuroplasticity,** the brain's ability to reorganize itself by forming new neural connections, is deeply affected by lifestyle changes such as diet, sleep, and stress reduction. During detoxification or cleansing, the body undergoes biochemical shifts (like balancing neurotransmitters or **eliminating physical and energetic toxins** from the body). This accounts for the sudden ability to overcome addictions, bursts of love that allow us to forgive certain things that once seemed impossible, and the eradication of other debilitating programmes.

- Then there's the **tryptophan/DMT pathway,** evoked by fasting, retention, bhakti and other "sacred secretion practises" laid out in many previous videos, books, and the Super Consciousness Awakening Course on **"Teach: able**." The tryptophan/DMT pathway is the driver of alchemical upgrades in the body, it is a major catalyst for the felt experience of enlightenment. It's no coincidence that melatonin is key to this chemicalization as melatonin secretions are stimulated by darkness. So, during the "dark days" of December (in the Northern hemisphere), when the natural man would have been encouraged into an organic state of "hibernation," they consequently would have been exposed to longer hours of darkness and thus heightened their opportunity to engage the tryptophan/DMT pathway.

In conclusion, it's crucial to observe the various time-phases associated with different bodily sheaths or aspects, and collective vs. individual consciousness. To summarise:

1. The collective luni-solar regeneration occurs every winter solstice (in your respective hemisphere).

2. The individual fluidic body is revitalised and renewed every lunar month.

3. The individual mineral body is revitalised and renewed every year on your birthday.

DICTIONARY OF CHRISTMAS SYMBOLS

Angelo Morphism

Christian mystics describe the "angelo morphism" transformation as an internal process where "light" is consciously gathered and assembled within the body. This relates to esoteric interpretations of scripture, where the body becomes a vessel for the Divine Light. Practitioners focus on harnessing spiritual energies, raising their internal vibrations, and working on their soul's purification. This idea mirrors the modern process known as "preserving and raising the Sacred Secretion" and other mystical traditions where energy centres (chakras), are awakened and aligned.

One of the most essential practices for achieving this transformation is said to be deep contemplative prayer, akin to the practices of the Christian "hesychasts." By quieting the mind and aligning one's thoughts with the Divine, the practitioner begins to focus inwardly, accessing the divine spark or light within. Mystical Christians often engaged in meditative practices that allowed them to experience a unity with God and gradually transform into beings of light, becoming closer to angelic forms.

The following points describe practises associated with angelo morphism:

- Purification of the body, mind, and soul through fasting and asceticism was also seen as a crucial aspect of achieving angelo morphism. The focus here is on cleansing the physical body to make space for divine energies. Similar to how angels are believed to be free of physical needs, ascetics aimed to diminish the body's desires, thus allowing the spirit to elevate.

- In some mystical teachings, practitioners use visualization exercises to facilitate their transformation. This involves visualizing oneself enveloped in divine light or becoming a radiant, angelic figure. These practices can be seen as a form of "inner alchemy," where the dense, material aspects of the self (such as ego, negativity, or impurity) are transmuted into spiritual light. The visualisations serve as a modality to literally cut the cords between debilitating programmes and conditions in the mind.

- The repetition of sacred names or phrases ("mantras" in other traditions) also played a role in this transformation. Christian mystics would chant the names of God or Jesus Christ repeatedly (as in the "Jesus Prayer") to elevate their consciousness and immerse themselves in divine presence. This practice would help to dissolve their egoic identity and awaken their angelic nature.

The Bible book of Revelation refers to angelo morphism as "building the solar body," also known as "soma heliakon." The reference to "solar beings" or the "solar body" highlights the sun's central role as a metaphor for divine illumination. The sun symbolizes the source of all life and enlightenment. Thus, becoming a "solar being" represents the human's journey toward spiritual illumination and unity with the divine. This transformation is linked to the Eastern Orthodox tradition -- "theosis." Theosis is the process of becoming divinized or attaining likeness with God.

Ancient mystery schools saw the soul's ascension as akin to the sun's journey across the sky. In Gnostic and Hermetic traditions, the soul's passage through higher spheres of consciousness was likened to the sun's trajectory, with the soul becoming brighter as it ascended closer to God, the ultimate source of light.

Christian mysticism, especially from early Church Fathers like Origen and Pseudo-Dionysius, includes the belief that humans can ascend to angelic states through rigorous spiritual discipline, mirroring the perfection and purity of angels. In this sense, humans are seen as capable of ascending to the divine hierarchy, transforming into beings of light who assist in the governance of the cosmos alongside angels.

For those looking to explore this subject more thoroughly, one key work that explores this theme is "Posthuman Transformation in Ancient Mediterranean Thought" by M. David Litwa. In which Litwa distinguishes "Angelification" (becoming an angel) from "Angelo morphism" (becoming like an angel). This work discusses how certain spiritual practices and ethical transformations were believed to lead one closer to the divine state, resembling angels in function and essence. It also examines ancient sources that described both angels and "daimones" (demons or divine beings) as part of this transformative process.

Another source, by C.H.T. Fletcher-Louis called "All the Glory of Adam," explores angelo morphism in "Second Temple Judaism," highlighting how ancient Jewish mysticism perceived this transformation as part of spiritual ascension, aligning with themes of regeneration, divinity, and enlightenment.

These works illustrate how ancient mystics and philosophers believed that transformation into an angelic or solar being could be accomplished through spiritual practices, meditation, ethical purity, and a focus on divine light.

The notion of Angelo morphism is deeply connected to the regenerative effect of the winter solstice. Just as the sun begins to ascend and return after the solstice, this celestial event is seen as a reflection of the internal process of purification and enlightenment. Through this regeneration, the body and soul become vessels of divine light, enabling one to ascend into a higher, angelic state.

Bethlehem

In Luke chapter 2, Scripture explains that Mary (See Mary) and Joseph (See Joseph) travelled to Bethlehem to birth Jesus, but because of the annual census happening there at the time, all the Inns were full and so Jesus had to be born in a stable (See Stable). "There's no room at the Inn" means, **"there's no room in you"** i.e., there's no space for light to come in and transform you, *"if your body is full of darkness, light cannot dwell there."* **Paraphrase Matthew 6:23.**

The word "Bethlehem" stems from the root word and Hebrew letter, "Beth" and the root "helm." "Beth" means house, body, abode, or dwelling place, and "helm" means bread or substance. The substance centre in the body is the solar plexus and the glands and organs which it innervates.

The solar plexus is where everything that we consume gets digested and processed, essentially making the "daily bread" or "substance" for the body. The body (Beth) strives to eliminate waste and keep our pH neutral. Excessive eating habits and alcoholism, promoted by "death culture" and the media in particular, leaves the solar plexus and its processes "backed up," making it increasingly challenging for us "initiates" to fully purify and prime our temple bodies in order to properly receive and assimilate the Creative Light within us.

When the solar plexus and the functions that it governs aren't on the back foot (so-to-speak), toxins are easily eliminated from the body, and Life Force Energy or Creative Light (processed from food, water, breath, and the atmosphere), in the form of electrons is assembled and kept for rejuvenating bodily processes, such as generating "new" cells or "infant," "baby" cells, *"Jesus is a germ of life."* G.W Carey in the spleen. The spleen, innervated by the solar plexus is an organ where new cells are produced and proliferated (See Manger). Thus, the temple-body is regenerated by degree from the inside-out.

In addition to this, the majority of the body's serotonin is produced in the solar plexus. Serotonin from the root word "sero" meaning "seed" (so, the "atoning" "seed") is the precursor to melatonin. Therefore, it is crucial for pineal health and metabolism. Pineal metabolism is the process whereby serotonin (seed-o-tonin) and melatonin are transformed or transmuted into substances such as DMT (the spirit molecule) and the other biochemicals of enlightenment which I've spoken about at length in previous offerings.

Boots and Stockings

Most depictions and illustrations of Santa Claus, or "Old Saint Nicholas" feature his highly symbolic "black boots." There are several layers to peel away in order to understand the true significance of this.

Firstly, in a symbolic sense, feet and different kinds of footwear tend to symbolically represent our connection to earth, grounding us to the material world, while at the same time carrying esoteric weight regarding the movement of spiritual energy within the body. In this way, Santa Claus' iconic "black boots" represent the descent of Spirit, Life Force Energy, or Creative Light into matter. The colour "black" symbolises what alchemists call "Negredo," the first phase of the "Great Work" (See Three Wise Men). Negredo, "the blackness" is said to be a starting point for the assimilation of Creative Light within, which again, is akin to the practise known as "preserving and raising of the sacred secretion" in modern times.

Creative Light descends from higher realms into the root chakra of the physical body, where it begins to take form. The Creative Light, equated with procreative energies and essences, penetrate into the physical body, where they can be outwardly ejected or preserved and reabsorbed toward regeneration and spiritual enlightenment. This energy, when properly directed and transmuted, becomes the very "gift of light" given to the initiate for spiritual growth.

The turn of phrase, "Fill your boots" refers to taking full advantage of a situation, but in an esoteric sense, it's a metaphor for channelling vital energy. Procreative energies and essences are life-giving substances, that help to maintain the entire electromagnetic "structure" of the body. In this way, "filling one's boots" suggests the idea of gathering and containing this powerful energy within oneself, not letting it dissipate, but rather allowing it to course upward and be refined through the centres of the body. Thus the "black boots" correlate with the base substance, akin to black coal (See Coal, Lead and Carbon), ready to be primed and transformed.

It is said that St. Nicholas placed gifts in people's boots (See Saint Nicholas) on the 6th of December. This date also coincides with the festival of Faunalia (See Faunalia), and is also seen as a time when light begins to triumph over darkness, culminating in the Winter Solstice and eventually the rebirth of the Sun.

This act of giving "gifts in boots" symbolically mirrors the "gift of light" descending into the material plane, on both a macrocosmic and microcosmic level. Just as St. Nicholas places gifts into boots, the Creative Light penetrates the lower centres of the body, the seat of procreative power. Here, Creative Light descends into matter (boots), offering spiritual gifts to the initiates who were known in Hebrew as "the children of Shekinah." The notion of an "initiate" being a "child" regardless of their age is a key factor in the inner alchemy, as we'll come to see.

In ancient alchemy, it was suggested that the initiate had to wear the "boots of Hermes" (Greek rendition) or the "boots of Mercury" (Latin rendition).

Mercury was not just the messenger god in mythology but also represented the "alchemical Mercury," the "vital essence" present in sexual energy. In this sense, "Mercury" was said to be the "metallic soul" of seminal fluids, representing the subtle, vital energies that sustain both physical life and spiritual awakening. Procreative secretions are rich in nutrients, proteins, and enzymes, they also have a distinct electrostatic charge and are viewed as containing the essence of Life force that can either be expended or transformed for spiritual growth.

> *"While dealing with the forms assumed by man, we must notice those vital secretions which form the physical conditions for reproduction of his kind. The seminal fluids are the most ethereal of all physical secretions and contain the very quintessence of human nature."*
> **Page 36, The Light of Egypt by Thomas H. Burgoyne**

Mercury's boots, and indeed Hermes's boots were traditionally portrayed as winged sandals, signifying swiftness and the ability to navigate both the material and spiritual realms, offering a cool resemblance to modern Santa Claus stories and linking the feet (grounding in matter) with higher spiritual flights.

The process of "elaborating Mercury" or transmuting this force into spiritual energy is the secret that ancient Medieval Alchemists guarded so closely. This process is sometimes described as the "Arcanum A.Z.F."

The Arcanum A.Z.F unveils the steps to this transmutation,

- The "A" stands for Aqua, or "water," referring to the "Metallic Radical Number" or "Exiohehari" -- the procreative energies and essences which are to be transmuted.

- The "Z" is Azufre, or "sulfur."

- The "F" is "Fire," or Fohat.

Without "fire," "water" (Mercury) cannot be elaborated. The entire alchemical process lies in the careful combination and transformation of these elements, taking the base essences and turning them into "spiritual gold" -- the true "gift" of the initiates (children).

The "Metallic Radical Number," Exiohehari, is the number 8 (See Circumcision and Reindeer regarding the number eight). In esoteric teachings, particularly within Gnostic alchemy, "Exiohehari" refers to the "glandular sexual secretions" viewed as the vital energy that can be transmuted for spiritual growth.

The number 8 symbolizes infinity and balance, and in alchemical terms, it represents the regenerative and cyclical nature of energy. It is often associated with transmutation and the flow of energy that ascends and descends within the spinal column (the symbol of the Kundalini).

To be clear, there is no actual physical "mercury" (quicksilver) in sexual fluids. What we now call mercury (Hg) is a toxic heavy metal, and it's not found in any biological fluids of the human body. The use of "mercury" is purely allegorical in the context of spiritual teachings, referring to the "fluidity", "adaptability", and "transformational" potential of procreative essences.

While there's no "mercury," per say, sexual secretions do contain important chemicals and nutrients that are essential for life such as phosphorus (plays a crucial role in energy metabolism), lecithin containing choline (a neurotransmitter that assists brain function), Fructose (a sugar that provides fuel for the body), Enzymes, Proteins and amino acids (important for cellular function), Zinc (integral for immune function and reproductive health), Vitamins and minerals (such as vitamin C and calcium).

In Kundalini yoga and tantric traditions, procreative energy is often compared to the "serpent power" that rises through the spine. The "mercurial" nature of this energy (fluid, transformative, and dynamic) mirrors the alchemical idea of "Mercury" (which flies up in its winged boots) as the essential, transmutable life force.

> *"When the sexual organism is evolved above the physical plane of its manifestation, the seminal fluids are absorbed by the magnetic constitution and the etherealized atoms help to build up the spiritual body of man. But when this is not so these seminal germs, if not passed off amid the other secretions from the body, live and germinate a swarm of elemental lifeforms which rob the organism of a portion of its vitality. To obey the laws of Nature is the only safe and sure road to evolve the spiritual senses of the soul."*
> Page 36, The Light of Egypt by Thomas H. Burgoyne

Candle

In many traditions, lighting a candle symbolizes the awakening of the soul, dispelling darkness and ignorance. Representing the joyful light of life, candles have long been associated with Christmas and other celebrations. Before electric lights, candles were placed on the branches of Christmas trees illustrating the emergence of new light at the time of solstice. Many cultures add candles to their birthday cakes, showing the number of years they've been alive, or the amount of times they've journeyed around the sun.

In the Bible book of Revelation, the "seven candlesticks" represent the seven prominent chakras of the body. When light is properly harnessed through right living, kundalini energy freely flows through the chakras. The root word "cand" in candle, comes from "candere" meaning to shine, and "kand" meaning to glow. "Kand" is etymologically related to "kund" in kundalini which means coiled or spiralled light.

The simple action of lighting a candle, can be seen as a metaphor for igniting or assembling the light within us. Christ Oil (CSF) or "Soma" parallels the fuel, or wax of the candle and the "solar seed," akin to Agni parallels the flame. In the Vedas, Agni is the fire principle, while soma is the water principle. Our temple body's need a balance of both Agni and soma to work at their optimum capacity. On a deeper level, Agni is said to be the fire of consciousness **that is reflected in** the Soma or water of bliss. In this way, Agni and Soma are two intwined aspects of God

(Brahma) and are another example of the life polarity (See Dual Life Force).

In the human body, fire and water are seen as opposites but also complementary. The balance between Agni (fire) and Soma (water) is crucial. Too much fire (fight, passion, intellect, structure) can burn out the body's energy reserves, while too much water (passivity, emotion, relaxation, aimlessness) without the tempering influence of fire can lead to stagnation or emotional overwhelm. Serenity is wonderful, but measured assertion is important too. Practices like yoga, particularly kundalini yoga, focus on harmonizing these energies. Pranayama breathing exercises can stoke the internal fire (Agni), while meditation and proper hydration restore the flow of Soma (the fluids that nourish and rejuvenate the nervous system). Encouraging the inner "flame" to rise, and the inner "water" to precipitate allows for safe, gradual and beautiful awakening experiences.

Candy Canes and Shepherds Staffs

Candy Canes are traditionally coloured with "red" and "white" stripes that spiral around its "staff" or "crook" shaped form.

Red and white are heavily symbolic in the "Great Work," also known as the alchemist's path to enlightenment (See Three Wise Men). Spiral emblems are deeply reminiscent of energy patterns, like the tesla coil and the coiled serpent of kundalini, or the winding paths of the Ida and Pingala nadis on the caduceus which is a symbol for healing and medicine, "by his stripes we are healed." Isaiah 53:5 KJV

In the body, the significance of red and white is prevalent with the blood systems. "Red" correlates with life-giving, oxygen rich red blood cells. Oxygen has 8 protons, 8 neutrons, and 8 electrons, 888 is the Greek gematric value of the name Jesus (Iesous). And "white" is reminiscent of the lymphatic system, historically known as the "white blood system" which correlates with the "Christ oil," and the "blood of the lamb or ram." As explained in previous books and videos, the CSF (Christ oil) ventricles are even shaped like the horns of a lamb or ram (See Coal, Lead and Carbon for illustration).

The shape of candy canes matches the "J" in the name "Jesus," and parallels the form of the shepherd's staff or crook, *"The Lord is my Shepherd, I shall not want,"* Psalm 23:1 (KJV) i.e., *"I am already abundant, because I know*

I am a child of God, the INFINITE SOURCE AND SUPPLY OF ALL." The form of a candy cane is also parallel to the 12th Hebrew letter "lamed" which symbolises the spine and specifically, the way that it "hooks" or tethers the spiritual/light body within us to the material body.

The spinal column, like the shepherd's staff, channels the divine energies of the universe. The spine is a tangible connection between the spiritual realm and material world. In this sense it is imbued with the "power God" – "Infinite True Source Love Light."

As an extension of gods power, Moses' staff allowed him to "raise the serpent" (initiate kundalini, assimilate the light within, or reach super consciousness awakening)! As a personification of the world's greatest hidden truth, when Moses lifted the energetic serpent up on his staff (spinal medulla), and when he used his staff to produce "water" from a rock (the pineal gland and philosophers stone) he illumined the minds of his people, allowing them to see their own potential. **The pineal gland and its calcite crystals is quite literally the philosophers stone that seeps "living water" or the biochemicals of enlightenment into body, thus revealing the secrets of the universe.** *"He only is my rock and my salvation,"* Psalm 62:6 (KJV). This mechanism is activated by energy through the "cane," "rod," or "staff" of the body.

In the Christmas story, the shepherd guiding his sheep with a staff is a metaphor for the higher self, guiding the initiate to their true potential (See Shepherds and Fields). Perhaps your higher-self led you to read this book? Shepherds lovingly herd their animals in the same way that our higher-self guides us to channel our lower nature, and in a physical sense "retain the animal seeds."

Another perspective on the "staff" or "crook" brings us to the Hindu God "Ganesha" who is also known as "Vakratunda," which means "he who straightens out the crooked." In the Bible book of Isaiah 42:16 we find a Scripture that resonates with this notion of healing and development, *"I will lead them in paths that they have not known; I will make darkness light before them, and crooked things straight."* Isaiah 42:16. Some people believe that this notion relates to terrestrial life and therefore ask for help with things like a successful marriage or business deal. This is great because asking (praying) and projecting faith forward are keys to manifestation, but there's a deeper hidden purpose behind the symbol of Ganesha too. "He who straightens the crooked" is he who straightens us, because we are all crooked to some degree; we could be crooked with pride, lust, or anger, or we could be crooked with cripling grief or social anxiety. Whatever the case, invoking Ganesha is said to help with healing, realigning, and removing obstacles. In this way, Ganesha symbolises the aspect of God (in and through all) who puts obstacles or lessons in our path in order to teach us about God and straighten our "crooks."

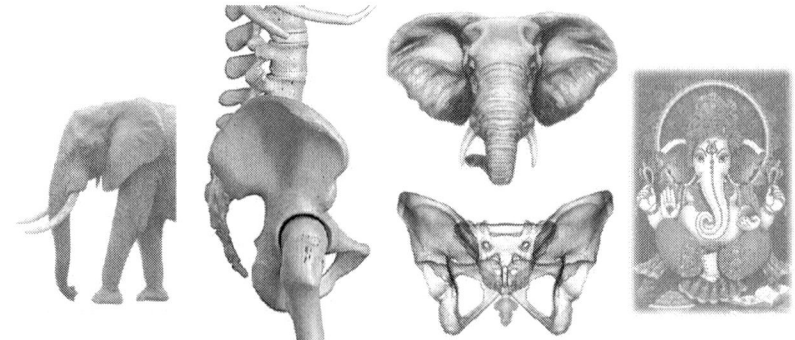

The hidden meaning of Ganesha's trunk is seen in the way its form and mechanism resembles the preserving and raising of vital energies

and essences in association with the sacral chakra and its lifting force. Ganesha, the elephant, has the power (with its trunk) to inhale (retain) fluid (procreative essences), lift them up and release them over its head in a washing and cooling ritual. If you've ever watched an elephant bathing, you'll know that it's a beautiful sight to behold! This imagery shares a beautiful resonance to the raising and invigorating of the Christ Oil that showers and cleanses the body and soul.

Many other deities throughout history and across many cultures have possessed staffs and canes also. For example, Osiris, Horus and Khnum are all depicted with a Crook and Flail, the crook traditionally being assigned to masculine, exuding energy (solar) and the flail representing feminine, receptive energy (lunar). This bears a striking parallel to the inner polarities of the Ida and Pingala nadis associated with pituitary and pineal energies and essences.

Christmas Tree, the Tree of Life

The tree of life, signifying a map of the human body is a universal symbol that appears in hundreds of places, religions, and traditions throughout history. Some prominent examples of this imagery include,

- "Es Hayyim" Kabballah's tree of life.

- "Etz Chaim" the Biblical tree of life.

- "Yggdrasil" the Nordic tree of life.

- "Bodhi" the Buddhic tree of life.

- "Kalpavriksha" or "Kalpataru" the Hindu tree of life (including the chakra system).

The imagery of the tree stems from the human body and its inner workings. Many of you will know that the pneumogastric nerve (CNX), as a channel for breath (pneuma/spirit) into the body, has been dubbed "the tree of life" in esoteric studies. In a broader sense, the spine can be viewed as a tree trunk with the nerves being branches. The way we decorate our Christmas trees with rows of lights on wires very much reflects the nerves of the body which are like electrical wires carrying energy or light to all parts of the body.

Another parallel between tree symbolism and the human body is vital/life fluid. Trees, particularly in their trunks, contain "sap" also known as "resin," and sometimes referred to as "oil.' Humans, particularly in their spines contain lymphatic fluid esoterically known as Christ oil (CSF is a part of the lymph system). Both sap and lymph are vital fluids that help their respective organism to grow and sustain itself.

Further similarities between these vital fluids (tree sap and lymph) include their roles in the following functions:

1. **Fluid Balance:**

In both trees and humans, fluid balance is essential. Tree sap circulates water and nutrients to maintain the tree's health, while the human lymphatic system manages fluid levels in the body, preventing tissues from swelling and keeping the internal environment stable.

2. **Waste Removal:**

Tree sap removes waste products from plant cells, transporting them out of leaves and bark. Similarly, the lymphatic system clears toxins and cellular waste from the body's tissues, filtering them through lymph nodes to prevent infection and inflammation.

3. **Energy Transportation:**

Both photosynthesis and ATP systems supply essential energy for their respective organisms.

- **In trees,** photosynthesis converts sunlight into chemical energy (specifically, carbon-based glucose) which is stored in sap.

- **In humans,** the lymphatic system transports absorbed fats, which are metabolized into energy (ATP) used by the cells.

4. Immune Function:

Tree sap contains antimicrobial compounds that protect the tree from infections and diseases. The lymphatic system houses immune cells (such as lymphocytes) in lymph nodes, which help detect and fight infections, playing a crucial role in the human immune response.

5. Cellular Regeneration:

Sap delivers nutrients to tree cells, aiding the growth and repair of damaged tissues. In humans, the lymphatic system provides nutrients to cells and removes waste, helping in tissue repair and regeneration after injury.

6. Hormone Delivery:

Just as sap can carry growth hormones and signals that affect the growth and development of trees, the lymphatic system is involved in the transport of various signaling molecules and hormones that regulate processes like immune response and metabolism in humans.

7. Lunar Influence:

The moon influences tree sap flow -- traditional beliefs suggest that sap rises more during certain lunar phases, like solstice. Similarly, the moon affects human cerebrospinal fluid (CSF) and lymph. This lunar influence impacts fluid flow, energy levels, cognition, and even mood.

These points highlight the fascinating parallels between tree sap and the human lymphatic system, verifying the importance of tree symbolism in ancient world religions and philosophies.

Since many religious and other secret orders decided to veil the knowledge of the alchemy of ascension in pine tree and pinecone symbolism, pine trees have a distinct relevance at Christmas. Of course, pinecones represent the human pineal gland and Christmas trees depict the body.

The chakra system also comes from tree imagery. Each coloured chakra, energy centre, or nerve plexus coincides with an endocrine gland. For example, the pineal gland corresponds with the crown chakra. The endocrine system is vital in Angelo Morphism, or assimilating the Light Body because glandular secretions drive our overall picture of health. Each and every chemical released second, by second affects our alchemical state (biochemistry) in real-time.

When endocrine secretions are imbalanced, we experience the results in many ways. For example, a slow metabolism illustrates potential issues in the thyroid gland, and anxiety maybe the result of adrenal gland imbalance etc. But when the initiate begins to reflect on their ways, and perhaps spends time in meditation, or improves their diet, and carves out time to prioritize self-care by using other spiritual practices as well…then, the secretions of the endocrine system will begin to harmonise -- giving an increased feeling of healing, relief and lightness. This "felt" affect accentuates by degree based on input and devotion. Self-care is not "selfish." "Self" implies "other," just as "in" implies "out" and "dark" implies "light," *"A new commandment I give you, love one (self)* ***and*** *other."* John 13:34 (KJV).

When endocrine secretions are harmonised, the chakras of the body are naturally aligned and there's no longer any conflict between *what we think* and *how we feel*, or between how we act and how we feel -- we become empowered to just be ourselves: at one with truth, knowing that all things work themselves out for our highest good when we allow it to be so.

> *"If you think of yourself as anything less than the perfect child of the perfect parent, you lower the thought standard and cut off the influx of thought from Divine Mind."*
> Pages not numbered, "Christian Healing: The Science of Being" by Charles Fillmore 1909.

At the height of spiritual awakening, the pituitary gland stimulates the pineal gland to release the biochemicals of enlightenment. These molecules of bliss, vision, healing, and vibrant knowing are tiny spheres of life-enhancing goodness and can be viewed as the "baubles" that we traditionally use to decorate our "pine trees" or "spine trees" at Christmas.

Chimney

The human body has been likened to buildings for centuries. For example:

- The Masons are literal builders and "builders" of light bodies.

- The Christian Bible says, *"your body is the temple of the Holy Spirit."* **1 Corinthians 6:19**

- Islamic Sufi Scripture says, *"Your body is a house, and your heart is the door."*

- In Buddhism the body is likened to a pagoda.

- In Vastu Shastra (Indian architectural science), the human body is likened to a house or dwelling that needs to be aligned with cosmic forces.

The "Chimney" of the "house body" is a channel for Creative Light, this imagery is parallel to the trunk of the Christmas Tree which is also a conduit for Life Force Energy and vital essences. The chimney can further be seen as the shaft of energy that resides at the centre of your electromagnetic torus field (See Shepherds and Fields). **I have a children's picture book available called "Christmas Magic – The Cosmic Story" that includes many coloured illustrations of Christmas symbols in alignment with sacred science.**

In the body, the entrance to Santa's Chimney is the fontanel of the skull. This place is also known as the "Door of Brahma" and "Thura Iesous" which means "Door of Jesus."

When the initiates chakras are aligned and cosmic energy flows unobstructed, they are essentially on the "nice list" and Santa Claus delivers the divine gift of life, presence, or "presents" down the chimney of the temple body (See Presents, Presence and Gifts).

The term "spiritual" comes from the Latin, "spiritus" and the Hebrew "pneuma" meaning "breath." When we breathe, we conduct a vibrational connection that moves through us. The current of CSF in the spine or "chimney" is invigorated by proper breathing, which can be practised with breath exercises known as "pranayama's." A famous line from the poem "A Visit from St. Nicholas" by Clement Clarke Moore says,

"Laying a finger aside his nose and giving a nod up the chimney he rose!"

A popular yogic breath technique for raising energies and essences associated with the spine is alternate nostril breathing, in which you use the mudra (hand posture) where one finger is placed on either nostril as you breath. Was Clement Clarke familiar with the ancient mysteries? Perhaps he was aware, like so many members of secret "brotherhoods" are that St. Nicholas is a modern parable for Creative Light or Kundalini falling and rising through the spine (See Saint Nicholas).

Circumcision

In Luke 2:21, Scripture states that Jesus was circumcised on the 8th day -- after his birth on Christmas day (See Reindeer regarding the number eight). Aside from the physiological act currently assigned to the term "circumcision," the secret act of circumcision is deeply symbolic and represents a process of purification, regeneration, and inner transformation within the human body, particularly in the heart. In Romans 2:29 (KJV), the Apostle Paul says,

"But he is a Jew who is one inwardly; and circumcision is that of the heart, in the Spirit, and not in the letter."

Paul is emphasizing the fact that the original circumcision may not have included the severing of outer body appendages, as we've come accustomed to believing, but a spiritual one that occurs within the heart. *Note: I am not against anyone who has been circumcised in the other sense, the reported benefits and religious reasons are understandable.* However, the act of circumcising of the heart is about becoming spiritually renewed and aligned with God's will. It's a transformation from the inside out, where one's heart is attuned to divine love and wisdom.

In a physiological and symbolic sense, this mirrors the purification of blood and energy as it moves through the heart. Just as the physical heart pumps life-giving blood to the rest of the body, the spiritually circumcised heart pumps divine energy, love, and wisdom into the being of an individual. Biblically, this inner circumcision is described as the removal of spiritual "impurities" to open the heart to the divine.

The heart is often seen as the "centre" of the body. It is the place where spiritual transformation takes place. In this sense, the "circumcision of the heart" symbolizes the refinement of the emotional and spiritual body. The heart, which represents the emotional core of a person, is purified through "Bhakti" a spiritual practice realised in the practical application of unconditional love and all that it represents. Due to our past hurts and traumas, we can find it difficult to step into the full frequency of love that's described in 1 Corinthians 13 (KJV), but as it says in Romans 13:10 (KJV), *"love is the fulfilment of the law."* **Meaning, love is the way to ascension, not just in a mystical sense, but in the physiology of the body, transcendental love is the true catalyst for the sacred secretion of the biochemicals of enlightenment.**

When the heart swells with love, serenity, benevolence, and particularly the acceptance and surrender of self and circumstance to the divine flow, it stimulates the release of oxytocin by the pituitary gland. This mechanism literally activates pineal metabolism (the upgrades of serotonin and melatonin into DMT and the biochemicals of enlightenment). The "washing of the heart by oxytocin" is equivalent to the mystic concept of "washing the Jesus seed." Just remember, hatred, revenge, frustration and other similar frequencies don't release you from relationships and circumstances, they actually contractually bind you to them. The art of accepting life's lessons and then "letting go" or surrendering them to the one amenable law of justice – God, is a factor in the disposition of bhakti (compassion of Christ) and is necessary for the proper assembly of light within.

In the process of the circumcision of the heart, "fleshly" or worldly attachments are removed, and the heart is opened to the higher spiritual truth. This can be understood as the separation of the "gross" from the "subtle" -- a key step in the alchemical process. In the context of the body, this means removing the "gross" aspects of the heart, such as greed, hatred, and attachment, to reveal the pure, subtle essence of love, compassion, and divinity.

In many mystical Christian traditions, the heart is seen as the "throne" of Christ. This means that Christ, or Christ consciousness, takes residence in the heart when it has been properly purified through spiritual practice. This is the ultimate goal of the circumcision of the heart -- to make the heart a fit dwelling place for divine love and wisdom. Light is dimmed by shadows; therefore, we must devote ourselves to turning up the brightness of love and consequently shedding a light in the dark, thus literally dispelling (dissolving the spells and illusions) of shadow.

The eighth day after birth holds deep significance in many mystical and spiritual traditions, including Christianity. Also representing the symbol of infinity, the number eight often symbolizes new beginnings, resurrection, and regeneration. The seven days of creation correspond to the completion of the material world, and the eighth day symbolizes transcendence -- moving beyond the material into the spiritual realm. In this sense, the 8th day is a day of renewal and rejuvenation, marking the start of a new spiritual life. It may be significant, if undertaking a solstice fast to note that the 8th day (after Christmas day) is known as "new year's day" in many places around the world.

As well as being the day when babies are circumcised, the eighth day is traditionally the day they are officially named. In ancient Jewish tradition, a child wasn't fully named or integrated into the community until after the ritual of circumcision on the 8th day. Naming someone signifies more than just giving them an identity -- it's the act of imbuing them with purpose and connecting them to their destiny. In the case of Jesus, the great "Je suis," "I am" His name was a prophecy in itself, revealing His spiritual role; this is equally true for each of us.

Esoterically speaking, naming is related to the vibration or essence of the individual's spiritual purpose (words hold energetic signatures). The act of naming after circumcision symbolizes the moment when the divine mission becomes clear, much like when the soul fully begins to integrate with the body and express its purpose. In the microcosmic body, this relates to the way in which the purification of the heart, via the washing of oxytocin, leads to profound mental and spiritual clarity (heart/brain cohesion). When the initiate experiences this stage of the alchemy of ascension, their path and destiny become crystal clear -- suddenly they know "thy self" and understand their purpose, and identity in life.

Claustrum

The Claustrum is said to be the entry point of Spirit or Life Force Energy into the body, and an on/off switch for consciousness. Some of you will know that in secret anatomical studies there's an intrinsic link between this enigmatic sheet of neurons (the claustrum), and Santa Claus (See Santa Claus).

The name Santa Claus shares the same root as the word "Claustrum." "Clau" or "Klau" means "closed in" as in CLAUstrophia, "cloister", "seclusion", or "cave," and caves share the characteristics of grottos i.e., "Santa's Grotto". In the majority of Christmas Tales, Santa is described as living in a mysterious grotto, in an isolated or secluded region of the North Pole. The same rings true of the Claustrum in the brain which is tucked away and concealed by the temporal, parietal and frontal parts of the operculum.

Another root word associated with Claustrum and Claus is "lau" meaning "praise," "gratitude," and "joyful expression" as in the Latin term "Laus Deo" -- Praise to God! This root is echoed in the words LAUghter and appLAUse.

More compelling still, is the fact that "Mare Clausum" means "closed sea" -- *"a sea under the jurisdiction of one nation and not open to others."* **A Thesaurus of English Word Roots by H Danner.** This brings to mind the image of an individual sea or circuit within the human body such as the nervous, circulatory or "salt-sea" lymphatic-water system. Saint (Santa) Claustrum (Claus) at the "North Pole" (See North Pole) of the body conducts this "sea" and is surrounded by the "white matter" of the brain, which may be where the imagery of snow in Christmas tales stems from. A further link can be drawn between all the cells (neurons) of the Claustrum that work in unison or perform many synchronised tasks and the way in which Santa's Elves are depicted in the beloved Christmas renderings.

In Latin, the claustrum is known as "claustrum hematoliquorosum". Again, "Claustrum" means cloister, enclosure, barrier etc. and "hema" means blood. Additionally, "liquor" means spirit; therefore, "claustrum hematoliquorosum" can be transliterated to "blood-to-spirit barrier" -- this is true, since the claustrum is also seen to act as a barrier between blood and cerebrospinal fluid (CSF) -- CSF is a filtrate of blood. In God Man: The Word Made Flesh, Dr George Washington Carey says, *"It is from the claustrum that the wonderful 'Christ oil' is formed."* In plain modern terms this means, "Creative Light" (electromagnetic energy) acting on the substances of the brain forms cerebrospinal fluid (CSF) -- "Christ Oil."

"Creative Light" is one unified substance but contains male and female aspects (electricity and magnetism), hence the term "electromagnetic energy" (Light). When this Light enters the "North Pole" of the body and is receives by the Claustrum it is divided into two aspects by the pineal (electric solar) gland the pituitary (magnetic lunar) gland. Both aspects of Light manifest in chemical form within us (See Dual Life Force, Mary and Joseph).

"Man, as the Microcosm, possesses the properties of all things including those of magnets. He is endowed with magnetic power, which is subject to the same laws in the small world as it is in the great world. Man is

polar and has polar attractive and repulsive magnetism. He has two poles like the earth, from which circulates a north and south, an attractive and repulsive magnetism. The backbone in man is like the earths equator and divides him into two hemispheres with opposite magnetism."

Page 280, Kiesewetter's Version of Philosophia Moysaica by Gouda 1638

Coal, Lead and Carbon

Santa Claus, also known as Father Christmas, is known to give coal to "naughty" children at Christmas. Santa's "coal" is parallel to the alchemist's "lead" which can be refined into "gold," and to the biblical "carbon 666" that has to be refined in order to build the solar body (soma heliakon). Strong's Bible concordance details "coal" as a synonym for carbon. Indeed, coal, carbon, and lead are all synergistic symbols for the base substance or "first matter" that must be transmuted on the spiritual path. They are the "live embers" or fuels that we burn for life.

Origin of Symbols.

Coal releases traces of "mercury," also known as "living silver" upon refinement, thus providing a clever, secret, allegory for the inner alchemy of ascension. This alchemical code also appears in the Bible book of Isaiah where it says, *"give unto them beauty for ashes"* Isaiah 61:3 (KJV)

In the ancient metallurgical process known as "cupellation," gold and silver were refined from impure metals like lead, zinc or tin. The base substances (impure metals) were heated in a cupel by means of a blast of air. The base metals, were thus oxidized and absorbed, leaving an un-oxidizable, noble metal (gold or silver) behind. About seven and a half centuries before the birth of Christ, Isaiah referred to this process as follows, *"And I will turn my hand upon thee, and purely purge away thy dross, and take away all thy tin."* Isaiah 1:25 (KJV).

Like the refinement of coal and lead, the purifying of carbon creates a more valuable substance also – diamonds! Carbon has to be carefully, and painstakingly refined in order to create diamonds. Buying a diamond ring to wear on your finger is easy, but building a diamond soul takes time.

> *"To make your soul a diamond soul is to possess the Philosophical Stone, to be a resurrected Master with dominion over the four elements, because you are in the very centre of the cross, X, Chi and from that centre you command the water, the air, the fire and the earth, because you are the vehicle of that light, which is in the centre of the sun, in the centre of the earth, in the centre of the Pleiades, in the centre of the galaxy, in the centre of the universe."*
> **Audio Course. The Path of the Bodhisattva, Anonymous**

These are all wonderful metaphors for the inner alchemical process of ascension, but without knowing what refining "lead into god," "coal into mercury," or "carbon into finer substances" really refers to in the body, the initiate is still left in the dark.

Processes of Refining Carbon

The science of The Nativity of Christ is a graduation, a system of awakening the solar power or Creative Light that is latent within each one of us. The Light expands depending on your energy, thoughts, emotions, and actions -- so, your level of devotion. These factors determine how the biochemistry (alchemy) of your body changes and upgrades to reflect them. As well as previously explored chemical changes brought about by the preserving and raising of the sacred secretion, there are various processes involving carbon in the body, each one can be seen as a true biochemical parallel to the symbolic explanations. An introduction to the element of carbon will provide a good foundation to understand these processes clearly.

After oxygen, **the second most abundant element in the human body is carbon-12,** which has 6 protons, 6 neutrons, and 6 electrons (666). After hydrogen, helium, and oxygen, which are all gases, **carbon-12 is the most abundant element in the universe!**

<u>All organic minerals contain carbon</u>, it's really important to understand what is really meant by this. So, let's look at **the difference between organic and inorganic Minerals.**

- **Organic minerals** - Were once <u>living</u> or are <u>living</u> and <u>can bring life to cells.</u> **Organic minerals contain carbon,** and their electrons spin clockwise, just like those of the human body.

- **Inorganic minerals** - Were <u>never living</u> and <u>can NOT bring life to cells.</u> **Inorganic minerals do not contain carbon.** The body treats these metals like toxins. These materials are tightly held together; they cannot be easily broken down. Their electrons spin counterclockwise, out of sync with the rest of the body.

With this in mind, we see how carbon is crucial for life. Carbon is the backbone of all the organic compounds and structures in the body. It's unique ability to bond with many other elements, such as hydrogen, oxygen, nitrogen, and phosphorus, allows for the formation of DNA and RNA -- the fundamental carriers of life's genetic code! In this way, carbon-12 is a crucial element in forming life as we experience it.

Carbon is born from sunlight. In fact, the very processes that produce carbon on Earth originate in the nuclear fusion of stars, including our local star (the sun).

> *"Hydrogen is formed into helium, and helium is built into carbon, nitrogen, iron, sulphur etc. EVERYTHING WE ARE MADE OF."*
> Page 2, The National Geographic: How 40,000 Tons of Cosmic Dust Affects You and Me by S Worral 2015

The energy of carbon is *compacted into matter* or is materialised and transmuted in the body through various metabolic processes (as we will come to see), allowing the body to grow, repair, and sustain life. Carbon not only facilitates the formation and development of DNA but also plays a role in many other bodily functions such as,

- Being present in CSF (Christ Oil) -- hydrocarbons are present in the glucose and lipids, plus amino acids within CSF.

- Carbon plays a role in cell birth and proliferation (regeneration).

- Carbon plays a role in the calcification of the pineal gland and other vital channels of the body.

- Carbon is present in seminal fluids.

- The respiratory system produces carbon in the form of CO_2.

Each of these carbon featuring mechanisms plays a role in the alchemy of ascension and can thus be seen as part of the overall "carbon into light" or "lead into gold" transformation.

Carbon in DNA

DNA is essential for all life; every living cell, of every living organism contains DNA. DNA is the "never-ending" code for life and evolution, and carbon acts as the element that allows this code to be expressed in physical form. The twisting double helix of DNA is formed by its **carbon**-phosphorus structure. Esotericists have said that the double helix of DNA rises from the "water of life" (see Mary) like two serpents rising from the ocean. If DNA were a spiral staircase, the carbon-phosphate molecules would be the handrails. Specifically, the carbon element of DNA is a "5-**carbon**" pentose-sugar called deoxyribose. Deoxyribose is a tiny pentagonal molecule; pentagons are found throughout nature and are revered in art and architecture.

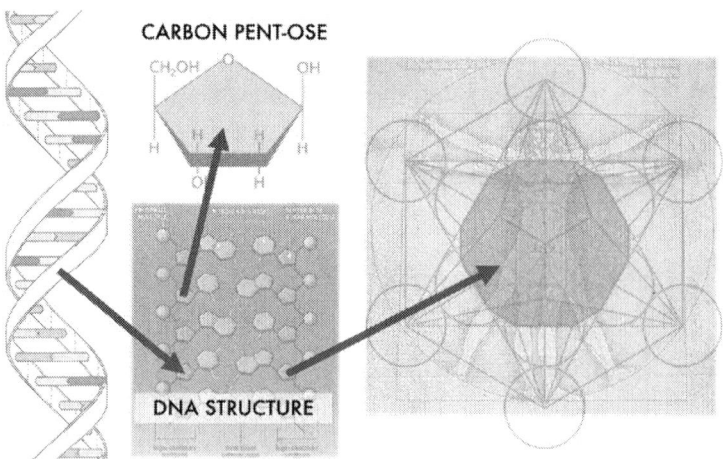

If you've read my previous books, you'll know that the DNA double helix forms a ratcheting dodecahedron (See Saturn, Santa and Satan) with 12 pentagonal sides. The word "car" as a name for a vehicle or mode of transportation is synergistic with the syllable "car" in carbon -- carbon is a transport system for life. The 12-sided dodecahedron is often regarded as the "ascension vehicle," and each of its sides is a pentagon. With all this in mind, it's clear to see why the ancient's equated DNA with the dodecahedral ascension vehicle and how carbon is an essential composite of this so-called "car." DNA serves as both the foundation or blueprint for physical life and the medium through which we rise to higher consciousness. Since DNA is born out "in" or "out of" the "water of life" (see Mary), perfecting those waters energetically and physically assists with DNA repairs and upgrades.

Carbon in CSF and the Lymphatic System.

Hydrocarbons are organic (living) compounds made up of carbon (C) and hydrogen (H) – "CH". They are the simplest types of carbon compounds and serve as the foundation for more complex molecules. Hydrocarbons can store a significant amount of energy (from sunlight), which is released when the carbon bonds are broken during metabolism. This is crucial for powering the body's cells and its biological processes.

One type of hydrocarbon that is found in CSF is Glucose which provides a source of energy for the brain. Cerebrospinal fluid (CSF) rises from the base of the spine to the brain, nourishing and supporting its function. This mechanism happens in tandem with Kundalini on an energetic level and Glucose helps to fuel this process.

Amino acids, the building blocks of proteins also contain carbon, some travel via CSF to nourish the brain and other parts of the nervous system. Finally, CSF carries certain lipids that contain hydrocarbons (chains of carbon and hydrogen).

Hydrocarbons especially in the form of glucose and lipids, are broken down to provide energy for the brain and nervous system. Esoterically these hydrocarbons represent "stored light" which the body, particularly through cerebrospinal fluid uses to maintain cognitive function, and support spiritual development.

The term "Christ Oil" refers to this sacred fluid, which is believed to hold the essence of life. The esoteric teaching holds that as this fluid rises, it undergoes a form of spiritual transmutation, elevating the individual's consciousness and connecting them to higher realms of existence. Just as hydrocarbons release energy when their bonds are broken, the carbon-based compounds in CSF (like glucose) undergo metabolic transformations to release light and energy, thus fuelling both bodily function and spiritual ascension.

Carbon in Cell Birth and Proliferation (Mitosis and Regeneration).

Carbon is sometimes viewed as the *"element that binds the physical world to spiritual realms"* Page 16, Physical Spirituality: Changing the paradigm by Michael Abramowitz 2018. Just as carbon bonds atoms and structures in the material world, carbon in a metaphysical sense is thought to connect the spiritual essence (life force) with the material body. Carbon has unique structural and bonding properties. Carbon is essential for the architecture of molecules and also the organisation and stability of living cells.

- **In atoms**, the nucleus is surrounded by electrons in different energy levels or shells. Carbon plays a vital role by creating stable covalent bonds between atomic nuclei, essentially linking one atom to another.

The strength and versatility of these carbon-based bonds allow atoms to combine into long chains or rings – crucial for building organic compounds. **In this way, carbon serves as a link between the core (nucleus) and the outer structure (case).**

- **In cells,** carbon-based molecules help connect the nucleus of the cell to its outer boundary, the membrane. This allows the cell to function as a cohesive unit. **The fusion between the inner nucleus of the cell, where the "solar essence" resides, and its outer layer where the "lunar essence" resides, is fundamental for cellular generation and regeneration (mitosis) which promotes health along all lines.**

> *"In other words, the **"solar germ"** -- electric, pineal potency, unites with the **"lunar germ"** -- protoplasm, pituitary potency, and the breath (supplied by the vagus) to form stem cells."*
> Page 38, The Cell of Life: Awakening and Regenerating by Kelly-Marie Kerr 2022

The nucleus of a cell is often considered the "control centre" where genetic material resides. This can be interpreted as the "core" or spiritual essence of the cell. The "outer case" of the cell—the membrane—represents the physical boundaries that hold this spiritual core. Carbon, as a unifier, connects these two dimensions: the physical body (represented by the cell membrane) and the spiritual essence (represented by the nucleus).

Carbon and Calcification

Decalcification is another process, involving carbon, that aids spiritual enlightenment. Practitioners of esoteric disciplines often engage in techniques such as fasting, meditation, and consuming specific diets to **decalcify the pineal gland and restore its function, thus opening the door to spiritual**

light. Solstice is an optimal time to ensure your body is free from calcified build-up.

> *"The pineal gland is a small conical, dark grey body situated behind the extremity of the third ventricle, in a groove between the nates, and above a cavity filled with sabulous matter composed of phosphate and of carbonate of lime. It is supposed by modern anatomists to be the vestige of an atrophied eye (third eye)."*
>
> **Pages Unnumbered, The Initiation of John by James Pryse**

The calcification of veins, organs, the brain, and specifically the pineal gland happens due to Calcium Carbonate build up. The carbon in calcium carbonate takes the form of a "carbonate ion", where one carbon atom is bonded to three oxygen atoms. This carbonate ion binds with calcium ions to form calcium carbonate. In this sense, breaking down calcium-carbonate (lime-scale) in the body is symbolic of the alchemical process of turning lead (calcified or "petrified" matter) into gold (spiritual light).

Exposure to sunlight promotes the production of vitamin D, which plays a key role in calcium regulation. This is important for preventing excess calcium build up in the body. The carbon-based mechanisms that process sunlight and nutrients on a cellular level help the body regulate calcium metabolism, which indirectly supports decalcification. In other words, get outside more, and remember to always sit near a window. Decalcification and detoxification go hand-in-hand. A detoxification programme, like the Daniel fast or a juice fast also helps to break down calcium carbonate in the pineal gland. Decalcification involves a detoxification process, similar to how cells detoxify by neutralizing free radicals (through antioxidants like melanin).

> *"The wise know of three sorts of gold. The first is an astral sort, whose centre is in the sun, the rays of which impart light to all the surrounding stars and also to our own human sphere and earth; it is a fiery substance and always fills the whole universe in an incessant ebb and flow (owing to the movements of the sun and stars) by the emission of solar particles. It pervades everything in heaven above and in the interior of the earth. We constantly absorb this astral gold (prana or vapor of the Od) with our breath and these astral corpuscles (cells) penetrate our bodies, which also exhale it without intermission."*
>
> Page 39, ABC of the Philosophers Stone printed at Leipzig by an unknown German savant

Carbon in Seminal Fluids

In many spiritual and medical studies, seminal fluid is considered a vital life force, and it is rich in carbon-based compounds. Preserving this fluid is key in overcoming the "666 beast" or the lower instincts associated with carbon-12. The formation, or image, created by the shape of the procreative organs near the lower chakras can be seen to resemble a goat or other horned "beast." Many worrying images and artworks have been inspired by this resemblance.

> *"The pentagram with one point up is the symbol of white magic which works in harmony with the law of progression. The black magician, who works against nature, subverts the life force and turns it downward through the lower organs. The pentagram, turned with two horns up, represented the symbol of black magic."*
>
> Page 56, Ancient and Modern Initiation by Max Heindel 1929

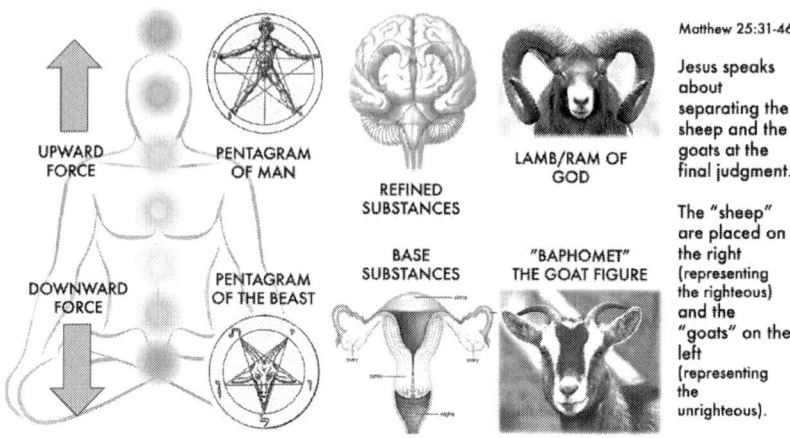

The element of carbon is often associated with the root chakra, as our connection to earth or materiality. By preserving and raising procreative energies and essences, we *"overcome the beast"* i.e., we transcend our base desires and retain life-giving molecules in the body to be used for higher purposes.

Seminal fluid is rich in carbon-based compounds that play essential roles in reproduction, vitality, and overall health. Here are some examples of key carbon-based compounds found in seminal fluid.

1. Fructose – a simple sugar that provides energy (fuel) for many bodily processes.

2. Citric Acid – helps to maintain pH balance.

3. Prostaglandins – hormone like substances derived from fatty acids that assist immune (lymphatic) function.

4. Spermine – a polyamine crystal helps stabilize DNA and prevents oxidative damage.

5. Zinc – has many useful functions in the body including being critical for immune function.

6. Choline – a nutrient that supports cellular health and brain function.

7. Carnitine – plays a role in transporting essential fatty acids into mitochondria and supports the overall energy availability for reproductive cells.

When seminal fluid is conserved and not wasted, the raw carbon-based compounds (as well as phosphorus and lecithin), can be metaphorically "refined" or reabsorbed into the body for detoxification, regeneration, rejuvenation, cognitive "enlightening", and many other health promoting purposes. The seminal fluid is redirected inward and upward, nourishing the brain, nervous system, and spiritual centres such as the pineal gland.

The carbon-based compounds in seminal fluid serve essential biological functions, but they are also viewed as vehicles for spiritual ascension in esoteric traditions. When conserved and "refined," these compounds are transmuted into higher forms of energy that nourish not just the body, but the soul. Through practices like celibacy, meditation, and energy transmutation, the initiate can ascend from the raw, physical realm represented by Carbon-12 (the beast) to a higher state of spiritual enlightenment. In this way, the body's most fundamental elements become tools for mastering both the material and spiritual aspects of existence.

Carbon and Breath

The respiratory (breath) system provides another example of carbon processes in the body. Carbon dioxide, the byproduct of cellular respiration, is necessary for life, but in excess it can lead to various health issues, such as acidosis and impaired oxygenation of cells. Alchemists referred to carbon dioxide as "fixed air" and knew that in unhealthy levels it inhibits the inner alchemy of ascension.

In other words, an overload of CO_2 signifies stagnation and death (lead), while practices that promote proper respiration, and carbon dioxide reduction promote the attainment of "gold."

Mildly reduced carbon dioxide levels elevate brain and lung pH levels causing pH dependent enzymes to encourage endogenous (self-produced) DMT formation. DMT is one of the biochemical of enlightenment. Two key factors for carbon dioxide reduction in the body, are as follows:

1. Proper breathing, if you're naturally a shallow breather, retrain your respiratory system with pranayama's (yogic breathing exercises) that can help regulate and reduce excess CO_2 in the body.

2. Fasting or reducing food intake, carbon dioxide is produced in the body during digestion, if your digestive system is on the "back foot" due to excessive eating, carbon dioxide levels in the body will increase.

These practices, along with dietary changes aimed at reducing acid-forming foods, are seen as essential steps in transmuting the lower, dense forms of carbon (coal) into lighter, more ethereal states (presents/presence).

Through discipline, insight, and the proper application of spiritual practises, the initiate can transmute the "lead" of carbon into the "gold" of enlightenment, overcoming the limitations of the material world and achieving true spiritual freedom.

Cracker

The Christmas cracker is a festive item that produces a loud "crack" when pulled apart. The crack may represent the moment of transformation from darkness (the longest night) to the re-emergence of light. In esoteric traditions, sound often represents creation (cymatics) or cosmic change, with the "bang" symbolizing an initiation or new beginning, similar to spiritual rebirth fuelled by the alchemy of ascension.

Just as alchemy aims to transmute base materials (like "lead" or carbon) into gold, the "crack" can be seen as a metaphor for breaking through physical limitations to reveal spiritual truths, "revelations," or enlightening knowledge.

The two people pulling the cracker from opposite sides can represent the duality of "masculine" (electric) and "feminine" (magnetic) energies or polarities within the cosmos and within the body (See Dual Life Force). The process of pulling the cracker, which combines force and tension, can symbolize the merging of these dualities into unity, a core theme in alchemical teachings. The surprise inside can be seen as the mystical "treasure" that's found in the "chest" or "chestahedron" of the heart (See Sleigh Bells) which is revealed during inward transformations.

Traditionally, a Christmas cracker contains a small gift, joke, or message. These messages are usually rolled into a scroll, which is again reminiscent of the heart which is a rolled or spiralled organ. This is probably linked to the much sought after "book or scroll of love/wisdom" symbolised in dozens of ancient writings and artworks such as, "The Throne of the Last Judgment" (11th-century mosaics) which depicts the book or scroll as an essential tool in the "ascension kit" (Etimasia).

The book of love represents hidden knowledge or the divine truth that is revealed after undergoing the initiatory process of unlocking the sacred heart (See Circumcision). In alchemical and spiritual traditions, the seeker undergoes trials (symbolized by the pulling apart of the cracker) to unlock inner wisdom or a gift of higher understanding. This also mirrors cosmic processes, where the universe itself "cracks open" or the "veil tears" to reveal immortal secrets.

The Christmas cracker could also signify the birth of stars or cosmic processes. Just as pulling the cracker creates a moment of explosive force, in the cosmos, stars are born through similar moments of intense energy and fusion. In the microcosm cell division visually resembles the process of star birth. The cracking could represent the energy of creation itself, mirroring the alleged Big Bang or the celestial forces at play during solstice. The act of pulling a cracker might be an unconscious echo of these grand cosmic events that lead to creation and transformation both in the sky and within our bodies. As the challenges of life bear down on us, it inspires the upward force to "pull us through" to the "other side."

Each of these points connects the seemingly simple Christmas cracker with deeper esoteric, alchemical, and cosmic processes, making it much more than just a holiday tradition.

Dual Life Force

Although it may not be obvious from the outset, many Christmas symbols from around the world illustrate the underlying power of dual forces.

Here are a few examples:

Yin and Yang in Winter Solstice:

The interplay of darkness and light during the solstice reflects the balance of dual energies. In esoteric traditions, this symbolizes the dual forces of life—light and dark, male and female—working in harmony to create renewal.

The Star of Bethlehem:

A guiding symbol for the wise men, the star represents the unity of opposites (See Star of David). It metaphorically illustrates the balance between the earthly (physical) and the celestial (spiritual) realms.

Holly and Ivy:

Traditionally used in Christmas decorations, holly (representing masculine energy) and ivy (feminine energy) symbolize the harmonious relationship between opposing forces. Together, they signify fertility, growth, and the regeneration of life, much like the regenerative forces present in light and dark energies during solstice celebrations.

In a broader sense, the dual forces echo throughout all aspects of life and many varied teachings from around the world.

Here are some examples:

The Kundalini Serpent:

In Kundalini yoga, the dual energies—often symbolized by two serpents coiling up the spine—represent the balance of masculine (Shiva) and feminine (Shakti) forces. This idea of merging these energies at the crown chakra is also parallel to the imagery of the Ida and Pingala nadis.

The Ankh:

The ankh symbol combines the feminine loop and the masculine cross, symbolizing the unity of life forces. In Egyptian esotericism, the ankh is a symbol of life and vitality and the balance of cosmic forces required to sustain life.

The Black and White Horses of Mithra:

In the ancient Mithraic mysteries, the god Mithra is sometimes depicted riding a chariot pulled by one black and one white horse, symbolizing the dual forces of light and darkness. This balance is essential for cosmic order, representing the interplay between opposites, much like the energetic balance in light and life force.

Understanding the dual forces is key to regeneration and spiritual rebirth, because they must eventually be "balanced" or harmonized in order to be transcended. The duality is apparent in the word Christmas which underscores the interplay between the sun and moon during winter solstice. The duality in the unified substance of light is necessary to create the 3D experiential realm that we call "reality." It's echoed through every layer of creation from the microcosm to the macrocosm:

Subatomic Level:

The scientific term for "light" is electro/magnetic energy. The duality in Light is **electricity** and **magnetism.**

Atomic Level:

The first element is hydrogen, comprised of one proton (+) and one electron (-). In atoms, "opposite charges attract," and "like charges repel." This means:

- Positive charges (such as protons) attract negative charges (such as electrons). This attraction holds electrons in orbit around the nucleus of an atom.

- Negative charges (electrons) repel other negative charges, which is why electrons tend to spread out around an atom.

- Similarly, positive charges (protons) repel other positive charges, contributing to the strong nuclear forces that help bind protons together in the nucleus despite their repulsion.

This principle is fundamental to how atomic and molecular structures form and is a key feature of electromagnetism, one of the fundamental forces of nature.

Cellular Level:

In cells, the Nucleus and Nucleoli is mineral dense (positive or "solar" in nature) whereas the watery surrounding of cytoplasm (soma) is said to be negative or "lunar" in nature. So again, we see dual forces at play. Every cell is bipolar (luni-solar) featuring the polarities of attraction and repulsion.

Microcosm (Biochemical Level):

Pineal secretions are viewed as positive, electric, solar in nature. Pituitary secretions are viewed as negative, magnetic, lunar in nature. This is the duality between our two master glands.

Macrocosm:

The sun and moon create an electromagnetic charge, much like an enormous version of a hydrogen atom. This is the dual force residing over earth.

Egypt

Matthew 2:13 (KJV) explains that after Jesus's birth, Mary and Joseph had to flee to Egypt to protect their baby under the advice of the "Angel of the Lord." (See Gabriel, the Angel of the Lord).

In sacred anatomical studies, Egypt symbolises the lower part of the body below the diaphragm, and in *God Man: The Word Made Flesh* Doctor Carey says that *"the salvation of the ego happens in the midst of Egypt."* Specifically, Egypt correlates with the sacral chakra located in the lower abdomen or reproductive area (the red sea). Crossing the red sea means sacrificing the ties that bind us to limited thoughts, emotions, and behaviours. When the "Jesus Seed" or cell arrives in the procreative energy centre it meets the "ens seminis" (seminal fluid) the -- "animal seed." At this point during the cycle, the bodies carnal urges heighten, and self-control is a challenge. This is why the old-testament exodus from Egypt story signifies the freeing of the "I am" spirit from the prison of sense consciousness. Christ consciousness, and indeed the "Jesus seed" have to transition through the "prison" of the lower chakras, and procreative energies and essences have to be preserved in order to be reabsorbed and raised (liberated). In the Bible book of Jonah, the "prison" is depicted as a giant fish, *"Now the Lord had prepared a great fish to swallow up Jonah. And Jonah was in the belly of the fish **three days and three nights."*** Jonah 1:17 (KJV). The "Three days and three nights" that Jonah was inside the belly of the fish, is yet another example of the 3.5-day time phase associated with the sacred secretion.

In relation to the celebration of Saturnalia (See Saturn and Saturnalia), which also happens during the timing of winter solstice and Christmas, the Anahuac allegories describe the Holy Spirit *"giving her children away to be swallowed by Saturn."* Again, this illustrates Creative Light descending into the root and sacral chakras where it must be preserved and processed, but in this rendition, it is described as being "swallowed by Saturn." (See Herod Kills the Children and Saturn Eats the Children). Contrary to some wicked, delusional and literal interpretations of these allegories, their origin does not pertain to performing any harmful or damaging rituals. These parables, with their weird fantastical imagery were written to veil the inner alchemical process of enlightenment and ascension from the masses, it's an utter travesty if anyone ever took their meanings literally. *"Woe unto them that call evil good, and good evil; that put darkness for light for darkness"* Isaiah 5:20 (KJV).

> *"According to tradition, energy assimilation begins with the reproductive organs, which are responsible for physical activity. If all the psychic energy remains in the reproductive organs, the individual will become over-preoccupied with sex. When the energy is raised to the Lyden gland, sexual impulses will be purified, and the energy vibrations prepared for further elevation.* **Nevertheless, the lyden is still located in the lower region of the body and is responsive to the emotions, particularly those of a negative type.** *The individual must desire to lift the prana still further to the adrenals, where a choice can be made between succumbing to the emotions or purifying (letting go) of the*

> *self/ego so the life force can ascend to the thymus region, where true balance between the lower and upper glands takes place."*
> Page 119, Centring: A Guide to Inner Growth by S Laurie and M Tucker.

Dormant Kundalini energy, often depicted as being coiled 3.5 times at the base of the spine, is said to be energetically sealed within the "Lyden glands" of the sacral chakra until it undergoes a process of awakening, stimulation, or indeed activation. The 3.5 coils of the kundalini "serpent", point to the 3.5 days that Jesus spent in the tomb prior to his resurrection and the time the moon spends in each sign during its cycle (the sacred secretion practice time), this also coincides with winter solstice as we've seen. In "Xxenogenesis Nuclear Fusion," the writer "Xxey" explains that there are both monthly and bi-yearly opportunities to *"fuse the lunar and solar germs within,"* although "he" doesn't elaborate on this point, it makes sense that, as well as our usual sacred-secretion time phases (discussed many times in previous offerings), the winter solstice (December for the Northern hemisphere and June for the Southern) are the other two time-phases optimised by cosmic alignments (See Timing).

According to Harold Percival in *"Thinking and Destiny"* the "sacred secretion" or "Christ seed" is travelling through the lower chakras during this time phase (when the moon is in your sun sign), meaning that cosmic influences endow the lower centres during these times, making it a prime-time to "save-seed." Due to the proximity of the sun and moon in December (particularly in the Northern Hemisphere), it's logical that astral influxes are extremely potent then too.

Of course, these are the minimum windows to practice retention because any increased duration will add to the concentration of life force (Ojas) in your temple-body and have positive effects throughout the body and experience of life too. This topic is covered in The God Design: Secrets of the Mind, Body, and Soul in more detail, but for ease here are some of the known scientific benefits of seed retention once more:

- Increased serotonin levels, serotonin is a precursor to DMT and the other biochemicals of enlightenment.

- Decreased Prolactin levels, excess Prolactin causes various problems such as: depression, anxiety, headaches and even weight gain.

- Dopamine Balance, too much or too little dopamine is detrimental. Too much drives addiction, compulsion, and aggression whereas too little dopamine leads to apathy and the inability to love. However, dopamine balance fuels healthy motivation, focus and excitement for life.

- Improved manifestation and spiritual vision, procreative essences fuel the imagination and build magnetism within thus assisting the law of attraction.

- The electromagnetic force in procreative essences supports regeneration at a cellular level.

Solomon exchanges his "lead" or carbon-12 (666) for gold (a finer substance) -- as procreative essences are reabsorbed into the body at "Egypt," the root and sacral chakras and raised toward the "receptacle of gold" (pineal gland) it fuels the chemicalization or manifestation of the biochemicals of enlightenment.

Going back to a more modern, scientific perspective -- When asked by a patient whether or not semen retention was effective Doctor Raymond Bernard replied:

> *"You ask whether the draining from the body of lecithin and phosphorus through the sexual act will hinder the highest intellectual achievement and debilitate body and brain.*
>
> *Most definitely this is the case.*
>
> *Read my article on "Do Neuroses and Psychoses have a Chemical Origin?", in which I show that the loss of these nerve-and-brain foods through sexual indulgence in any form deprives the nerves and brain of needed nourishment and leads to nervous and mental disorders.*
>
> *Our insane asylums are now overfilled with the victims of thoughtless sexual indulgence which has withdrawn valuable nutrients from the brain and disordered its functioning. These pitiful individuals, when in possession of their normal brain structure, never realized that with each discharge of seminal fluid, they are pouring forth the very substance of their nerves and brain, until a time is reached when their brain is so sapped of lecithin that it ceases to function.*
>
> *Measurements have shown an actual decrease in the lecithin content of the brains of the insane. This was due to previous sex indulgence, as a result of which the sex glands took up the blood's lecithin to replace expended fluids."*

> Page 4, "Science Discovers the Physiological Value of Continence" By Doctor Raymond Bernard

With all this in mind, Egypt is a significant "place" on the journey of alchemical ascension. Retaining vital energies and essences is seen as key in the regeneration of body, mind, soul, and spirit. Particularly during winter solstice and when the moon is in your sun sign each lunar-month.

Here are a few practical guidelines to assist the art of retention,

1. Mindfulness allows you to observe and redirect your mental energy, preventing it from getting entangled in low vibrational frequencies, negative or excessive sexual thoughts. Regular meditation on the heart chakra will promote the upward movement of these essences.

2. Maintain a healthy and balanced lifestyle that includes regular exercise, proper nutrition, and sufficient sleep. Physical well-being contributes significantly to mental and emotional balance, reducing the likelihood of impulsive, mood driven behaviours.

3. The procreative essences express themselves in our work and actions so channel their intelligent energy into art, music, writing, or any hobby that captures your interest. These essences also fuel your ability to be a powerful manifestor, so spend time flexing the muscle of your imagination and join the collective consciousness in building a brighter world for us all!

4. Foster healthy relationships and social connections. Engaging in meaningful conversations can contribute to emotional well-

being and reduce the desire to "connect" or fulfil yourself in other ways.

5. Engage in practices like Qigong or Tai Chi, which involve breath control, meditation, and slow, deliberate movements aiming to balance the body's vital energy (Chi) and promote overall well-being, including the harmonious circulation of sexual energy.

6. Explore the philosophy of Karezza, a gentle, bonding form of intimacy that prioritizes emotional connection over orgasm.

7. Incorporate specific yogic practices, like bandha (energy locks) into your routine to help regulate and redirect the flow of energy within the body. There are practical exercise videos on my YouTube channel to help you.

If you do decide to explore any of these techniques, consider learning from experienced teachers or practitioners and always approach such practices with respect and a commitment to your overall well-being.

Faunalia

The definition of a "Faun" is an "imaginary" creature that is like a small man with a goat's back legs, a tail, ears, and horns. The figure of "Pan," also known as "Faunus" was illustrated as a Faun. Faunus is similar to Mr Tumnus in C.S Lewis's "The Lion, the Witch, and the Wardrobe," and synergistic with the figure "Julbock" -- the Nordic Yule goat.

The "Faunalia Festival" traditionally held on December 6th (the same day Saint Nicholas allegedly left gifts in people's boots (See Boots and Stockings), holds a symbolic connection to the "inner alchemy" or biochemistry of enlightenment. Particularly when viewed through a lens of ancient cosmology, biological shifts, and vital fluids, as related to celestial movements leading up to the winter solstice. Here are some reasons why this mythological figure, festival, and time of year align with concepts of inner transformation:

"Faunus," also known as "Inuus" or the "fructifier" was a Roman god of fertility, symbolizing the procreative force in nature, animals, and human beings. In the body this can be seen as a metaphor for the cultivation of seminal energies and essences, often referred to as Qi or Chi in Eastern traditions, which is understood to undergo subtle transformations during different seasons.

"Each year a spiritual wave of vitality enters the Earth at the winter solstice to impregnate the dormant seeds in the frozen ground, to give

> *new life to the world wherein we live, and this work is done during the winter months, while the Sun is passing through the zodiacal signs Capricorn, Aquarius, and Pisces."*
> Page 36, Ancient and Modern Initiation by Max Heindel 1929

The fertility aspect of Faunus as "Inuus" is tied to inner biological shifts. As the winter solstice approaches, the outer world enters a period of dormancy, yet the inner world of human beings is cultivating and conserving vital energies or "assembling light," much like a seed preparing for eventual growth and renewal.

The time leading up to the winter solstice is associated with deep biological shifts both in nature and within human bodies. The winter solstice (the longest night of the year) is a moment of pause and reflection, often tied to the rejuvenation of internal processes. Faunus, as the god of shepherds and herds (Shepherds and Fields), is tied to the natural rhythms of life and the care of "flocks," symbolic of the "inner shepherding" of one's vital forces. His festival, Faunalia, coinciding with early December, represents a period of gathering inner strength and nurturing life forces within. This guidance suggests the careful cultivation and management of life forces -- especially sexual or procreative energies -- during the dark period before the solstice, when such energies are said to be most vulnerable to dissipation but also most potent if conserved. Thus, devoting time to "sacred secretion" or regenerative spiritual practises particularly in the time leading up to solstice prepares the body for elevating shifts.

The Roman association of Faunus with fertility aligns with the idea that during this period, as the sun approaches its lowest point, celestial movements mirror an inner process. The descent of the sun into darkness represents the withdrawal of energy inward, allowing time for the inner alchemy to occur. This time is ripe for the cultivation of spiritual fertility, where internal energies are refined and transformed.

Pan (the Greek counterpart to Faunus), represents a deity of the wild, unrestrained natural forces, symbolizing the primordial forces within human beings associated with the "carnal" mind centred in the lower regions of the body. In inner alchemy, this raw, chaotic energy can be harnessed and refined into something more subtle and spiritual. The time leading up to solstice is a period for taming or transforming these wild inner energies, preparing for the "rebirth of the sun" in the sky, and the sun/son in you.

> *"Verily, verily, I say unto you, He that believeth on me, the works that I do shall he do also; <u>and greater works than these shall he do;</u> because I go unto my Father."*
> John 14:12-14 (KJV)

Faunalia, occurring in early December, would have been a festival marking the completion of the agricultural year and preparing for winter's inward turn. This can be metaphorically understood as a "cleansing process"—just as fields lie fallow, human beings can purify and gather their inner energies, especially vital fluids, as a preparation for the solstice. The festival served as a ritual precursor to the introspective work that follows during the darkest days of the year. This period, then, is a time of inner alchemy where, similar to agriculture, the body and mind undergo cycles of purification, renewal, and gestation.

The dual nature of Faunus as both the "wild Pan" and the "fertility god Inuus" reflects the alchemical principle of polarity—the reconciliation of opposites (See Saturn, Satan and Santa). Pan represents chaos, desire, and instinct, while Inuus represents fertility and regeneration. This duality aligns with inner alchemical processes, where the alchemist works to reconcile lower, raw energies (represented by Pan) with higher, refined spiritual forces (represented by Inuus). The process of transformation becomes especially potent during the period leading to the solstice, when light and dark are in dynamic tension.

Again, the notion that vital fluids are influenced by celestial movements at this time fits with the alchemical view that the body mirrors cosmic rhythms and the implicate order in scientific terminology. As the sun reaches its nadir, the inner world also undergoes a cyclical shift, encouraging a time of deep inward focus, conservation, and eventual transformation of vital energies.

In summary, Faunus (as Pan and Inuus), the festival of Faunalia, and the celestial movements leading up to the solstice represent a period of inner alchemical transformation. "Faunalia" marks the time when life giving molecules begin to impregnate all of nature, including our bodies in preparation for their full manifestation in spring. In preparing our bodies for this "seeding" period, we are essentially preparing our "soil" and creating the prime conditions for our inner Christmas tree to blossom and "light up."

Gabriel, the Angel of the Lord

In Matthew 1:20, the etheric messenger that visits Joseph (See Joseph) to announce the immaculate conception is called the "Angel of the Lord." Although, in the gospel of Luke the visiting angel is specifically named, "Gabriel."

In Gnosticism and the Essene gospel, Gabriel is the angel of water. Water is the element of the sacral chakra and has to do with the vital fluids of the body -- the "emotional-liquid-soul" body. In The Light of Egypt by Thomas Burgoyne, Gabriel is equated with the moon. This assignment further links Gabriel to water, since the moon governs the fluids of the earth and body.

The significance of the name Gabriel or Geburael is that it represents the "perfect man" i.e., the body, mind, and soul purified and primed in order to become a portal or vessel for understanding and receiving higher truths. The fluidic body is indeed the lens for spiritual promptings or for divine messenger "angels" to appear through.

The "Angel of the Lord" terminology used in the book of Matthew, identifies this messenger with "God" or "True Source Love" itself. This is because Angels are akin to angles of photon light coalescing in various forms in order to speak to us through the mind's eye. And the word "Lord" is a modern translation of YHWH or YHVH the divine name for the "unknowable one," the true I AM -- God!

It's the "Angel of the Lord" that appears to Moses through the burning bush, another rendering of the pineal and nervous system (tree/bush of life) set ablaze with spiritual fire or a passion to know God. The messages received by both Joseph and Moses are examples of downloads or spiritual prompts from the Most-High Intelligence, the Pure Light, the All Knowing One that resides in and through all things.

When we preserve procreative energies and essences, primarily from the "watery" sacral chakra, the channels of the body are cleansed from the residue of toxic substances, emotional debris, thought imprints, and degenerative energies. This facilitates seership and receptivity to hear and discern the voice of God, Divine Mind or the "Angel of the Lord" offering guidance and truth.

Giving and Generosity

One of the main traditions of Christmas is the giving and receiving of presents (See Presents, Presence and Gifts). Giving and receiving is a divine idea that helps make a connection with the underlying "Spiritual Substance," "True Source Love," "The Infinite Supply" -- "God."

> *"Every good gift and every perfect gift is from above, and* **cometh down from the Father of lights,** *with whom is no variableness, neither shadow of turning.*
> **James 1:17 (KJV)**

The same germinative force, "Christ" that fills the cosmos, nature and our souls stirs our spirit and fosters altruistic activities at this holy time of year. The endless resource, "God" flows endlessly from the unseen to the seen, animating every tangible life form as we experience it. Toys, gadgets, and all other material goods are simply expressions of limitless energetic supply, the only limits are the ones we create with our minds. Even money itself is a material counterpart of the divine current (currency). If you need prosperity, ask yourself, "what have I got to give?" Pray to be shown how to give, what to give, how to serve etc. and your prospering idea, your true destiny aligned purpose will come through you. The "final word from God to humanity" is given in Colossians 1:25 (KJV), ***"FULFILL THE WORD OF GOD. Even the mystery which has been hidden from ages but is now made manifest to his saints to whom God would make known the riches of the glory of this*** *mystery, which is **CHRIST IN YOU, THE HOPE OF GLORY**.*" The application of this one passage changed my entire life, giving everything to God is the same as giving everything to yourself. Going against the God in you, the truth in you, skews your integrity, and when your integrity suffers the blossoms (manifestations) of your life show up in utter disarray.

We can all choose to be "Santa Claus" this Christmas because the One Spirit, True Source Love, the GIVING Spirit lives in everyone. We can choose to let it flow for ourselves, and the ones we love *"love one another."* John 13:34 (KJV). Remember it says in James 1:17 (shared above), *"with whom is no variableness,"* -- "no variableness" means God doesn't change, natural law doesn't change, cosmic principles do not change, the law of giving and receiving (attraction) is steadfast, and so whatever you believe about yourself, and the world comes true for you. If you believe that the world is against you or bad, you will find something to impede you at every turn. But if you believe there is love and endless support in the world, then it will turn up for you abundantly, even when faced with hardship. The key is asking the univariable, supreme, amenable law of God for the ultimate solution and knowing that "he" WILL deliver. God is love, and God is ALL, therefore -- ALL IS LOVE (everything else is ILLusion, springing from the recesses of our own distorted programmes).

Once you know who and what God really is, the Infinite Giver of Life in all its fullness, you are ready to uncover life's greatest gift. It's not really a gift to be given, but rather to be revealed or uncovered, because it's always been with you. The origin of the giving and receiving practised at Christmas is a mimicking gesture, replicating the giving nature of God, *"freely ye have received, freely give"* Matthew 10:8 (KJV). The ability to both give and to receive freely is an illustration of faith, a demonstration that you, as an individual understand the infinite, endless source and supply of all -- God.

Jesus performed many miracles through his understanding of Abundant, Limitless, True Source Love... he knew it could heal the sick, recover the sight of the blind, multiply substance (fish and loaves). He was a metaphysician who understood that God is both the giver and the gift, his life aligned in service allowed him the authority (knowingness) and faith so that he could easily do those things through God. This gift lies in you also, you have the shining light of Christ within you. It multiplies and beams brighter in your heart when you are full of love, joy, appreciation and forgiveness, and the more illustrious your inner light shines, the more your metaphysical abilities become apparent.

The world is full of distractions, particularly at Christmas and these distractions are designed to lure us away from who and what we truly are, and what we're destined for (See Saturn and Saturnalia), but in the purest form, "Santa Claus" is the perfect example of the giving spirit, just as Jesus is the perfect example of the Christmas spirit. They both give freely in the spirit of true generosity and love in alignment with the abundance of God. Everything we have to give, <u>absolutely everything we have to give came from God</u> -- the giver and the gift. Without the animating power in and through all they'd be nothing, so by choosing to be the secret giver, you choose to align with the infinite power of God.

Grottos and Caves

When exploring the image of the grotto or cave there are a few parallels to bear in mind. First, the location of Christ's birth is sometimes depicted as a cave. Secondly, the tomb in which Christ's "dead" body was placed is also referred to as a "cave" in some crucifixion renditions. Then there's Santa's secret Grotto, and the cave of Brahma, both esoterically associated with the claustrum in the brain (See Claustrum).

Caves, like tombs, are places of darkness and shelter, but also of transformation. They can be seen to represent a container for the divine mystery of life and death. This mirrors the phenomenon of light emerging from darkness, much like the rebirth of the Sun at the Winter Solstice.

Several solar deities across various mythologies are associated with caves, tombs, or similar symbols that represent death and rebirth. These symbols often illustrate themes of resurrection, transformation, or the cyclical journey of the Sun. Here are some examples:

- In Roman mystery cults dedicated to Mithras, a solar deity, the cave held great symbolic importance. Mithras was often depicted as being born from a "rock or cave," representing his cosmic origin and connection to the Earth. The cave also symbolizes the cosmos, where initiates of the Mithraic mysteries underwent rituals related to spiritual rebirth. These rituals are parallel to what's now known as "dark room technique" and there's a video on my YouTube channel, specifically explaining the practise of "light deprivation" and the way initiates use it to heighten their spiritual senses. Mithras' cave setting serves as a metaphor for both the tomb and the womb, symbolizing the death of old forms and the birth of new, similar to Christ's tomb and resurrection narrative.

- Osiris, an Egyptian god of the underworld and resurrection, was associated with tombs and burial sites. His dismembered body was placed in a tomb by his wife Isis, only to be resurrected. This myth is an allegory for the solar cycle: Osiris, representing the Sun, "dies" each day and is reborn. His tomb, often symbolized as an "underground crypt," signifies death but also the promise of renewal.

- Horus, the son of Osiris and Isis, is associated with the rebirth of the Sun and is often depicted as emerging from the underworld after battling Set, the god of chaos. In some versions of the myth, Horus's rebirth can be likened to an emergence from a tomb or cave-like place after the struggle with Set, symbolizing the return of light after darkness.

- The Sumerian god Tammuz (also known as Dumuzi) is closely associated with the cycles of life, death, and rebirth. His myth tells of his "descent into the underworld," where he dies and is mourned, only to be resurrected through the efforts of his lover, the goddess Inanna (Ishtar). The underworld, in this case, serves as both a "tomb or cave and a place of transformation." His resurrection is tied to the return of fertility and the Sun's life-giving power.

- Krishna, an incarnation of Vishnu, is associated with caves in certain stories. For example, Krishna hid in a cave to avoid the wrath of King Kamsa as a child. Caves in Vedic symbolism often represent "spiritual retreats" or places of transformation, where one undergoes internal change. The cave metaphor in Krishna's life has been used esoterically to describe the journey of enlightenment and rebirth, which is akin to the solar journey through darkness into light.

- The Phrygian god Attis is a vegetation god who dies and is resurrected. He is associated with cycles of nature, especially the death and rebirth of the Earth. Attis is said to have died beneath a pine tree (See Christmas Tree, the Tree of Life), and his body was later placed in a cave, where he miraculously revived.

- Persephone's descent into the underworld and eventual return to the surface is often depicted as a journey of death and rebirth. While she resides in the underworld (a metaphorical tomb) for part of the year, her return heralds the rebirth of the Earth's fertility. Again, highlighting the Sun and the solstice, where the Sun "dies" and "resurrects" with the changing of the seasons.

- In some accounts, the Sun god Apollo retreats during the winter months to Hyperborea, a mystical land where he rejuvenates and returns with new vitality in the spring. The "Delphic Oracle" where Apollo speaks through the Pythia was often envisioned as a cave, linking it to hidden knowledge and rebirth of wisdom, aligning with esoteric traditions of solar rebirth.

- The Roman "Sol Invictus," or the "Unconquered Sun," was celebrated on December 25th. Although there is no literal tomb for Sol Invictus, the metaphor of the Sun's burial in darkness is central to the Roman story. The death and rebirth of Sol Invictus are linked to the return of longer days and the resurgence of the Sun's strength.

In each of these myths, caves, tombs, or the underworld represent periods of death, reflection, or stillness, after which the deities, like the Sun at the Winter Solstice, emerge transformed or reborn. Of course, these examples also align with personal spiritual transformation, where the soul undergoes a symbolic death before experiencing enlightenment or rebirth.

Jesus Christ

Due to the format of this book, some of the points to be made in this entry are covered elsewhere in the introduction and other entries. For the sake of clarity and credit, I decided to keep an entry solely dedicated to perhaps the most universal Christmas Symbol of all --Beautiful Jesus Christ – the Creative Light, the man, the myth, the legend – the oil!

This is a VAST topic, with many overlapping ideas, so I will do my best to keep the perspectives as concise as possible without losing any of the main themes and without belittling the miraculous beauty that Jesus Christ encapsulates.

The cosmos includes many incredible layers of creation from the tiny, microscopic phenomena of the microcosm to the inspiring enormity of the star nurseries and stellar "objects" of the macrocosm. Then of course there are multiple layers in-between that all play a synchronous role in maintaining the material world as we perceive it. For this reason, it's paramount to explore Jesus Christ in relation to the most prominent layers of creation including:

- Jesus in association with the sun in the sky

- Jesus as a historical person

- Jesus as the I AM or as Consciousness

- Jesus as an Oil or Seed (Word)

- Jesus in relation to Kundalini.

Jesus Christ the Sun (Son) of God:

If you've heard of the "gospel in the stars," then you'll be well aware of this correspondence. But here are a few points to highlight the correlation between Jesus Christ and the Sun in the sky. In John 8:12, Jesus – the SON, is referred to as the *"Light of the World."* This is also true of the SUN which is of course the primary source of light on Earth. This cosmic principle is highlighted at Christmas, when the SUN goes down through the Southern CROSS constellation, which is parallel to Jesus, the SON'S crucifixion on the cross. For approximately three and a half days thereafter, the astronomical phenomenon known as "sun-pause" occurs, this is when the SUN is said to "go dark" or "lay in a tomb" (just like the SON did). On or around December 25th the SUN "restarts" and begins its upward trajectory – this is associated with the resurrection of Jesus the SON (and other solar deities featured in different cultures).

Another parallel is Jesus (the SONS) 12 disciples which can be seen to reflect the SUNS 12 zodiac signs. The fact that many old churches were built with windows specifically coloured, shaped, and angled to absorb and filter specific creative SUN influences (photonic energy) while people worship the SON and listen to sermons about the SON shows a deep reverence for the power of the SUN!

The SUN forges oxygen atoms (888) and nitrogen atoms (777) in its core – the form and value of both these creative elements also relate to the gematria of the name Jesus Christ – isn't that uncanny! When the suns light is absorbed by the body it forms nitric oxide, a molecule of health that the body cannot function without.

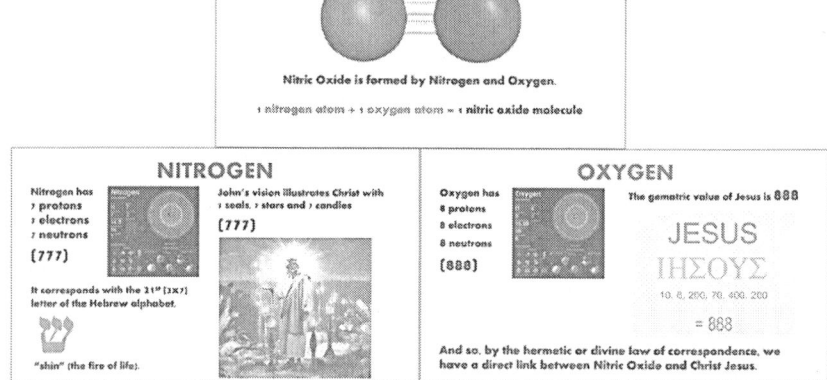

This is all very compelling in highlighting the macro and microcosmic reflections of Jesus's identity.

Jesus Christ as Consciousness:

The SUN is not merely a stellar "object" (as science puts it), but an intelligent, divine, creative force or consciousness. Since the sun in the sky pervasively powers and animates all life as we know it, we *could* also say that it enables us to be conscious or to have consciousness. Consciousness is really the power to have thought or the ability to reflect and perceive "reality" -- the seemingly simple capability to consider and say the words "I AM," "JE SUIS," JESUS" is actually a complex miracle! Since we're made, *"in the image (imagination) and likeness/sameness as God,"* it makes sense that, like God, we too "image" and think reality into being through consciousness as individual "sons."

> *"O, Almighty God, I am thinking Thy thoughts after Thee!"*
> Page 112, The Harmonies of the World by Johannes Kepler, 1619.

The suns radiant energy nourishes and sustains us, awakening consciousness within us. Like a divine source of light, the SUN generates and illuminates our souls, guiding us on our spiritual journey. In the SUN, we find the essence of life itself, endless-miraculous-creative-energy. It forges the atoms that construct "reality" -- these atoms are in all and through all, including being within every cell of our temple body's, again making us individual SONS in the image and likeness of Source. This reminds us of our interconnectedness with all of creation.

Jesus Christ the Person

Research, along with wonderful personal experiences of healing, and transformation gives me the opinion that the Bibles Jesus Christ "person" is the amalgamation of two major aspects.

1. "He" is a personification, symbol and metaphor representing the sacred sciences and divine principles serving to illustrate our own spiritual nature and capabilities (The symbol of his 33 years of life falls into this category).

2. "He" was an actual person, a "mystery man" -- not known by the name "Jesus Christ" until much later. A metaphysician so aligned to True Source Love (God) that his capabilities knew no bounds; he was a Christed or Anointed one so rich in Love and Wisdom that he sought to share his knowledge with the world and was adored far and wide for it. This same person was

considered a threat to the tyrannical authorities that attempted to delete him from history.

Let's explore --

ASPECT 1: A Personification, Symbol, and Metaphor.

> *"It will amaze the reader to see how skilfully the Masters and writers saved their Sacred Science from destruction and preserved it, in symbol and allegory, in the Fictitious and Fabulous life of Jesus Christ."*
> Page XIII, Who Was Jesus by Hilton Hotema

Etymology tells us that the name "Jesus" from the root "Ya" or" Ye" means I AM, and that "Christ" (the status) means oil or anointing. This name deliberately points to something broader than just one individual being. And this notion is further validated in John 14:12 (KJV),

*"Verily, verily, I say unto you, He that believeth on me, the works that I do shall he do also; **and greater works than these shall he do.**"*

Here, the character/person "Jesus" is telling us that we too have the potential to perform miracles and to transform the solar energy inside atoms to shift realities and heal illusions with our minds, AND on an even greater scale than he did! So, "his" power was never proclaimed to be limited to just one person. The "I am" is in and through all of us.

ASPECT 2: (of the personal Christ) The Master and Metaphysician

Exhaustive research shows that the mystery man that the writers of the New Testament, under the rule of the emperor Constantine, most likely based the life of their "Jesus Christ" on is "Apollonius of Tyana." *"The Life of Apollonius of Tyana,"* by Philostratus explains how the New Testament writers incorporated similar miraculous deeds and teachings originally attributed to the sage and master Apollonius of Tyana into the narrative of Jesus Christ. And Dr Hilton Hotema describes how Apollonius's name was replaced with the name Jesus,

> *"The fourth gospel (John) was compiled from a biography on Apollonius, written by Damis, a Greek historian. The compiler had orders to delete the name Apollonius wherever it appeared and insert the name Jesus. Then the original manuscript was to be destroyed, but it was not."*
> **Page 4, More Pious Fraud by Dr Hilton Hotema**

"Yeshua," "Yahushua," "Apollonius," later dubbed "Jesus" was said to be a Nasarean Essene believed to be the Messiah. This Messiah had many run-ins with the religious rulers of his day (the Pharisees and the Sadducees). The Essenes were (are) known as "the immoveable light race." They practised certain types of asceticism (veganism and chastity) in isolation and studied the sacred sciences of nature -- including celestial prophecy and star mapping, plant medicine, energy healing, sound healing through chanting and reading spiritual texts, and purifying themselves toward ascension (See Angelo Morphism). They did not worship at the temple in Jerusalem, because they believed the priesthood had been corrupted, and they did not perform animal sacrifices. Apollonius has been linked to the Qumran Essenes where the Dead Sea Scrolls were discovered, but there were other practising Essene groups in places like Mount Carmel as well.

Through his practises, "Jesus" or "Apollonius" was a great metaphysician, directly aligned with the infinite power of True Source Love -- God, which allowed him to perform many miracles. Unfortunately, it seems that by the switching of names and the deletion of certain Scriptures any obvious wisdom or knowledge that could empower or inform the average person about their own divine nature was lost and forbidden. These altered teachings made people look outside of themselves, rather than focusing within and attuning their own metaphysical capabilities.

> *"The emperor Constantine would invent a new religion, sell it to the people of his vast realm, and by this means **destroy the Ancient Arcane Science.** The Masters were too clever to be outwitted by Constantine. They met him at his own game, prepared the New Testament as he directed, -- but skilfully made the gospel Jesus play a double role. For the exoteric, he was the Lord and Saviour of humanity; but for the esoteric, he was a symbol of cosmic principles and spiritual processes. There was nothing new in that. **The writings of the master's always contained dual messages,** -- one intended for the profane (general population) and one intended for the initiates and disciples."*
>
> Page 28, The Apocalypse: A Series of Special Lectures on the Revelation of Jesus Christ, 1892 by J M Roberts

Dr Hilton Hotema summarises the life of Apollonius of Tyana, the inspiration for the Bibles Jesus Christ as follows,

> *"1. He was the most wonderful man the world had ever known,*
>
> *2. He lived the greatest life that history records,*
>
> *3. He changed the destiny of man and was worshipped by millions,*

> *4. Then he became the most feared man of any man that ever lived,*
>
> *5. His very name was erased from the pages of history,*
>
> *6. The encyclopaedias declare that he was only a mythical character,*
>
> *7. Because of him people were slaughtered, cities depopulated, and blood flowed in streams, (Leaders of the Crusades were ordered to bring back the mystery man dead or alive).*
>
> *8. His writings were burned, and men were forbidden to speak his name,*
>
> *9. He then became the God of a new religion under a new name (Jesus Christ),*
>
> *10. That caused the crash of the greatest nation on Earth and a reign of darkness that lasted for a thousand years."*
>
> **Page 27, Awaken the World Within by Hilton Hotema**

With all this in mind, it can indeed be seen that Jesus Christ -- the greatest, noblest, wisest, most compassionate, and powerful man that ever lived, AND his life and works are an amalgamation of two aspects 1) The sacred sciences (veiled in symbolism), 2) History.

This does not diminish the importance or power that the Bibles Jesus encapsulates, just because the name was changed, and the stories were altered doesn't mean that the miracles, and incredible acts of unconditional love, and ultimately full transcendence are any less real or any less inspiring. In fact, Jesus Christ being both symbolic of sacred sciences AND based on a sole individuals' achievements in the realms of metaphysics makes the teachings even more profound as something we can embody and aspire to.

> *"Through mental (thought) energy or the dynamic power of the mind, man can release the life of the electrons secreted in the atoms that compose the cells of his body... ...you weren't born to die. You were born to harness your full atomic capabilities!"*
> Page 4, The Twelve Powers of Man by Charles Fillmore

It's through the sacred sciences that healing, and "resurrection" or transcendence become possibilities, for example research shows different accounts of ascended masters that attained such seemingly impossible feats -- Ramtha, from "The White Book", claims to have transcended death, taking his physical body with him and traveling through different dimensions. Figures like Saint Germain and Sanat Kumara are also considered ascended masters in Theosophical teachings, having achieved spiritual mastery and ascension beyond physical death. According to some Taoist legends, the ancient Chinese philosopher Lao Tzu is said to have ascended to the stars, and Mahavatar Babaji is described as an immortal yogi who has transcended death and continues to guide spiritual aspirants toward enlightenment. His story is popularized in the "Autobiography of a Yogi" by Paramahansa Yogananda. Each of these figures represents the idea of transcending physical existence, often through inner spiritual transformation, the practice of sacred knowledge, or through mystical and esoteric traditions. Their stories are used to illustrate the potential of the human soul to rise above material limits.

Arguably, the dual aspects of symbol and fact intwined in the story of Jesus Christ have affected the world and our collective consciousness more profoundly than any other. Jesus Christ is the embodiment of unconditional love, and that's something to aspire to! The effect of thinking or meditating on such a high power literally shifts the alchemy of the body – and that's sacred science in play!

> *"Contrary to Jesus' life, Apollonius's life is well documented. He is a well-known historical character and son of wealthy parents. He had stored his vast intellect with the religious doctrines of the whole world, from Spain to India, and his life extended well over a century, one author asserting that he lived to 130. Like a luminous meteor he traversed the earth, in constant intercourse with kings and the powerful ones of the world, who venerated and feared him. If he ever met with opposition, he triumphed over it majestically, always stronger than his tyrants, never subject to humiliation, and never brought into contact with public executioners."*
>
> Page 32, The Apocalypse: A Series of Special Lectures on the Revelation of Jesus Christ, 1892 by J M Roberts

Jesus Christ the Myth

A wonderful book by Kersey Graves called "Sixteen Crucified Saviours" highlights the fact that history documents many Christ-like characters in different cultures all throughout history including, but not limited to:

- Thulis of Egypt

- Prometheus of Caucasus

- Atys of Phrygia

- Mithras of Persia

- Osiris of Egypt

- Krishna of India

Many people are unaware that before Constantine's Christianity and the introduction of Jesus Christ there were at least 15 other "saviours" who were said to be crucified and resurrected from the dead. Some were also said to be born of immaculate conception like Jesus, and many allegedly share the same birthday (December 25th). Graves lists an astonishing 346 similarities between Christ and the Hindu God Krishna. This all highlights the way in which their "lives" parallel solar/sun cycles and therefore signify sacred sciences and divine principles.

These saviours all symbolise or mirror the divine power of both the sun of the macrocosm and the tiny, miniscule suns (electrons) of our individual solar body's.

> *"Know ye not that ye are the temple of God, and that the Spirit of God dwelleth in you?"*
> **1 Corinthians 3:16 (KJV)**

Jesus Christ -- the Seed (Word), Oil, Fish and the Kundalini.

> *"In the beginning was the Word, and the Word was with God, and the Word WAS God."*
> **John 1:1 (KJV)**

This clearly states that the WORD and GOD are the same. Then we have Luke 8:11, *"Now the parable is this: the Seed IS the Word of God."* Illustrating, that the SEED is also the same as the WORD which again, is the same as GOD! In other words – GOD, SEED, and WORD are synonymous or synergistic. So, when John 1:14 (KJV) says, *"And the Word was made flesh"* in reference to Jesus, it's also saying -- "The SEED was made flesh," or "GOD was made flesh."

The "Word", "Seed", or "God" becomes flesh via the majestic "oil" also known as Christ Oil, Soma, or Chrism. This substance is 1) inside EVERY cell of our body, as cytoplasm/protoplasm, 2) outside every cell of your body, as the extracellular matrix, 3) inside the spinal cord as CSF, 4) inside the brain as glymphatic fluid, and 5) throughout the body as "lymph fluid," which includes bone marrow and the substances in the spleen. Historically these fluids weren't differentiated with varied labels like they are in the modern world but where all classed as the "white blood" system, the "blood of the lamb." In other words, this majestic "oil" is the lymphatic system in all its various manifestations (spleen, marrow, CSF, glymph etc.).

> *"If we analyse this material point at which all life starts, we shall find it to consist of a clear structureless, jelly-like substance resembling oil, albumen, or egg white. It is made of carbon, hydrogen, oxygen, and nitrogen. Its name is protoplasm. And it is not only the structural unit with which all living bodies start in life, but with which they are subsequently built up. 'Protoplasm' says Huxley, 'simple or nucleated', is the formal basis of all life. It is the clay of the potter."*
> **Page 319, Manly P Hall, The Secret Teachings of All Ages**

In this excerpt, Hall highlights the fact that this "Christ" substance is the basis for all manifest life, and that it contains carbon, hydrogen, oxygen, and nitrogen. Remember, the structure of those last two elements relate specifically to the name Jesus (Oxygen 888) Christ (Nitrogen 777) -- the SON or SUN. And of course, all four of the elements that make up "protoplasm" are made from miniscule SUNS called ELECTRONS,

> *"ALL LIFE DEPENDS ON A SMALL TRICKLE OF ELECTRONS FROM THE SUN."*
> **Pages Unnumbered. Introduction to Submolecular Biology, by Nobel prize laureate Szent-Gyorgyi**

The SEED, WORD, OR GOD becomes "flesh" (manifest) via the "oil" because all those miniscule SUNS (electrons) forming the "oil" are poised and ready to merge and coalesce into DNA and consequently create all the cells of the body from the inside out! This explains how not only mystically, but scientifically also, "Jesus Christ" is also a symbol for the innate "God" power in and through all of us.

> *"I have said, Ye are gods; and ALL of you are children of the most high."*
> **Psalm 82:6 (KJV)**

We are all ONE with Jesus Christ, the Sun and Son – we are all sons, and reflections of the living God (True Source Love). *"In him was life; and the life was the light of men."* John 1:4 (KJV)

Synergistically all these multiple "layers of Christ" further relate to "Kundalini energy". As explained on previous pages, Nitric Oxide is made up of Oxygen 888 the so-called Jesus Atom and Nitrogen 777 – the Christ atom.

> "Tingles and bubbles are always associated with increased kundalini flow. There is some indication that the tingles are **associated with increased nitric oxide.**"
> Page 43, The Biology of Kundalini by Jana Dixon

Nitric oxide is essential for the metabolism of ALL CELLULAR GENERATION and REGENERATION. So, with enhanced nitric oxide flow, comes the stimulation of kundalini (the Holy Spirit/Jesus Christ within).

Jesus Christ as the "fish" also resonates with the procreative energies and essences of the body. Seminal fluid and lymph fluid are very similar in composition and are also inexplicably interwoven. Any excess seminal fluid, i.e., procreative substances that are not "wasted" or expelled from the body are available to be reabsorbed and transported away by the lymphatic system. Lymphatic vessels then carry the seminal fluid to nearby lymph nodes which act as filtering stations, where lymphatic fluid, including absorbed seminal fluid, is examined for pathogens, cellular debris, and other foreign substances. After filtration, the cleansed lymphatic fluid, which now contains the absorbed seminal fluid, is returned to the bloodstream through the right lymphatic duct. From there, the fluid is circulated back into the bloodstream, where it can be redistributed throughout the body. The filtered seminal fluid enriches and improves the quality of lymphatic fluid, blood, and consequently other parts of the body because it contains various nutrients, hormones, and other bioactive substances that contribute to our overall health and vitality (the awakening and regenerating of the temple body).

Historically the lymphatic system was known as the "white blood system," and was revered for its marvellous role in the temple body. The "white blood system" mediates between manifest and unmanifest worlds because its where stem cells (the new life of the body) are born, proliferated, and differentiated. Some experts in the esoteric field regard the purified and charged "white blood system" as being part and parcel with John's vision of Christ and the ascension body,

> *"I turned to see the voice that spoke to me,*
>
> *And being turned, I saw seven golden candles;*
>
> *And in the midst of their blazing light*
>
> *I saw someone like a son of man,*
>
> *Clothed in white, white as the snow.*
>
> *And his voice filled the air with the sound of rushing water;*
>
> *And in his hands were seven stars,*
>
> *And when he spoke, his face was streaming light,*
>
> *Blazing and golden like a thousand suns."*
>
> **Essene Book of Revelations**

The layer of the micro-macrocosmic creation that see's Jesus Christ as "The Cell of Life" born in the manger every 29.5 days has been discussed at great length in The Cell of Life: Awakening and Regenerating which is devoted to that topic, and is also explained in the "Manger" entry of this book, but it's important to again highlight the perspective that "Jesus Christ" is also found on this interconnected level of perceived reality too. *"Jesus is a germ/seed of life,"* G W Carey.

In conclusion, the multifaceted character of Jesus Christ encompasses various layers of interpretation, each revealing profound insights into the nature of existence and the human experience.

- From the cosmic perspective, Jesus Christ is intricately linked with the sun, symbolizing divine light and life-giving energy.

- On a metaphysical level, Jesus Christ represents consciousness itself, the divine spark within each of us that connects us to the source of all creation.

- Historically, Jesus Christ is a figure shrouded in mystery and symbolism. While some aspects of his life may be based on historical events, others are allegorical representations of sacred principles and universal truths.

- The figure of Jesus Christ is also intertwined with ancient wisdom traditions and mythologies.

- Jesus Christ embodies the concept of the "Word" or divine Logos, the creative force that gives birth to all life and the symbolism of the "Seed" or "Oil" represents the sacred essence within us.

- The fish symbol, another emblem of Jesus Christ, represents abundance and fertility, reflecting the procreative energies and their potential to lift health and consciousness to profound new levels.

- Jesus Christ is associated with Kundalini energy, the primal life force that resides within us and is roused to life by our devotion to truth and love.

In beauty and essence, Jesus Christ embodies the interconnectedness of all life, the all-pervasive creative love that promotes life and wellness. On every level Jesus Christ is a signpost on the eternal quest for spiritual awakening and enlightenment. Whether viewed from a cosmic, spiritual, historical, or symbolic perspective, Jesus Christ continues to inspire and guide humanity on its journey of self-discovery and gracious transformation.

Joseph – Jesus's Father

In Matthew 1:20, the "Angel of God" tells Joseph not to be afraid and to take Mary as his wife, because the child, conceived in her is produced from immaculate conception.

Mary is the "pure water" of the soul (see Mary – The Virgin Mother), making Joseph the pure "electric" potential or spirit of the universe and body. Mary and Joseph, "water and spirit," are examples of the two poles of dual life force (see Dual Life Force). It states in the Bible that, spiritual rebirth and baptism occurs only by "water and fire/spirit". Water coincides with the pituitary gland and the moons (masa's) cooling, filtering, forming, and ever renewing influence, and fire or spirit coincides with the pineal gland and the suns (Christs) empowering, continuous life force. This reminds us of the baptismal opportunity presented with the word and event called "Christ-Mas."

In the Body, Joseph coincides with the pineal gland – the piezoelectric sunshine gland, the gland that receives and circulates solar light through the body. This "fire of life" is what mingles with the "pure water" (Mary) of the body to create new cells. In "The Perfect Way," Anna Kingsford assigns the pineal secretions to the nucleoli and nucleus of each cell (where Mary is the soma/cytoplasm). In the entry for "Coal, Lead and Carbon" we explored how carbon is the key element implicated in drawing these to "Mary" and "Joseph" substances together.

In Genesis 49:22, Joseph is called *"the fruitful branch by the water well."* This imagery illustrates the antennae (branch) of the pineal gland reaching into the pool (ventricle) of CSF surrounding it, which is part of the lymphatic system. Many worldly "antennae" such as the Eifel Tower, and the Burj Khalifa are replicated after this divine bodily blueprint. Manly P Hall calls the pineal "antennae" the "Holy Spear," and many spiritual practices are designed to increase the vibratory frequency of this gland, and the piezoelectric crystals contained within it in order to experience the "falling veil" or to witness the connecting link between human and divine consciousness.

To be "reborn of fire" is to come into the realisation or consciousness of divine law. Meaning, through "bhakti" analogous with the "compassion of Christ" you've embodied truth and raised the vibratory frequency of all your cells and atoms. By realising the truth of your abundant, fully creative nature as a being of unconditional love and limitless potential you consequently upgrade the alchemy of your temple body, and the pineal gland is stimulated to release the biochemicals of enlightenment. Simultaneously, the "veil" falls and all kinds of "revelations" about supernatural phenomena are witnessed.

Julbastu (Sauna)

The "Julbastu," or Christmas sauna, is a deeply rooted Scandinavian tradition that dates back to pre-Christian times. In Finland and Sweden, the sauna (or "bastu") was a sacred place used for both spiritual cleansing and physical regeneration. During the Christmas season, it was customary to purify the body and spirit in a sauna before the holiday festivities, symbolizing a fresh start, both physically and spiritually. This tradition is closely tied to the ancient Norse Yule celebrations, which centred around the winter solstice, a time of renewal and rebirth as the sun returned.

The sauna was considered a sacred space in Nordic and Baltic cultures, and it was often associated with rites of passage, healing, and spiritual practices. Invoking a centred, relaxed and transcendent state, the sauna was seen as a place where people could commune with nature, their ancestors (passed and present), and the divine. It was thought that spirits could enter the sauna, and special rituals were performed to invite health, protection, and good fortune for the coming year.

The sauna became a key part of the Christmas season after the Christianization of the region, symbolizing the purification of body and soul in preparation for the celebration of Christ's birth. It was often used on Christmas Eve, and entire families would partake in the ritual to cleanse themselves before attending church or beginning their festivities. There are many Biblical scriptures that refer to cleansing rituals performed by heat, for example:

> *"But who can endure the day of his coming? And who can stand when He appears? For He is like a refiner's fire and like launderers' soap."*
> Malachi 3:2 (KJV)

This verse uses the imagery of fire as a purifying force. Although it's metaphorical and refers to the true inner process of detoxification and purging, the refining fire can be linked to the outward heat of a sauna, which can aid cleansing and purification of both body and spirit.

Health Benefits of Saunas:

- **Detoxification:** The lymphatic system is responsible for removing toxins and waste from the body. Saunas promote sweating, which aids in the excretion of toxins, including heavy metals and metabolic waste. The heat from the sauna helps increase circulation, encouraging lymphatic flow and allowing the body to detoxify more efficiently.

  Since the lymphatic system doesn't have its own pump, like the heart does for the circulatory system, it relies on muscle movement and heat to stimulate flow. The heat from a sauna can help dilate blood vessels and encourage the movement of lymphatic fluids, helping to reduce swelling and improve immune function. A lesser-known way to help clear the lymph is via "bio-photonic energy lymphatic detoxification (BELD)" a therapy hailed for its ability deeply cleanse any blockages in the cellular terrain of the body.

- **Relaxation and Stress Relief:** Saunas are known to reduce stress by lowering levels of cortisol, the body's main stress hormone. Heat also encourages the release of endorphins, which are natural pain relievers and mood enhancers. This can help calm the nervous system and promote relaxation, making the body more resilient to stress and anxiety.

  Some research suggests that exposure to heat in a sauna can promote the production of heat shock proteins, which play a role in protecting and repairing cells, including neurons (brain cells). This could potentially support the regeneration of the nervous system and improve overall cognitive function.

- **Improved Circulation:** The increased circulation caused by the heat in a sauna delivers more oxygen and nutrients to tissues and cells, promoting faster healing and regeneration. This can also improve skin health by stimulating collagen production and enhancing the skin's ability to repair itself.

- **Autophagy:** Regular sauna use has been linked to autophagy, the body's process of cleaning out damaged cells and regenerating newer, healthier ones. This cellular "self-cleaning" process is crucial for maintaining health and longevity, and saunas can help stimulate this natural detox and regeneration mechanism.

- **Boost to Immunity:** The heat and steam in a sauna can also stimulate white blood cell production, which boosts the immune system's ability to fight off infections. This is particularly useful during the winter months, when cold and flu viruses are arguably more prevalent.

The combination of the physical detoxification, emotional relaxation, and spiritual purification offered by a sauna session during the Christmas season taps into the ancient belief in the body-mind connection. Just as the sun is reborn during the solstice, the individual is also "reborn", and cleansing is an integral part of the rebirth process. Thus, Julbastu can be seen as a useful practise for promoting the inner solstice. Julbastu at Christmas is a powerful ritual of renewal and cleansing.

King Herod

King Herod is the villain of the Biblical Christmas story. Matthew 2:13 describes the "Angel of the Lord" telling Joseph that Herod is seeking the baby Jesus's whereabouts in order to destroy him.

The name Herod stems from the roots "he" and "rod" i.e., "his-rod." Rods, staffs, candy canes, and shepherd crooks are all synergistic with the spine in the body and the axis of the universe in the macrocosm. He-ROD signifies the material aspects of the spine and central nervous system which are programmed by divine (natural) law and cannot be hacked i.e., it cannot deviate from law (Torah). In other words, its set by the limitations of material form and must be transcended.

"Herod" is the "King" of the body because it rules over it and supersedes other bodily functions. Only by right living, thinking, and feeling can we prevent the baby Jesus (seed or cell) from being destroyed by the "downward" force of Herod. The "Christ Seed" of super consciousness awakening is the highest concept of life that man can possess, but "Herod" calls for the destruction of that essence thus preventing the literal mitosis and regeneration of body cells from the inside out i.e., spiritual rebirth.

"If your consciousness is established in materiality (Herod) and has no expectation of spiritual life, the germ is destroyed and passes away -- this is the death of the first born of the Egyptians. If the mind is set on higher things, then the germ is saved from destruction; it is retained in

> *the organism, goes through a regenerating process, is multiplied, and eventually strengthens the whole man."*
> **Page 727, The Metaphysical Bible Dictionary by Charles Fillmore**

Via retention and spiritual practise, Herod must be overcome. As the initiate master's their inner alchemy, the spine transforms into a rod of ascension, channelling the mystical dance of Kundalini energy (Creative Light) into all the cells and atoms of the body. The celestial current on the energetic plane, is akin to Christ Oil (CSF) on the chemical plane -- in a clear and truth-aligned vessel it rises and anoints the brain, illuminating the path of limitless potential and unconditional love.

> *"The generative urgency, which, when we are loose, dissipates and makes us unclean, when we are continent invigorates and inspires us. Chastity is the flowering (**bud**ding, **Bud**ha mind); and what are called genius, heroism, holiness, and the like, are but various fruits which succeed it."*
> **Henry David Thoreau**

When an initiate (child of Shekinah) first discovers this knowledge, they are enthusiastic about awakening and developing their inner self and excitedly start talking to others about it and wanting them to follow the same path. But these teachings are for *"those with eyes to see, and ears to hear,"* and even if the individual believes that their friend or acquaintance is ready for this knowledge they may well not be.

Then the initiate finds that other people's energies, responses, and scepticisms start to form doubts in their own mind. This is another example of Herod, the opposing force. Herod also represents the outside (material) world on the sensory plane, and there is an egotistical, self-preserving "Herod" inside the mind of every single person. It's challenge enough to overcome or reconcile with our own personal Herod without worrying about others, and by natural law we deal with the outer Herod's in properly dealing with our own inner Herod. As within, so without -- this process starts and ends with you.

With all this in mind, we can see why, to a degree, and particularly at the beginning of one's path, it may be wise for the initiate to keep their mystical experiences to themselves. Unless being specifically asked to share. It's been advised that in order for each person to truly help humanity, that first of all, the Lord (Creative Light) needs to grow, mature and produce **unswerving faith** inside the individual before they take their teachings to the world (if they still feel compelled to do so).

Lucy's Day

St. Lucy, or Santa Lucia, is a significant figure in Christian and pre-Christian traditions, with connections to both Christian martyrdom and ancient pagan symbols of light. St. Lucy is believed to have been a Christian martyr from the 3rd century, known for her unwavering faith and refusal to marry a pagan man. According to legend, she gave her dowry to the poor and was tortured for her beliefs, leading to her martyrdom in 304AD during the Diocletian Persecution.

St. Lucy's Day, celebrated on the 13th of December, aligns with ancient pagan celebrations of light and winter solstice traditions. In Scandinavian countries, this holiday incorporates elements of pre-Christian winter solstice rituals, which honoured the return of the sun and the lengthening of daylight. St. Lucy is often connected with deities or personifications of light in various cultures, such as the Norse goddess "Sol," representing the sun.

Lucy's name comes from the Latin "Luci" as in "Lucifer" and "lux," meaning light. In Scandinavian customs, she is depicted with a crown of candles, symbolizing the triumph of light over darkness during the long winter months. This reflects halo symbology and perhaps the "crown of thorns" worn by Jesus.

Jesus' "crown of thorns" is akin to the "crown of life." When light assembles in the body it forms an actual halo (light ring or sphere). The physiological alchemy (biochemistry) that causes the halo, is an alteration and accumulation of mineral salts in and around the brain. Some of the saints' "halos" were so vibrant they even became visible on the outside. Some esotericists believe that the "crown of thorns" is a deliberately disturbing illustration, made to be a misleading symbol that veils the inner alchemical process of enlightenment. Sometimes divine secrets were hidden behind vulgar masks to deter curious minds and maintain control. "Kalium" is the thorny bush used to make Jesus's crown of thorns, and kalium is also the former name for the mineral potassium. This is a deep alchemical symbol.

> *"Another way of saying "crown of thorns" would be "halo of potassium" – the name Kali, short for Kalium comes from the name of the thorny bush that was burned to make potash (potassium)."*
> Page 100, "Elevation: The Divine Power of the Human Body" By Kelly-Marie Kerr

Potassium AKA "Kalium" brightens the synapses of the brain. Thus the "crown of thorns" is the "halo of enlightenment" -- the "illumined" or "Christed/Anointed" mind. It is almost certainly a reference to thorny kalium bushes and the inward transmutation that involves sodium/potassium channels which are the bodies bioelectricity. According to Strong's Bible concordance (Entry 1253), Potassium or Potash is represented by the word "Lye". "Lye" stems from the root "barar," meaning "to purify or select." The Book of Isaiah mentions the burning of calcium and potassium in verse 33:1 (KJV), *"And the people shall be as the burnings of lime (calcium), as thorns (Kali – potassium) cut up shall they be burned in the fire."*

St. Lucy is often represented holding a dish with her eyes on it and wearing a crown of candles (halo) on her head. The platter of eyes comes from the legend that her eyes were gouged out as part of her martyrdom but were miraculously restored. Her connection to sight and light makes her a patron saint of the blind and those with eye-related illnesses. If

Lucy holding her outer two-eyes on a plate is an emblem for the inner solstice, I'd assume that this illustration highlights the prevalence of the one-inner-eye (third) eye -- when the illusion of reality, fed by the outer eyes disappears. Closing our two outer eyes, stimulates melatonin release, and looking toward the third eye (light of the chamber) in meditation promotes supernatural sight and spiritual vision.

St. Lucy (or Santa Lucia) embodies the merging of Christian martyrdom with ancient solstice traditions, serving as a symbol of light and hope during the darkest time of the year. Her celebration marks both spiritual and natural regeneration, reflecting light's overcoming of darkness.

Manger

Luke 2:11 tells us that Mary birthed her first child, wrapped him in swaddling clothes and laid him in a manger.

The microcosmic "manger" is in the spleen, which is supplied and vitalised by the nerves of the solar plexus (see Bethlehem). **The spleen is part of the lymphatic system, a key player in the purification of the temple body.** Specifically, the spleens "germinal centre" where cells (seeds) are generated is the "manger" where the "Jesus seed" is "born."

> **"This gift is, the everlasting life, the psychophysical Christ germ seed of immortality.** *And when the majestic, priceless Christmas present is used wisely, according to the nuclear physics laws, it shall return you to your original state of divinity, the union with the Spirit of God, the creator. That is what the coming of the Christ unto woman and man means."*
> Pages Unnumbered, 144 Cubits Books I – Xxenogenesis by Xxey.

The pituitary (Mary) and pineal (Joseph) streams flow down from the brain through the left and right sides of the autonomic nervous system, also known as the Ida and Pingala Nadis to the solar plexus and specifically into the spleen.

> *"...The spleen mysteriously creates cells; it does this by enclosing a minute body from the cerebrum within a case. Thus, within the spleen is formed the TRUE PHYSIOLOGICAL SEEDS (CELLS) OF THE BODY..."*
> Page 111, Zodiac, and the Salts of Salvation by G W Carey

The spleens germinal centres are sites of multipotent stem cell production. Therefore, the esoteric Jesus-Seed, "Germ" or "Cell" of Life is parallel with stem cells generated in the spleen.

Multipotent stem cells are infant (baby) cells which have the ability to become many types of bodily cells, thus through their production we are replenished, invigorated, and renewed at a cellular level (from the inside out).

In the diagram, the "SOLAR GERM – Electric, Fire "Joseph" - pineal potency" is labelled "c/d" and the "LUNAR GERM – Magnetic, Water "Mary" pituitary potency" is labelled "a/b".

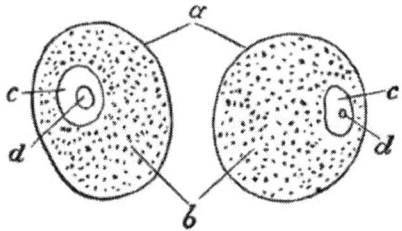

Cells of Round or Oval Form.
a, Border of the cell or cell-wall; *b*, cell substance;
c c, nuclei; *d d*, nucleoli.

Carbon is one of the elements that helps fuse these two potencies, and together they form stem cells, or the "Jesus seed" born in a manger (spleen) in the town of Bethlehem (the solar plexus) every 29.5 days, when the moon is traversing through your sun sign (See Regeneration Calendar), and additionally during solstice when the fluids of the body are stimulated by cosmic movements.

This is what being reborn of water and of fire means on a physiological level -- the mitosis and regeneration of the body from the inside (cellular level) to the outside!

Mary – The Virgin Mother

The virgin mother of the Christmas Story signifies what mystics call, the "water of life" -- "the mother substance."

In many cultures it is a spiritual belief that ocean water is the essence of all life. Foetal development occurs in the pure water (amniotic fluid) of the womb and the cells of the body develop in the pure water (Lymph -- including CSF, Marrow and Glymph). The concentration of "salt-water" inside cells is similar to that of the worldwide ocean. Water is the divine creative substance, the immaculate mother of all things, even air (vapour) is a higher potency of water.

> *"There is nothing from which flesh and blood can be made, but this one universal air (water), energy, or spirit, in which man has his being."*
> Page 32, The Zodiac and the Salts of Salvation by G. W. Carey

In Luke 1:30 the "Angel of the Lord" tells Mary not to fear and that she will conceive and birth a son named Jesus. The Jesus "baby," "fish," or "seed" (cell) is born in the living water of "Mother Mer" (Mer means sea). This sentence sounds mystical, but when we consider the two sides of the DNA "ladder" or double helix emerging in spirals, circling like swimming fish as they rise from the creative water (cytoplasm) in cells, suddenly the imagery comes to life and makes plain sense! DNA is literally bathed in "seawater," which plays a crucial role in establishing DNA's winding structure.

Mary is Mother Earth, Mother Nature, the pure (virgin) substance -- "Prima Materia" or "First Matter." "She" corresponds with the watery soul body (Lymph and all its forms), pituitary secretions, and the "soma" or cytoplasm/protoplasm of every cell.

> *"This is the water of life which so often occurs in mythological stories, the alchemist's aqua vitae. The "water" is 'our heavenly fluid' which does not wet the hands. It is not the ordinary sort."*
> Page 113, a Rosicrucian Notebook by Willy Shrodter

When we purify the vital fluids of our bodies, they become virginal or "chaste" – primed for regeneration, and the birth of new cells ("baby" stem cells). The state of our internal waters affect the DNA produced in cells, and therefore the cells themselves. Water changes quality according to the information it takes in. Any Disney fans will recall Olaf from Frozen reminding us that *"water has memory"* and many of you will be aware of Doctor Masuro Emoto's water experiments that visually illustrate how the frequencies of thoughts, emotions, and sounds physically affect the structure and quality of water. The water of the body is our path to enhancing DNA. Everything we think, feel, say and do imprints on lymph fluid and consequently affects DNA construction. So, the yogic manta *"good thoughts, good words, good deeds"* is key to the spiritual path, and *"hear no evil," "see no evil," "speak no evil"* is an alchemical code to live by -- a masterpiece for hacking your inner systems and experiencing deep healing. The song "Unwritten" by Natasha Bedingfield explicitly highlights the opportunity we are given each morning, *"Today is where your book begins, the rest is still unwritten."* For these proven scientific reasons, singing praise and worship songs, chanting mantras of love and transcendence, reading the

Holy Scriptures, and many other spiritual practises are **sacred, potent, effective, transformational modalities.**

To properly receive and assimilate the Creative Light within, we should not only purify ourselves physically, mentally, emotionally, and energetically, but we should also preserve our procreative energies and essences – i.e., prepare the "virgin" body. This is how our own matter (mother) can be impregnated by Creative Light (Kundalini). Retaining our procreative energies and essences, keeping our minds on higher ideas, and purifying ourselves body, mind, soul, and spirit is how we "sacrifice the animal" part of us and overcome the "carnal mind."

All the great prophets, avatars, and masters worked hard on their selves (their cells), so that the Creative Light, the true Christ (solar) mas (lunar) fusion could emerge in them little by little. This is what it means to "Christify" yourself and is the true definition of a Christian. It's a process that you work at, day by day -- the solstice process that you see in the sky has to be repeated in your individual body in order to understand the full potential of "Christmas Magic."

Mistletoe

Mistletoe is an evergreen plant that remains green during the darkest time of the year leading up to Winter Solstice, symbolizing life, vitality, and fertility. In many traditions, it is a reminder that life persists even in the depths of winter -- a time when the sun appears at its weakest.

In ancient times, mistletoe was revered as a sacred plant by Druids, native Americans, Celts, and Ancient Greeks. They believed mistletoe had a mystical connection to the divine, as it grew high in trees, seemingly between heaven and earth. During the solstice, it was harvested as part of rituals celebrating the rebirth of the sun and the victory of life after deathly winters.

Mistletoe was believed to guard against evil, misfortune, and dark forces, symbolizing our ability to transmute negative energies and assimilate light in the body. Mistletoe has long been used in traditional healing practices for its medicinal properties. It is known for treating various ailments, such as high blood pressure, epilepsy, and even cancer in modern-day alternative treatments (according to European accounts regarding anthroposophic medicine).

"In Switzerland and Germany sixty percent of all cancer patients are now prescribed mistletoe at some point in their treatment. Many receive it for weeks before surgery and most take it for years afterwards to help prevent recurrence. The test of time is also a test. Iscador is an integral

> *element of a wholistic treatment method called the anthroposophical approach to health and illness. This method addresses body, soul, and spirit of the patient, recognizing that every illness bears within it the seeds of change and the possibility for new direction. It includes full acceptance of proven scientific methods as well as homeopathy, anthroposophical medicine, phytotherapy, art therapy, massage, counselling and more."*
> Pages 15-16, Iscador: Mistletoe and Cancer Therapy by Christine Murphy

Some of the active substances in mistletoe that contribute to its healing effects include:

- **Viscotoxins:** Small proteins that are cytotoxic, which means they can kill cells, particularly they are used in cancer treatment as they can target and destroy cancer cells.

- **Lecithin**: Helps stabilize cell membranes, which is key for maintaining cellular health and preventing disease. Procreative essences are rich in Lecithin, and this is one of the reasons why retention has a vitalising effect on the body (See Coal, Lead and Carbon and Egypt).

- **Mistletoe Lectins:** These proteins are known for their ability to stimulate the immune system (lymphatic system). They are being researched for their anti-cancer effects, as they have been shown to inhibit tumour growth and activate immune responses.

- **Alkaloids:** Known for their ability to lower blood pressure and their overall calming effects on the nervous system.

- **Flavonoids:** Potent antioxidants found in many plants, including mistletoe, that help reduce oxidative stress and inflammation.

Mistletoe's unique combination of these bioactive substances contributes to its widespread use in alternative medicine, particularly in Europe, for treating cancer and cardiovascular conditions. Its energetic symbolism, connecting light and dark, is also aligned with its healing potential. This connection, especially during solstice times, reflects mistletoe's traditional role in harmonizing bodily energies and balancing health. Mistletoe's ability to harmonize and balance energy mirrors the balance that is restored during the solstice, and the opportunity for detoxification and regeneration at this time of year. During winter, when sickness and lack of sunlight weaken the immune system, mistletoe acts as a restorative herb, boosting vitality and the immune system. Its use in treating conditions like arthritis and as an anti-inflammatory highlights its role in promoting warmth, circulation, and overall healing in the coldest, most stagnant season.

Kissing Under the Mistletoe

In Norse mythology, mistletoe was associated with peace and reconciliation, and kissing under it was thought to foster goodwill, love, and harmony. Over time, this evolved into a Christmas tradition symbolizing affection, love, and the joy of the season. Making peace and releasing old energetic contracts of conflict, frustration, or anger etc. sets the heart free to swell and stimulate oxytocin release, which as I've said elsewhere is the catalyst for pineal metabolism. Similar to the "X" used for "Christ" in the abbreviation "Xmas," the "X" symbol is used to illustrate kisses, and kisses are a form or energy exchange. Kissing under the mistletoe signifies the fusion of the pineal (solar gland), with the pituitary (lunar gland) as they come together in "holy matrimony" akin to the "alchemical wedding."

Mistletoe remains a potent symbol during the Christmas season, but it's true potential and meaning has sadly been lost or diminished. Thankfully, the traditional re-use of mistletoe throughout the generations has preserved its legacy, and once certain harmful pharmaceutical medicines are exposed, natural remedies will prevail once more.

Nasarean (Nazarian)

> "The greatest teaching of Jesus the Essene, the nearest to us of the great masters, is that of the sevenfold peace. This sevenfold peace is revealed in the seven beatitudes of the Sermon on the Mount. It means harmony or peace with the body, with the mind, with our family, with mankind, with the earth, with all the kingdom of the earthly Mother, and with the kingdom of the heavenly Father. All-sided harmony is the sevenfold peace, one of the most sublime revelations of all ages. When the master revealed this greatest of the Essene traditions in all its wonderful simplicity, he established his claim to be one of the greatest teachers of all times on this planet."
>
> Page 22, The Essene Jesus by Edmond Bordeaux Szekely

The Essene order of the Blue Rose refers to the Nasareans as "Essenoi" and "Therapeutae" -- ascension healers who knew the art of raising themselves up the "golden ladder." Indeed, ascension to higher states of consciousness and the assimilation of the light body is the main topic of the Holy Megillah -- the Nasarean Bible of the Essene Way.

The Essenes or "Nasareans" believed in connecting the physical and divine realms through practices that symbolically mirrored the growth of the soul towards enlightenment, often correlating their path with seasonal cycles such as the solstice, a time of inward reflection and renewal.

Experts on Essene history, such as Greg Braden and Edmond Bordeaux Szekely claim that the Essenes were forced to hide their teachings and live in seclusion. It's said that the Essenes were often seen as heretical by mainstream religious authorities in the Second Temple period. Their mystical and ascetic practices, such as emphasizing direct spiritual experiences and communion with divine forces, threatened the established religious order. This led them to withdraw from mainstream society to avoid persecution and maintain the purity of their teachings. During the Roman occupation of Judea, the Essenes and Nasareans were particularly vulnerable due to their beliefs and opposition to foreign rule. The intense political and military pressure exerted by the Romans caused these communities to retreat into more isolated areas, such as the desert regions near the Dead Sea (as seen with the Qumran community).

The Essenes are believed to have safeguarded esoteric knowledge, including mystical interpretations of scripture and advanced healing techniques. To prevent this knowledge from being corrupted or suppressed, they would only share their teachings with trusted initiates, often living in seclusion to preserve their spiritual traditions. The Essenes practiced strict purity laws, avoiding the cities and choosing secluded areas like caves and remote communities to prevent contact with what they viewed as the moral and spiritual corruption of society. Their lifestyle of withdrawal also helped protect their meditative and ascetic practices (fasting, vegetarianism, periodic chastity, and period light deprivation), which were thought to be essential for their spiritual advancement.

Many believe the Essenes saw themselves as the guardians of ancient prophecies, which were hidden away from both Roman occupiers and mainstream religious groups. The famous Dead Sea Scrolls, found in Qumran, are often cited as evidence of their efforts to preserve sacred knowledge in isolation.

An example of a secret Essene spiritual practice is "angelic communion", a meditative practice involving daily prayers and contemplation to align oneself with the natural and divine forces of the universe. The Essenes believed in a strong connection between humans and angels, viewing the angels as intermediaries between God and man, and as forces of nature representing cosmic principles. Their teachings on angelic communion have been preserved in texts like the "Essene Gospel of Peace," which reflects their deep connection to nature and the divine order.

Another of their practices involved communion with the "seven forces of light," perhaps since the visible light spectrum includes seven prominent colours. Each day of the week was dedicated to communing with a specific aspect of creation or angelic force, such as the "Angel of the Sun," "Angel of Water," or "Angel of Earth." This communion was meant to harmonize the practitioner's body and soul with the rhythms of the cosmos, facilitating healing and spiritual ascent. The Essenes believed these spiritual exercises were crucial to maintaining their purity and achieving higher states of consciousness.

Naughty and Nice

> *"He's making a list and checking it twice; he's going to find out who's naughty and nice!"*
> Santa Claus is Comin' to Town. Song by John Coots and Haven Gillespie in 1934.

Children are told that Santa's elves watch their behaviour and relay messages back to Santa Claus about who is being "naughty" and who is being "nice". In this allegory, the Elves are all-seeing and all-knowing, no child's mischief is overlooked. If the child's name ends up on the "naughty list" they are said to get coal (See Coal/Lead/Carbon), but if they're well behaved then their name goes on the "nice list", and they are said to receive plenty of presents or "presence."

This "law" of message-relaying by the "elves" relates to the autonomic functioning of claustral neurons (brain cells). The mind (North Pole), ALWAYS knows what's happening in the body (on Earth). Thus, the "naughty and nice" allegory can be seen as parallel to the measuring, judging or weighing system that is continually occurring in the human body. As described in the entry for "Christmas Tree," the chakras and their corresponding endocrine glands drive the overall picture of health for the body, mind, soul, and spirit.

Each one of our thoughts, emotions, and actions causes AUTOMATIC changes in the body's alchemical state. Our choices literally drive the generation or degeneration of our cells (ourselves). In the same way that children can't escape the watchful eyes of Santa's elves, we cannot escape the autonomy of the body. If our thoughts and emotions are "off-key" so will our overall picture of health be. We can either prime our bodies to receive and assimilate Creative Light (Presents/Presence) by being "nice," or we can intoxicate and degenerate it, creating "coal" through acting "naughty."

Some examples of alchemical states that may block the "niceness flow" include:

- ROOT CHAKRA: Fearfulness and fretting -- the Bible says, *"for the thing I greatly feared is come upon me, and that which I was afraid of is come unto me."* Job 3:25 (KJV) Meaning, when we exude fear, fear manifests and returns to us by natural law.

- SACRAL CHAKRA: Guilt -- obvious things such as stealing and cheating create guilt and its chemical counterparts in the body, which can block the "niceness flow." Even on a subconscious (unfelt) level, guilt wreaks havoc on the body. Disproportioned guilt projected on to us by others is inhibiting too, don't absorb other peoples distorted views of you.

- SOLAR CHAKRA: Shame -- can fester and tie the psyche in knots. Shame produces all kinds of manifestations in our alchemy. For example, shame can unbalance cortisol, epinephrine and Pro-inflatokinem leading to insecurities, distrust, embarrassment and even paranoia). Consequently, the way we perceive the world may change also.

- HEART CHAKRA: Grief, sorrow and sadness held in the heart all block the flow of "niceness," we must learn to let go and find thankfulness for life's challenges, lessons, and losses. In the film *The House with a Clock in Its Walls* (2018), Cate Blanchett's character, named **Florence Zimmerman**, loses her magical abilities due to the trauma of losing her family saying, *"My magic doesn't work anymore. Not since I lost my family."* This line encapsulates Florence's grief and emotional struggle, which has rendered her magic ineffective. This represents the emotional toll trauma can take on one's abilities -- both "magical" and otherwise. Letting go is essential for alignment (the only way out is through, so don't be afraid to face and feel every emotion -- in a safe space of course).

- THROAT CHAKRA: Deception -- it's "naughty" to lie or be deceptive, even if you think you're getting away with something, intelligent Creative Light lives IN you and knows exactly how you really feel about things (autonomic chemical secretions), and what really happened. Lying to others (and indeed to ourselves), is a foolish practise that sends ripples into the collective consciousness -- eventually those ripples catch up with the perpetrator.

- MIND AND CROWN CHAKRAS: Attachments -- feeling powerless to change situations and ourselves due to the illusions of the outside world. Material forms are holograms reflecting the state of our inner being. Releasing attachments and realising our creative, limitless potential (for the good of all, or not at all) allows for the ultimate niceness flow of presents (presence)!

These seven aspects of consciousness also coincide with the "seven deadly sins" and their inhibiting action in the body.

Having an attitude of assurance, or an inner knowing about our health, prosperity and abundance will enable us to maintain divine order, firstly within ourselves and consequently in our outer circumstances. Being honest with ourselves and others, and always willing the best for self and others, sends love-filled ripples into the cosmic ocean. With an abundant, unconditional-love mindset comes an abundant and love-filled life. Faith that our needed good is ALWAYS available glitches us onto a whole new reality strand that is aligned in the "niceness flow." Our trust in the perpetual flow of good will lie not in the accumulation of *things* but in the quickening of our consciousness of abundance. It's funny how little you want when you realise how abundant you are.

With all this in mind, the "naughty and nice list" can be viewed as the automatic bodily measure of energy, thought, emotion, and action -- The alchemical state that we choose to dwell in determines where we each reside on spectrum of repulsion (naughty) and receptivity (niceness).

North Pole

All living organisms are surrounded by their own electromagnetic torus field. Tiny creatures emit miniscule toroidal fields, and enormous entities emit huge toroidal fields. The shape of each individual torus field resembles a ring donut.

All electromagnetic (light) torus fields, no matter how small, or how big have a North Pole and a South Pole. The poles are vortexes that direct Life Force Energy (Creative Light) into the organism that they are surrounding. These vortexes have also been described as "plasma fountains."

In the macrocosm, the North Pole is said to be located in international waters where the earths surface meets its axis i.e., where the horizontal plane, meets the vertical plane and it spins vital energies, and creative elements into earth.

> *"The aurora borealis stands as the emblem for the magnetic attraction of Earth on spirit, the Christ soon to be born in the manger of the goat (Capricorn); the descent of the Holy Ghost into material form, so that heavenly truth may illuminate the drear speculum of earthly thought with the divine iridescence of celestial light."*
> **Page 127, The Light of Egypt by Thomas H. Burgoyne**

In the microcosm, the North Pole is located at the top of your head, it spins vital energies, and creative elements into your body. Physiologically, the entry point for energy into the body is seen as the fontanel, known as the "little fountain" of the skull. Below is one visual example of the macrocosmic parallels that occur between Earth and the boy, there is an entire video dedicated to this on my YouTube channel called, **"INNER ALCHEMY, Parallels Between EARTH and the BODY, Macrocosm Vs. Microcosm, The Brain & North Pole."**

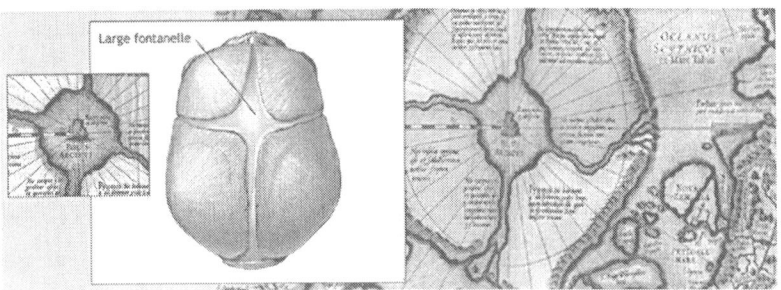

Fontanelle of the Skull beside Ancient Depictions of the North Pole.

Other secret names for the North Pole of the body include:

- The "door" or "opening" of Brahma.

- Thura Iesous (meaning, the door of Jesus).

- Laodicea (the seventh church of Revelation) Read ELEVATION: The Divine Power of the Human Body for further information.

- Kether (the highest Sephirot on the Kabalistic Tree of Life).

- Sahasrara (the crown chakra).

- Bai Hui (a major Taoist energy point associated with the reception of cosmic energy).

- Thousand Petalled Lotus (Buddhic symbol for the crown of the head, where the awakened mind resides).

Santa Claus is said to live in the "North Pole" because it's the entry point for electromagnetic energy which is "Creative Light" (Presence -- Presents) into Earth and our bodies. Electromagnetic Energy enters your own North Pole at the crown of your head and spirals down through your spine, just like Santa Claus coming down the chimney.

Directly under the fontanel, inside the skull, is a lobe called the "insula." "Insula" is the Latin word for "Island" and the insula's historical name is "Island of Reil." The "Island of Reil" is parallel to the "Isle of Patmos" where St John had his revelation or vision of the regenerated man (Christ). Read Elevation: The Divine Power of the Body for more about John and his revelations. This "island" is the central lobe of the cerebrum and according to Harris. E. Santee and George. W. Carey was otherwise known as the "POLE." Among medical students It's considered to be very mystical because there is so little information about its function and structure. In modern science, the term "pole" is assigned to three bodies: the frontal pole, the temporal pole, and the occipital pole.

Oil and Cerebrospinal Fluid

Cerebrospinal fluid (CSF) is a clear, colourless liquid that surrounds and protects the brain and spinal cord. It acts as a cushion, but more importantly, it provides essential nutrients and removes waste products from the brain. CSF circulates through the brain and spinal column, playing a key role in nourishing the nervous system. It's composed of water, ions, proteins, and a small amount of glucose, which, as a carbohydrate, contains carbon (See Coal, Lead and Carbon).

In esoteric traditions, CSF is referred to as "Christ oil", describing a divine, life-giving essence. It is seen as the "carrier of light and consciousness", moving up and down the spinal column. "Protoplasm" or "cytoplasm," the fluid inside cells that contains life-giving nutrients and energy, is similar in composition and nature to CSF. It is often described as the "substance of life," and as it circulates, it nourishes and sustains the central nervous system, allowing for higher states of awareness and spiritual growth. This precious "oil" of which the Bible speaks flows from "Santa Claus", the Claustrum (See Claustrum) down through the spine or "pine tree" bringing life to all its all its members, *"Thou anointest my head with oil."* **Psalm 23:5 (KJV)**.

> *"This oil is the most sacred substance in the body – it is the quintessence of Gold – the "Gold of Ophir" – most truly a rare gift.* **Santa Claus is thus the giver of the supreme gift in the human body, the oil for the perpetual lamp."**
> Page 109, God Man: The Word Made Flesh by G. W Carey

The "oil" for the perpetual lamp is Cerebrospinal Fluid (CSF). Synergistic names and forms of this life-giving substance include -- Lymphatic Fluid, Spinal Marrow, Cytoplasm/Protoplasm, Chrism, Liquid light, Amrita, Ambrosia, Soma, Gold, Christ Oil, Anointing Oil, Mineral Oil, and the Oil of Gladness.

> *"CSF is a STORAGE FIELD (See Shepherds and Fields) and CONVEYER of light energies."*
> **Doctor Zappaterra in the Science and Nonduality Lecture.**

Unpacking this quote really allows us to understand the transference of "Creative Light" into the body:

- If something is a *"storage field for light energy"* it means, it's directly **capturing or receiving light in its various aspects and holding it for the body.**

- If something is a *"conveyer of light energy"* it means its **translating that light for use in the body.**

This highlights the absolute magnificence and indispensable nature of this "Holy Oil," and in his research and experiments, Doctor Mauro Zappaterra has demonstrated that CSF literally is the crystal/CHRISTal-clear water or oil of life! Like a river of lightning, CSF IS THE MOST ELECTRICALLY CONDUCTIVE FLUID IN THE BODY and our breath charges it with every inhalation, just like a breeze stoking a fire. This explains why sacred secretion practices like breathwork, and yoga are so effective for assembling light in the body; the breath charges or excites CSF allowing it to convey more light energy. When CSF is cleansed from the residue of toxic thoughts, emotions, and chemicals it reaches its highest potential and becomes the amrita or nectar of the Gods. *"We have drunk Soma and become immortal; we have attained the light, the Gods discovered."* **Rig-Veda, Book 8, Hymn XLVIII. Soma.**

This substance is the life source that flows through our brain and spine! In Colossians (2:10) St Paul speaks of Christ as the "head", to which all parts of the church are fixed and nourished. This is parallel to the physical fact that from the brain, CSF or Christ oil nourishes the entire body also.

Man is a microcosm, whatever exists in the outer universe exists in him also. "Oil" or "PETRoleum" is a major commodity on earth, so major that countries wage war over it!

And so, it is in our bodies… The Oil or "PETRoleum" within us is of irreplaceable value and the lures and temptations of the exterior world wage war on its frequency and purity. Exploring the composition of the word "petroleum" gives deeper insight to the nature of this sought after substance and how it mirrors CSF in the body.

"Petr" means "rock" or "mineral" -- as in "rock salt," "mineral salt" or "cell salt".

"Oleum" means oil.

Petroleum is mineral oil.

Like petroleum, CSF also contains minerals (cell salts), and CSF bathes the philosophers stone (rock), thus CSF can be viewed as a "mineral oil" also. *"…and the rock poured out rivers of oil"* **Job 29:6 (KJV).**

Our inner "petroleum" (CSF) flows around the brain and through the 33 vertebrae of the spine. The Biblical Christ lived for 33 years, "his" oil was "whole" or "holy" because he kept his body, mind, and soul in a state of love (high vibes) and purity. As the saying goes, *"Cleanliness is next to Godliness."* His life and teachings illustrate the type of transcendence; peace, love, and super consciousness that we can embody to bio-hack our DNA toward enlightenment.

In the body, the mineral based "Christ Oil" on the chemical layer of creation is parallel with the "kundalini" of the light body. In the petroleum industry, nitrogen is used to draw oil up from under the ground. A reflection of this happens in the temple-body when nitric oxide (nitrogen and oxygen) helps to raise, and foam CSF in kundalini awakenings. Breath work also assists with nitric oxide production and circulation -- we can enhance nitric oxide (NO) via deep nasal breathing.

> *"The kundalini utilizes that which is termed spinal liquid. It actually ionizes CSF and changes it molecular structure and consequently the basic DNA structure of the entire body."*
>
> **Page 243, A Beginners Guide to Creating Reality by Ramtha**

In human anatomy, we observe with wonder and awe how the nerves, muscles and other systems of the body are all centred and anchored to the spine. The spine is a delicate, yet resilient instrument or "rod" of splendor that can bend and twist similarly to the movement of a snake and is filled with the replenishing "water of life," "Mineral Oil," or CSF. According to King Solomon, CSF is the material counterpart of the "silver cord" in our microcosmic temple body's. The "silver cord" is our connection to the universal macrocosm as is this divine fluid. As the conveyor of light (electromagnetic energy) and a medium for cell birth or production, our lives and bodies are continually "manifesting" or generating from CSF and the mystical "silver cord".

Cerebrospinal fluid was historically known as "spinal marrow" -- it is part of the lymphatic-water system, as is all other bone marrow, and this glorious substance in its various forms and consistencies; from thick, squidgy marrow to fine, runny oil is where the stem cells of the body are born, proliferated, and differentiated... Meaning, all of the billions of stem cells that make you who and what you are form and develop in or by this Divine Substance!

Cells of all kinds literally form from the mineral cell-salts present within CSF, lymph and marrow. The word "salt" is derived from the word "cell," and the French word for salt is "sel". The root "hal" as in Halo also means salt, in chemistry "halogens" are formers (GENerators) of mineral salts (hal). In the "Sermon on the Mount," Jesus says that salt and light make life on earth worthwhile. Salt is necessary for life. Consider the beating heart, the heart beats because of a chemical exchange between sodium and potassium salts.

All the mineral salts in "Christ Oil" are "builders" (masons) of cells and therefore, builders of bodies. This is the reason why secret brotherhoods have many codes symbolizing the magical fluid that births the cells life. For example, the master's lost word "MVABAVN" means MAHABONE or MARROW BONE and Free Masons are taught the "MAHABONE" handshake signifying the power and intelligence of this divine liquid, oil, or marrow.

The Bible calls "mineral oil" (CSF/Lymph/Marrow), *"living water"*, and *"water springing up into everlasting life"* and the primitive Christians, the Essenes dedicated their lives to maintaining the purity and frequency of their internal crystal streams making them the immoveable light race of powerful ascension healers -- all healing, purification and regeneration is aided by the living water. Just think of the saline (salty) mineral IV solutions given to support lives and or detox patients in hospital.

As part of the lymphatic system, CSF assists with immune functions, helping to detoxify the brain by absorbing and removing toxins and the metabolic by-products of our thoughts and emotions. Our incredible spines bear the weight of our entire bodies at the same time as being a pipeline for the most crucial liquid in the body -- literally ALL voluntary and involuntary motion depends on mineral oil (CSF)! Cerebrospinal fluid flows through all the nerves of the body in its various forms, and **breath is the crucial mechanism that enables it to move,** this is why kundalini yoga's mulabandha (root lock) and other breath exercises are celebrated for assisting CSF and lymphatic flow.

As stated in "ELEVATION – The Divine Power of the Human Body," the CSF ventricles, shaped like a lamb or rams' horns are often equated with the microcosmic "throne of God". CSF is "the blood of the lamb." The "inferior waters" are the seminal fluids in the lower (goat) end of the body, and the "super waters" are the CSF and lymphatic substances of the upper (sheep or ram) body. See "Coal, Lead and Carbon" for an illustration of these two concepts.

> *"And he showed me a pure river of water of life, clear as crystal, proceeding out of the throne of god and of the lamb."*
> **Revelation 22:1 (KJV)**

As mentioned in the "Timing" chapter and "Introduction" at the beginning of this book, there is an intrinsic relationship between our inner Christ Oil reservoirs and the moons motions and conjunctions with other celestial bodies. This relationship is what creates certain favorable time-phases for cleansing and advancing along your spiritual path. *"The natural man receiveth not the things of the Spirit of God,"* 1 Corinthians 2:14 (KJV). Meaning, when our carnal mind and urges dominate in mind, body, and soul our waters cannot be fully detoxified and charged by the moons gracious cycle.

As a certain controversial Doctor once said,

> *"The Herculean task or great work which everyone must perform, eventually, is the purification of this material, for then it becomes the Christ or Holy Oil."*
> Page XV, The Zodiac and the Salts of Salvation by G W Carey

Spiritual awakening is largely a remembering and reactivation of our innate human power, and this remembering is facilitated by the health, purity, and vibrancy of our internal river of life (Christ Oil).

> *"Then will I make their waters deep, and cause their rivers to run like oil, saith the Lord GOD."*
> Ezekiel 32:14 (KJV)

Presents, Presence and Gifts

The true Christmas gifts that are brought down the chimney by Santa bring life to every facet of the human vessel: body, mind, soul, and spirit (See Chimney). The "presents" that the myths speak of is really the Holy Presence bathing the macro and microcosms at this wonderful time of year, "Holy" as in "whole" means complete, and not lacking anything, i.e., abundant.

In this day and age, people have forgotten the true meaning of the word "gift." True gifts are powers obtained by the Creative Light. Some gifts are available to use and hone from birth, whereas others must be earned. Matthew 18:3 states, *"Except ye be converted and become as little children, ye shall not enter the Kingdom of Heaven"* this highlights the importance of chastity, purity, innocence, and unwaivable faith. These characteristics are prerequisites to the proper absorption and assimilation of light within. The initiate receives spiritual enhancements (gifts) according to their transformation by Creative Light.

Buddha curated a childlike mind; hysterically joyful, beautifully appreciative, zestfully excited, adorably generous, relinquished and surrendered, at ease, unaware of so-called "evils," blissfully naïve and basically impenetrable. In order for "Christ" to descend into you, you have to be united with your own individual Buddha, who gives you that illumination.

Spiritual gifts come from being in the perfect state of magnetism, faith plays a huge role in this phenomenon. Faith in terms of believing in the unseen and knowing with all your heart that 'Love conquers all things' is what it takes to shift into the ultra-magnetic state. It's true that we are supplied by infinite True Source Love (Creative Light), the inexhaustible substance, so why do we believe that we are limited beings? Is it because of past programmes and conditioning, or a vast forgetting of our infinite origin? Or does reality deliberately mask our abundance with its desire driven 'entertainment?' Whatever the reason, shifting into 'infinity consciousness' is a major key in the art of manifestation, simply KNOWING that all things are possible, and residing in that place of expectancy is TRUE FAITH!

Most young children, have faith in spades! Of course there are unfortunate exceptions, but generally speaking, before a child learns of disappointment and suffering they are more innocent and faithful in their worldly perceptions. When a child asks for something simple like a drink of juice, they innately know it's coming before their parent or guardian has even replied. They may even start dancing around singing, *"juice," "juice," "juice," "I'm getting the juice,"* thus, residing in the ultra-magnetic state, because they just know it's coming! I heard this analogy in a sermon many years ago, and the imagery stuck with me very vividly. Maybe it's because I've seen how my own child behaves when he knows something he's asked for is on the way, it's a state of pure faith and pure expectation. Similarly, observing a child eagerly anticipating Christmas, is witnessing the state of true abundance consciousness. In their minds, they've already received the "presents." When the initiate lives in that same frequency of awe, appreciation, and expectation for GOOD they too become ultra-magnetic. It's divine law! Praise and worship songs can induce this frequency, prayer and gratitude practises can induce this frequency -- in fact, many spiritual practises help us to 'get there.' *'There'* is the frequency that aligns with our divine inheritance.

Charles Fillmore explained that the fullness of the "Universal Law of Increase" in effect can be experienced by using our talents. When asked what he meant by 'talents' he replied that "belief" is the first, and most important "talent" that we have, because *"belief is faith in action"* -- the knowing and expectance of GOOD in all aspects of life.

> *"I know him in whom I have believed. I am persuaded that he is able, that he is willing, that he is eager, to give me whatsoever I ask."*
> **Page Unnumbered, The Science of Being: Christian Healing by Charles Fillmore**

The "Divine Economy" (Unity Metaphysics 2) teaching, which is available free online at truthunity.net really helps the initiate to grasp the idea of "giving" in alignment with "faith." Faithful people give more generously because they know that they're supplied by the infinite source of ALL! They also receive blessings more freely for the exact same reason. We must remember that because of God's limitless good will for us, the return is always greater than the investment as we generously use our gifts and talents "for the good of all, or not at all" as the caveat for keeping in alignment with the benevolent, gracious ray of True Source Love.

A gift with reservations is not a gift at all; it is a bribe. There is no universal law of increase unless we give freely (as God does for us), we must let go of the gift entirely to fully experience the universal scope of this law.

When giving becomes a pure expression of love and generosity, then we have willingly cooperated and raised ourselves up to the divine idea. We should then make room in ourselves for an additional experience: RECEIVING. Do not be reluctant to receive, or to know your worth. Freely give. Gracefully receive.

> *"The idea of giving and receiving is a divine idea that helps us make connection with the underlying substance, ever flowing from the Fountainhead, the Source. It is a divine idea that keeps the connection unbroken. If you need prosperity, ask yourself, "What do I have to give?" Pray to be shown how to give, what to give, how to serve. Your prospering idea will come through you. You will enlarge and increase the scope of your life and its interests and activities"*
> **Eric Butterworth, The Divine Economy, Unity Metaphysics 2**

We can learn an important lesson from the faith of the child who hangs his stocking by the fireplace for Santa Claus to fill with the gifts he has been asking for. Instead of trying to lessen the faith of the child in the unseen helper, it would be vastly beneficial to us if we learned from the child how to ask, and how to stretch forth the empty hand, and find it filled.

Looking at presents from a more alchemical perspective, highlights a link between "boxed presents" and the "cube of sacred geometry" often associated with the root chakra -- the fireplace at the bottom of the body's "chimney."

The word "Kaballah" stems from the root words, "Kaaba" meaning cube, and "Allah" meaning God or Creator. The purpose of Kaballah is to fulfil the path of "Meshach" meaning "oil." The "path of oil" is the preserving and raising of the sacred secretion also known as the inner alchemy of ascension, it begins with a "boxed gift" or cube in "Malkuth" (equivalent to the root chakra) and ends with the dodecahedron ascension vehicle associated with the third eye chakra, which then transforms finally into the sphere associated with the crown (See Saturn, Santa and Satan for illustration).

The image of the Kaaba or "box" transforming into the dodecahedron ascension vehicle is equivalent to the Bible book of Revelation's "mystery of the cross." A folded cross forms a cube, so in this version of inner alchemy, the cube of the root chakra unfolds into the cross of transformation as base matter is refined into spiritual substance. In other words, "Life" comes down the chimney of the body in "gift-wrapped boxes" or "cubes" (carbon 666) and the unwrapping of "presents" mimics the divine process of transmuting base matter into spiritual substance (gifts).

As a structure, the cubes' influence on light and sound dynamics is significantly restrictive. The sharp corners affect light distribution, creating shadows, and acoustically, the flat surfaces affect sound distribution, creating distortion. But when the cube unfolds into a cross, or morphs into a sphere light and sound are unbounded!

Reindeer

Santa's Sleigh" can be considered as a fantastical representation of the spiritual "Ascension Vehicle." The ascension vehicle is linked to DNA in the microcosmic body (See Sleigh), and to the cosmic spiral of the milky way galaxy in the macrocosm.

Just as DNA spirals within the body, the Milky Way Galaxy can be seen as a larger, cosmic spiral. The spiral arms of galaxies resemble the twisting double helix of DNA, suggesting a fractal relationship between cosmic structures and the body's microstructures. The idea here is that the galaxy itself serves as a macrocosmic "ascension vehicle," guiding the evolution of consciousness on a larger, collective scale, similar to how DNA governs cellular evolution within individual beings.

With these assignments in place, it begs the question: what do the reindeer represent?

The first thing to address when exploring this question is the fact that the creatures pulling Santa's sleigh weren't always reindeer.

Here are some examples of sleighs or chariots pulled by various creatures, across history, mythology, religion, and folklore:

- **The Deer Mother**
  Pulls her own sleigh.

The Deer Mother is an ancient goddess figure found in pre-Christian mythologies, particularly among Northern and Arctic European cultures like the Sámi and Siberians. **She is often depicted flying through the dark winter skies, pulling a sleigh filled with the life-giving light of the sun, symbolized by her antlers.**

- **Thor's Chariot**
  Pulled by: Two goats, Tanngrisnir and Tanngnjóstr.

In Norse mythology, Thor, the god of thunder, drives a chariot pulled by two goats that he could slaughter and resurrect at will. "Satan" iconography is largely associated with the face of a goat, or some other "horned beast." As illustrated in the "Coal, Lead and Carbon" entry, this image stems from the resemblance between the organs of the procreative region in the body and a goat's head.

- **Saturn's Quadriga (chariot)**
  Pulled by: Winged serpents or dragons.

In Roman mythology, Saturn, the god of time and harvest, is sometimes depicted in a chariot pulled by winged serpents or dragons, symbolizing cosmic cycles, transformation, and the mystical aspects of time. **As the god of time, Saturn can be seen to preside over the entire material realm which is restricted by time and space (spirit does not have such parameters).** In this way, solstice and all other cosmic movements can also be seen as influenced by Saturn (keeper of time).

- **Apollo's Chariot**
  Pulled by: Four horses.

The Greek sun god Apollo drives a chariot pulled by four horses, guiding the sun across the sky each day. **The horses were often depicted as fiery, symbolizing the sun's power and light.**

- **Chandra's Chariot**
    Pulled by: Two antelope or deer.

Chandra, the Hindu moon god, rides a chariot pulled by two deer (or sometimes antelope). In this rendition the animals are said to symbolise the moon's gentle, reflective nature.

- **Odin's Sleigh**
    Pulled by: Eight-legged horse, Sleipnir.

Odin, the chief god in Norse mythology, rides the **eight-legged horse** Sleipnir. **Sleipnir symbolizes speed, the ability to travel between worlds, and Odin's wisdom.** The number 8 is significant to DNA generation and regeneration as we'll come to see.

- **Dionysus' Chariot**
    Pulled by: Panthers or leopards.

In Greek mythology, Dionysus, the god of wine, revelry, and ecstasy, (all reminiscent of Saturn and Saturnalia) rides a chariot pulled by large cats such as panthers or leopards, representing his wild, unrestrained nature and connection to animalistic forces or "carnal nature."

- **Saule's Sleigh**
    Pulled by: Horned reindeer.

Saule, the Baltic goddess of the sun, is said to ride a sleigh pulled by female reindeer, flying across the heavens and symbolizing the winter solstice and the return of the sun's light. Interestingly, only female reindeer keep their antlers during winter. The femininity of the reindeer could point to the female characteristics of the moon, and how Santa (Solar Light) "rides" moon beams toward earth. **The moon is essential, it filters solar energy, making life on earth possible.**

These examples represent a diverse range of cultures, deities, and mythological creatures. Many of these chariots or sleighs carry deep hidden meaning, often tied to cosmic and biological forces, cycles of time, or spiritual journeys. Let's take a closer look.

The ancient "Deer Mother" figure predates Santa's reindeer. In various northern European and Siberian cultures, the Deer Mother was believed to fly through the longest night of winter (the solstice), carrying the life-giving sun in her antlers. This mythological figure is tied to the winter solstice, when the rebirth of the sun is celebrated. Her antlers, often seen as symbols of the sun's rays, were crucial in bringing light back to the world during its darkest period, this can be viewed as an early version of the "guiding light" depicted by Rudolph's glowing red nose. Saule, the goddess of the sun in Lithuanian and Latvian myths, was said to ride across the sky in a chariot or sleigh pulled by horned reindeer. **She would throw pebbles of amber (symbolizing the sun's warmth and light) into chimneys as gifts of light and warmth for the dark winter.** This image reflects the idea of Santa's sleigh and gifts descending down "chimneys."

The Roman god Saturn, closely associated with the winter solstice festival Saturnalia (See Saturn and Saturnalia), was often depicted traveling through the heavens on a type of chariot or sleigh called a "quadriga" pulled by winged serpents or dragons, presumably these creatures are yet more symbols for the twisting sides of the DNA double helix. Over time, these creatures morphed into the reindeer of popular imagination, this was likely due to cultural shifts and the spread of Norse and European winter mythologies. As explained elsewhere in this book, Saturn's affiliation with time and form reflects its seeming control over celestial and biochemical movements during the solstice.

Chandra, the Vedic moon god, is a significant figure in Hindu mythology and is often depicted as a radiant deity riding a chariot. As a moon god, Chandra is closely associated with the fluidic-soul body, lunar time cycles, emotions, and the direction of cosmic energies into earths electromagnetic field as well as into our own bodies. Chandra's chariot is traditionally illustrated as being pulled by "ten white horses" or "two antelope" (sometimes also referred to as deer, (yet another form of "horned beast"). The ten horses can be interpreted as the ten senses featured in Hindu philosophy, again linking Chandra to the control of the mind and emotions. Antelope or deer are symbolic of purity, and a connection to nature, particularly the moon's influence on the cycles of life and fertility, which includes the mitosis and regeneration of the cellular body. Chandra's presence in the sky was believed to influence the minds and moods of human beings on Earth, as well as plant growth, and tide cycles due to the connection with the lunar phases. This connection is scientifically known as the cranial respiration cycle, which loosely explained means "moon brain connection." The moons force affects all the waters of earth and indeed our bodies.

Chandra is also associated with "Soma," the divine nectar, synergistic with Christ oil. Soma is believed to be the source of immortality and vitality. In Hindu rituals, Chandra governs Soma, and the consumption of Soma is often linked with rejuvenation. Soma is the subtlest form of matter, it feeds the cells, RNA/DNA molecules and eventually becomes consciousness. Chandra's lunar light was believed to have protective and healing properties. This celestial role reinforces Chandra's importance in both physical health and the spiritual ascension process.

Chandra's chariot, whether pulled by deer or antelope, represents a graceful, flowing connection between the heavens and the earth, guiding both cosmic cycles and internal human processes. Other moon gods synergistic with Chandra include:

- Selene (Greek Mythology)
- Mani (Norse Mythology)
- Khonsu (Egyptian Mythology)

Many ancient gods and mystical figures have been depicted with horns or antlers, often symbolizing the sun, moon, or celestial forces. This can be seen in images of gods like Pan, Dionysus, and Cernunnos, who represent fertility and life. The ancient depictions of figures with horns link to the reindeer's antlers in Santa's sleigh mythology, representing a cosmic or spiritual connection.

Another interesting example of this seen with the Impala. As one of Africa's most agile, adaptable and elegant antelopes, the impala has naturally become a subject of stories, proverbs, and spiritual beliefs in African tales and folklore. The horned impala visually resembles the ganglion impar of anatomy, and the similarity in their names presents an interesting parallel. The Ganglion Impar is a small, unpaired structure found at the end of the sympathetic nerve chain, located in front of the sacrococcygeal junction (where the sacrum meets the coccyx). In addition to the resemblance between the impalas' horns and the form of the ganglion impar, the sacral bone that it's nerves (reins) weave into has 8 holes, which may relate to the 8 reindeer of popular tradition. In this scenario, "Rudolf," the ninth reindeer with "his" "bright red nose" may correspond with the ganglion impar, which could be seen to "light the way" for kundalini.

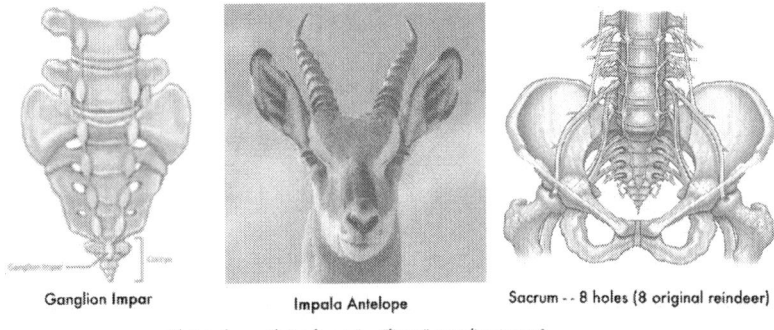

Ganglion Impar   Impala Antelope   Sacrum -- 8 holes (8 original reindeer)

9th Reindeer with "red nose" -- "lit up" ganglion impar?

The "horned beast" analogy derived from the forms and shapes of procreative anatomy isn't necessarily a 'bad' or negative symbol. As long as the correct interpretations are made, and the initiate takes care to liberate themselves from the influence of the carnal mind (beast) it can be a useful symbol.

The combination of ancient sun worship, esoteric interpretations of light assembly, and mythological animals blend together into the Christmas imagery we see now, with Santa's reindeer symbolizing both physical and spiritual guiding forces.

In esoteric interpretations that view Santa's sleigh as an "ascension vehicle," often relating to the dodecahedron shape formed by the ratcheting of DNA's double helix, the reindeer pulling the sleigh take on symbolic meanings tied to spiritual evolution, and inner alchemy. Here are a few possible representations:

- In this view, "Rudolph's red nose" could represent the awakened or activated crown chakra or "Bindu" point, a symbol of enlightenment guiding the ascension.

- Esoterically, the number 8 (as in the eight reindeer of modern Christmas stories) is often associated with "infinity", the eternal cycle of death and rebirth, and cosmic law, which are key themes in spiritual ascension.

With all this in mind, Reindeer allegories can also be compared to the forces that guide DNA activation and evolution. Since the sleigh is equated with the dodecahedral shape of the DNA helix, the reindeer might be seen as the energetic or spiritual elements that "pull" the DNA into higher configurations, assisting in the "ascension of consciousness" through the ratcheting of the dodecahedron (ascension vehicles) double helix. The reindeer then correlate with "guiding energies" such as light, sound, and vibration, that influence genetic activation, much like they propel the sleigh in through the sky.

The number of reindeer described in many versions of the Christmas story is 8. Interesting then, that the **DNA double helix makes a complete turn approximately every 8 base pairs or nucleotides.** This cyclic pattern suggests that 8 is significant to the structural geometry of DNA. This concept ties the number 8 to DNA's fundamental shape and its replication process. Furthermore, the double helix of DNA is often visualized as resembling a figure-8 shape when seen in cross-section or as it twists. This spiral or helical structure naturally embodies infinity (a concept symbolized by the number 8 in numerology), representing the ongoing process of life, replication, and genetic continuity. In addition to this, DNA contains 64 codons, which are sets of three nucleotide sequences that code for amino acids. Mathematically, 64 is 8 x 8, suggesting an inherent order and balance in the coding system that drives protein synthesis, linking the number 8 to genetic encoding and life's molecular foundation. Unbelievably, DNA in eukaryotic cells wraps around eight histone proteins to form nucleosomes, which organize the DNA into chromatin and allow for efficient packaging. This association with 8 histones further links the number 8 to the functionality and organization of DNA.

In other words, the number 8 is written all over DNA and its functioning, thus adding to the probability that Santa's "8 reindeer" are spiritually significant to our own DNA and ascension journeys, is this why we are so instinctively compelled by the Christmas drama?

Rice Porridge (Risgrynsgröt)

Historically, Risgrynsgröt (rice porridge) was a simple yet deeply significant dish in Scandinavian traditions, particularly associated with the Yule season. Its roots are much deeper than is widely known. Far more than just a "holiday treat;" it played a key role in **solstice cleansing practices.** Unlike the modern, sweeter version enjoyed today, early Risgrynsgröt was a minimalist dish, made with simple ingredients such as water and rice, and sometimes barley or oats.

The winter solstice marks a period of rebirth and spiritual renewal. Scandinavian cultures viewed this time as one of cleansing and preparing for the coming year, both physically and spiritually. Fasting was often practiced in the lead-up to solstice as a way to purify the body, and risgrynsgröt was served as a cleansing meal that would gently nourish the body without overwhelming it. It was light, easily digestible, and symbolically connected to renewal and rebirth, much like the solstice itself.

Early versions of risgrynsgröt were stripped of the richer ingredients we associate with today's recipe -- originally there was no sugar, and milk was not always included. Originally it served as a **"fasting food,"** used to reset and prepare the body before the "break—fast" feast to come. The simplicity of the dish made it a natural component of a solstice cleansing regimen, much like the **Ayurvedic dish kitchari,** which is used in Ayurvedic cleanses to reset the digestive system while providing sustenance.

Kitchari, made from rice, lentils, and mild spices, is known for its balancing and cleansing effects. Much like risgrynsgröt in early Scandinavian culture, kitchari serves as a dish that sustains the body while helping to remove toxins and reset the digestive system. Both dishes reflect the idea of nourishment without indulgence, offering a way to bring balance back into the body during cleansing or spiritual preparation. I recently shared a video called "The Immortal Body Cleanse" a practise borrowed from Secret Siddha Yoga, also known as Kaya Kalpa. The video shares the benefits and protocol for a 5-day master detox that the yogis and ayurvedic masters use to promote cellular clearance and regeneration (autophagy), rejuvenation, healing and longevity. **You can also download a free PDF guide at www.seekvision.co.uk.**

While risgrynsgröt today may have lost some of its original value, its roots as a cleansing food offer a glimpse into how ancient cultures used food in alignment with spiritual cycles, just as Ayurvedic traditions continue to do with dishes like kitchari.

In both cases, food is not merely nourishment -- it's a tool for spiritual and physical balance. By simplifying the recipe and focusing on its original purpose, you could even use risgrynsgröt today as part of a **modern solstice cleanse**, reconnecting with the ancient practices of resetting the body and preparing the spirit for the return of the light.

Santa's Sack

As the entertaining Christmas narrative goes, Santa's "sack" is large enough, or infinite enough to hold enough presents for <u>all</u> the children in the world! Yet somehow, it is still small enough to be carted around on a flying sleigh... The idea of "infinite space in a confined vessel" resonates with the fundamental principles of quantum physics, where subatomic particles hold tremendous energy, much like how DNA, despite its size, holds the blueprint for all life on Earth. *"There is enough energy in a single cubic meter of space to boil all the oceans of the world"* Albert Einstein.

Santa isn't the only beloved character with a magical sack, Mary Poppins also had a "carry on" sized carpet bag that could mysteriously hold items of vast disproportion. Both of these iconic symbols from popular culture illustrate the concept of holding infinite contents within a confined space. This reflects the idea that even within a material boundary (like a sack), there is infinite creative potential or energy, and similarly, the vastness of the universe is held within atoms.

Esoterically speaking, "cloth" is usually a symbol of the many "X" shaped chromosomes that make up our DNA. Chromosomes and cloth/fabric have a similar lattice appearance; DNA is the "fabric" of life (See Sleigh). "X" shaped DNA Chromosomes are the "sackcloth" and "garments" described in the Book of Revelation. "Sackcloth" is base matter, and the "garment of light" parallels refined substance i.e., charged DNA emitting increased photon light.

"Sack cloth" is transformed into "royal garments" or "raiment's" by Creative Light through the activation of DNA via epigenetics. Epigenetics emphasizes the role of external factors (like diet, stress, and environment) in altering gene expression. Epigenetics is a science that directly reflects the spiritual belief that one's inner state can be transformed through meditation, mindfulness, prayer, and other practices. Both modes of thinking agree that our state of wellness and physiology are altered by our thoughts, feelings and actions.

The book of Revelation, chapter 19:13-14 describes God as being "dressed in a vesture". A "vesture" is another reference to fabric (DNA), so in other words -- God is IN DNA -- i.e., "the presents (presence) are in the sack." Scripture says, the "vesture" is "dipped in blood" because DNA is inside the cells of the body, including blood cells. Thus, *"the life of the flesh"* truly is *"in the blood"*.

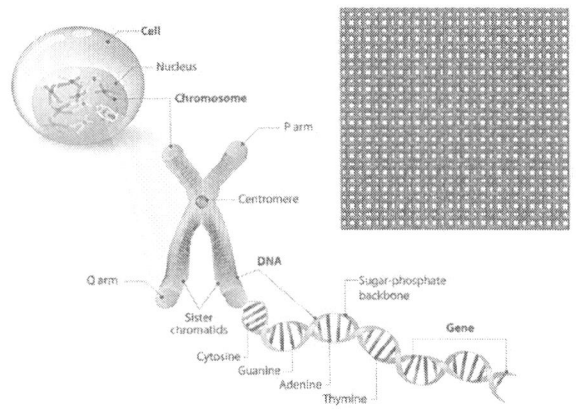

DNA - The Fabric of Life "God in every cell."

Chromosomes, although microscopic in size, contain the blueprint for all biological life. Their "X" shape links to the idea of endless creative light (energy) being stored in a seemingly finite vessel. This mirrors the idea that DNA holds the potential for evolution and transformation, storing not just genetic information, but the possibility for life itself to unfold in boundless forms.

The metaphor of chromosomes as "X" shapes resembling cloth, particularly in esoteric symbolism, presents a compelling connection between biological structures and mystical concepts. Chromosomes, shaped like the letter "X," are vital in the storage and transmission of genetic information, much like fabric or cloth, which weaves together fibres to create a unified structure. Therefore the "unified field" or "divine matrix" could be considered a macrocosmic "bag" or container holding infinite creative potential.

Saint Nicholas

It is largely believed that Santa Claus is an evolution, or modern version of a historical figure named "Saint Nicholas," or that the true origin of Santa Claus lies with Saturn, the planet of structure, time, and materialism (See Satan and Santa).

Another theory suggests that Saint Nicholas' origin isn't based on a real person at all, but rather an allegory for the natural cycles of winter solstice occurring both in the sky and in our bodies. It's helpful to explore historical accounts of a "Saint Nicholas" in order to unravel all these conflicting ideas and build a clear picture.

History

The evidence for the historical existence of a literal figure named Saint Nicholas primarily comes from written records and traditions that developed over time. However, there is no absolute empirical evidence in the modern scientific sense (e.g., artifacts with his direct name or undisputed contemporary accounts) that definitively prove his existence. The primary sources are hagiographies, which are biographies of saints written by later Christians, and these accounts often mix historical fact with legend.

In the Vedic Kathopanishad (believed to be written between 800 BCE and 200 BCE), we have the story of the Brahmin Vajasravasa who fathered a son called **Nachiketa, which is Sanskrit for Nicholas.** The story goes that the boy dies and goes to the abode of Yama, the "Lord of Death" associated with Saturn, where he lingers for three days (a significant time period, as explained elsewhere in this book).

When he returns, he is embarrassed to discover that he kept a Brahmin waiting. The Brahmin grants the boy three boons (favours) before he returns to life (resurrects) bearing gifts for his family. This story, known as "Amrita Manthan", is often depicted in ancient Hindu stories. **Sant Nachiketa (Saint Nicholas)** is depicted driving a chariot-like sledge loaded with favours for the good of mankind. **Flying a Vaanaprami (reindeer) through the air, Sant Nachiketa distributes the celestial gifts to mankind, including the knowledge of life after death.** Although there are many similarities to the Christmas narrative within this rendition, the details appear to pertain more to solstice and the rebirth of the sun, than a historical person.

Then next earliest written accounts of a "Saint Nicholas" allude to **"Saint Nicholas of Sion"** and **"Saint Nicholas of Myra"** (modern-day Turkey). These accounts were written by historians, detailing the life of a bishop and the miracles attributed to him, such as healing the sick, rescuing the impoverished, and even resurrecting children from the dead, all of which are reminiscent of Jesus Christ. One of the earliest texts mentioning Nicholas of Myra is from "Michael the Archimandrite" in the 9th century, but it was still hundreds of years after Nicholas' supposed life. Experts say, and medieval and renaissance artworks reinforce that these two saints Nicholas of Myra and Nicholas of Sion, were merged by the literary tradition, and the voids left by the life of the former were filled by the latter.

Allegory

Elsewhere in this book, we've discussed how Santa Claus, and Jesus Christ coincide with the natural cycles of winter solstice both in the macro and microcosms, but how does Saint Nicholas' story coincide with this? Is he parallel with Santa? Or has there been a merging of cultural traditions?

Remember, this time of year, "solstice" has long been associated with death and rebirth, as the Sun appears to "die" and then begins its ascension to longer days. Saint Nicholas' generosity and "gift-giving" could be symbolic of the sun's return, bringing life and abundance after the long, dark winter.

But what's really interesting is that **Saint Nicholas of Myra was known as "patron saint of the seas", "patron saint of sailors" and "patron saint of children."** These titles immediately bring hidden meanings to mind, Saint Nicholas being depicted as "saint of the seas" and "protector of sailors", can be **metaphorically linked to the idea of guiding and safeguarding "the fluids of the earth (macrocosm) and body (microcosm)".** In esoteric traditions, sea water on earth and in the body is seen as a carrier of Life Force Energy.

Saint Nicholas -- Patron of the Sea, Sailors and Children

Symbolically speaking, "seas" signify the salty oceans of the body i.e., vital fluids like CSF and lymphatic fluid. Thus, making Saint Nicholas a force that resides over or guides these currents. Specifically, the "salt" in the sea parallels mineral cell salts and seminal essences (Sea-men/semen) in bodily fluids, which many mystical systems view as crucial for spiritual development. Saint Nicholas, "Saint of the Ocean," presiding over the "seas" of the human body, could symbolize mastery over one's own spiritual essence which is carried through vital fluid. This assignment makes Saint Nicholas an indispensable factor for the regenerative opportunity available at this time of year when the energies of the cosmos align for inward reflection and rejuvenation. This further links Saint Nicholas to the moon which also presides over water (the fluidic, emotional soul body), and cycles of growth (waxing) and decay (waning).

This perspective is further supported by the fact that, just like Jesus Christ, Saint Nicholas was known for his supernatural ability to calm storms and save people from the sea. This reflects a symbolic mastery over the lunar forces and the "Sun's" victory over darkness and chaos as the solstice marks the return of light. In other words, their miracles are both allegorically linked to the cosmic movements of the Moon (which control the tides) and the Sun, which is metaphorically seen as navigating through the "storm" of the winter solstice before its rebirth.

According to legend, after Saint Nicholas of Myra was buried in his tomb, a miraculous liquid called "Manna" or "Myrrh" (etymologically similar to Myra) began to exude from his relics. The Manna is described as a clear, watery substance believed to have healing properties. Yet again, this imagery matches that of "soma," "Christ Oil," and "Amrita" etc. The Manna was reported to be collected by pilgrims and stored in vials. It was associated with various healing miracles and blessings for those who came into contact with it. However, scientific studies of the relics have not conclusively linked them to any historical figure such as "Nicholas" is alleged to be. This portrayal again points to the inner anointing that assigns Santa Claus and Saint Nicholas to Life Force Energy and the "Claustrum" of brain. The Claustrum is theorised to be the entry point of "Spirit" or "Life Force Energy" into the brain, acting as an on/off switch for consciousness (See Claustrum). Dr Carey says, *"It is from the claustrum that the wonderful 'Christ oil' (Manna) is formed."* "Manna" is also known as "Soma," "ambrosia," and the "nectar of the Gods." The root word "Nic" in "Nicholas" comes from the Sanskrit "Nec" meaning "overcoming death" -- "Nectar."

Esoteric theories suggest that Saint Nicholas' role as a "patron of children" parallels the preserving and raising of procreative fluids and essences (seminal fluids) i.e., the "chi" or "children" are the "seed that must be saved." Perhaps, the most famous legend about Saint Nicholas is about him saving three women from prostitution, which again exemplifies the practise of seminal fluid retention. According to the legend, Saint Nicholas threw **three** bags of "gold" (Creative Light) through the window, or in some renditions they were thrown down the chimney (See Chimney) of the sisters' home, in the dead of night. This can be seen to coincide with the approximate 3.5-day time phase associated with the practise of raising the sacred secretion (See Timing).

In "There is a Santa," renowned researcher and author, William J. Federer states that like Jesus, Saint Nicholas of Sion visited Golgotha (the place of the skull). If you're familiar with sacred anatomical codes or have read my previous books, you'll know that this fact alone points to Saint Nicholas as an archetype, or symbol based on the physiological processes of the body (and the macrocosmic processes that mirror them) rather than a historical figure.

The Manna Legends contributed to the growth of Nicholas' popularity in both the Eastern Orthodox and Western Christian traditions. His feast day on December 6th became a major religious celebration. December 6th is believed to be the day that Saint Nicholas left gifts in people's boots (See Boots). However, there are several alternative and hidden theories that link this date to broader symbolic, astrological, and alchemical interpretations. For example,

- The 6th of December is positioned as a lead-up to the winter solstice on December 21-22. This period is often viewed as a time of inner reflection and preparation for the spiritual renewal that occurs with the return of light. The theory here posits that the 6th could symbolize the first stage of the inner work that needs to be done before the solstice—the gifts may represent the early fruits of spiritual labour or insights gained as the year ends.

- One of the most visible meteor showers, the Geminids starts around early December and has been linked by astrologers and esoteric thinkers to the concept of divine gifts or cosmic blessings.

- The ancient Roman Festival of Faunalia (See Faunalia) occurred on December 5-6. Faunus is a Roman god of fertility, symbolizing the creative force in nature, animals, and human beings. In inner alchemy, this can be seen as a metaphor for the cultivation of procreative energy and essences, "Life Force," or "chi," which is understood to undergo subtle transformations during the seasons. The fertility aspect of Faunus is tied to inner biological shifts. As the winter solstice approaches, the outer world enters a period of dormancy, yet if the conditions are correct, the inner world of human beings can be seen as detoxing and cultivating vital energies, much like a seed preparing for eventual growth.

- Esoteric traditions have long observed that Saturn and the Sun also begin their "dance" in early December. It is believed that the energies of Saturn, planet of restriction and reduction heavily influence Earth at this time of year, creating a period where the coldness of Saturn teaches valuable lessons, leading into the rebirth of the Sun at the solstice. As the god of time and materiality, Saturn was seen as the silent puppet master ushering in solstice to the tick-tock of its clock.

With all this in mind, it can be seen that "Saint Nicholas" the reported origin of the "Santa Claus" tradition actually coincides with other "Sun Gods" such as Mithras, Apollo, and Sol Invictus who are also celebrated around the winter solstice, reinforcing the idea that Nicholas is part of a broader tradition of solar deities or figures representing the return of light. The notion of Saint Nicholas presiding over earths tides and the fluids of the human body draws on the metaphysical secrets of traditional figures that connects them with forbidden sciences equated with spiritual development, energy, and the body's inner processes.

Inversion

A more sinister perspective of Saint Nicholas, links him to what Charles Fillmore calls the *"Nicodemus state of mind."* The Nicodemus state of mind refers to the blind acceptance of religions or customs just because "our parents believed in them," or because a church elder told us to, Fillmore refers to this sort of conditioning as "a dark state," because there's no real understanding in it -- true knowing (gnosis) comes from experience and "cure-iosity."

This perspective aligns with the nonlinear Latin etymology of "Nic" meaning "to kill." We see this root in words like Nicaea, Nicolaitan and the English slang word "nick" meaning steal i.e., "he nicked it" means "he stole it." **The council of Nicaea veiled or 'killed' the expansion of consciousness by restricting (stealing) what the public were allowed to see and know, and the Nicolaitans beliefs and practices threatened to corrupt or degrade the collective spiritual consciousness by promoting ideas that oppose the forces of life, health, and regeneration.** The Nicolaitans were condemned in the book of Revelation (See **ELEVATION:** The Divine Power of the Human Body) for moral laxity, sexual immorality and idol worship. Their teachings encourage followers to indulge in the desires of the flesh (carnal mind), contradicting the true opportunity and purpose that presents itself at Christmas. The true linear etymology of "Nic" brings us to the word "Nicanor" which relates to the recognition of abundance, and the name "Nicolaus" itself means "conqueror" or "victor" in the metaphysical dictionary. Did the Romans deliberately demonise the word "Nicholas" in their development of Latin? Perhaps, but the interchangeable meanings also point to the polarised forces within all things (See Dual Life Force and Saturn, Santa, and Satan).

Santa Claus

The name 'Santa' is synergistic with "Holy," "Sainted" or "Saint" as in anointed *with oil*, or enlightened, which is synonymous with the term "Spirited" or "Spirit." It stems from,

1. The Hebrew root "Qados" meaning sacred, which is also used as a noun (name) for God -- Strongs concordance H6918. God is the unknowable Source from which "True Source Love", or "Creative Light" emerges.

2. The Sanskrit root "Sat" meaning "pure existence" or "truth."

These word origins again highlight Santa's hidden ties to the Life Force Energy that enters the North Pole of earths toroidal field, or the human toroidal field, depending on which perspective you're looking at.

The name Santa also coincides with,

- The Latin "Spiritus Sanctus," from the Greek, "Pneuma Hagion" meaning Holy (Hagion) Breath, Spirit or Force (Pneuma).

- The Portuguese "Corpo Santo" (Holy Spirit).

- The Spanish "Espiritu Santo" (Holy Breath).

Again, these names correlate with the pure (Holy) energy that invigorates all layers of creation from macro to micro, -- the cosmic energy that is particularly potent during the winter solstice.

Traditionally, Santa Claus is described as wearing **black** boots and a **red** coat with **white** trim. The Aztec equivalent of Santa Claus called Quetzacoatl or Ometecuhtli is also depicted wearing **black, white, and red**. These colours symbolise the three major phases of the alchemical path known as "The Great Work." These phases of the inner alchemy of ascension; Negredo (blackness), Albedo (whiteness), and Rubedo (whiteness) are explained in depth in the entry for "The Three Wise Men Part 2." The alchemists "Great Work" is akin to "Angelo Morphism", "assimilating the Creative Light within" and "the preserving and raising of the sacred secretion." The fact that Santa is illustrated wearing these highly significant colours immediately lends to his symbolic identity and role in the alchemy of ascension.

Regardless of where the Santa story is observed in today's world, "he" always possesses supernatural (godlike) abilities. Santa is thought of as immortal or "everlasting," able to be everywhere at once i.e., visiting all the houses of the world in one night (omnipresent), and all-knowing (omniscient) i.e., he automatically knows who is being naughty and who is being nice – like a unified presence behind all the workings of creation. When children write their lists to Santa, they are essentially practising the art of prayer, asking for their hearts desires and having faith that "Santa" will deliver.

Santa's Hat

Santa Claus is often depicted wearing, a tall, pointed hat. This type of hat, known as a mitre, usually symbolizes a saint's connection to divine wisdom and authority. Esoterically, Santa's hat could be seen as a symbol of the ascension of spirit or consciousness, especially as Santa Claus aligns with themes of magical ascension and spiritual enlightenment.

The putamen is part of the brain's basal ganglia, known for its shape resembling a pointed or "cone-like" form. In alchemical traditions, this structure is associated with inner mystical ascension.

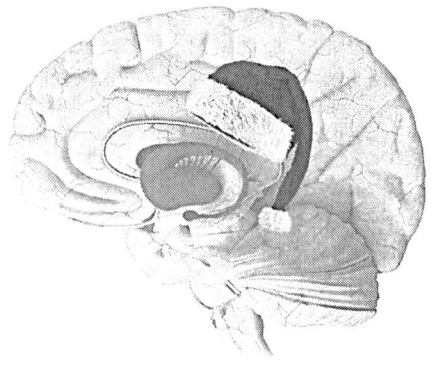

The Santa Claus hat, with its conical shape, mirrors this form and symbolizes the same "ascent" -- i.e., the rising of internal energy (spiritual or alchemical) to reach a state of enlightenment or higher consciousness. When placed on the head, the hat can be seen as a metaphor for "crowning" the ascent of consciousness and merging lower physical desires with higher spiritual ideals. Just as Santa ascends through chimneys, energy rises through the body's channels, specifically the spinal column, leading to illumination.

In esoteric anatomy, the putamen and other parts of the brain, like the pineal and pituitary glands, are critical in awakening higher states of consciousness. The "hat" or headwear of saints and religious figures is often seen as symbolizing the seat of higher wisdom and divine insight, corresponding to these regions of the brain. This reflects the inner alchemical process, where the putamen (alongside other brain structures) plays a role in transmuting physical matter (base consciousness) into spiritual gold (enlightened awareness).

These themes interweave religious symbolism, neuroscience, and esoteric practices, all pointing toward the idea of ascension -- both in terms of spiritual evolution and the literal rising of consciousness within the body. Of course, Santa Claus isn't the only iconic Saint or so-called enlightened being to have worn a hat such as this. Here are some examples of saints, deities, and scholars who traditionally wore "pointy hats," and how their head wear ties into their spiritual significance:

Zoroaster, the prophet of Zoroastrianism, is sometimes depicted wearing a pointed cap in ancient representations. Zoroaster's teachings focus on the duality of good and evil, and his pointed hat can be interpreted as a symbol of his role as a mediator between the spiritual and material worlds. The pointed cap in ancient Persian culture was also a symbol of wisdom and connection to the divine.

Many **Buddhist deities** and bodhisattvas depicted in the cave paintings of Dunhuang, China, wear "conical" or pointy hats. This reflects a mixture of Indian and Chinese Buddhist iconography. The pointed hats represent spiritual authority and heightened states of consciousness. The ascending form of the hat symbolizes the ascension of the mind and spirit to higher planes of existence.

Historically, wizards like **Merlin** and scholars in the medieval and Renaissance periods were often depicted wearing tall, pointed hats.

These hats symbolize their role as keepers of esoteric wisdom and hidden knowledge.

In some interpretations and artistic renditions, the **Norse goddess Freyja**, associated with love, beauty, and fertility, is shown wearing a pointed hat, similar to the wizard-like pointed caps. Freyja's association with magic (seidr) and transformation aligns with the pointed hat's symbolism of mystical power and divine connection, much like the wizards of later European traditions.

Many **Egyptian pharaohs** wore the crown of Upper Egypt, which is a tall, conical headdress, pointed at the top. The crown of Upper Egypt symbolized the pharaoh's divine right to rule and their connection to the gods. The pointed form of the crown was seen as a channel or antennae through which divine power flowed to the earthly ruler (See Joseph for more about Antennae).

It's likely that all of these figures, and many others attained the inner anointing powered by the basal ganglia and other parts of the brain implicated in the preserving and raising of the sacred secretion and the release of the biochemicals of enlightenment.

Saturn and Saturnalia

The Roman Saturnalia, "the festival of Saturn" is traditionally celebrated over the period of a few days, from December 17th to December 23rd, these dates clearly coincide with the timing of Christmas and Winter Solstice.

In the analogy where the Sun signifies spirit, Saturn represents matter. Opposing the Suns force of expansion, life, and abundance, Saturn's force resonates contraction, death, and restriction. In the solstice cycle Saturn plays a significant role. The Sun's descent into darkness, is a period that's said to be governed by Saturn's cold, slow, reflective energy. As mentioned earlier in this book, **Saturn's role as the 'keeper of time' illustrates "his" role in overseeing the whole solstice drama.** Only after its descent into the Saturnian realms of limitation and endings can the Sun be "reborn," symbolizing the triumph of light, life, and consciousness over darkness and ignorance. This interplay between Saturn and the Sun mirrors the eternal cycles of death and rebirth, not only in the cosmos but within human life as well.

Initially, Saturnalia lasted one day "the darkest/shortest day" of the year. On this day people celebrated Saturn's role in the solstice process, seeing Saturn as the ruler of time and cycles and respecting Saturn's part in incubating the sun ready for rebirth.

But, during the time of the Roman Empire an inversion occurred. **First, the festival of Saturnalia was extended to last for several days,**

and second, devitalizing practises such as drinking alcohol, gorging on food, riotous living, and defiling the body became traditions associated with "the Feast of Saturn/Saturnalia." This can be seen as the birth of "death culture" and trends that propel dis-ease, discomfort, and degeneration. This inversion of the true solstice practise stems from Roman governments who sought to lead the general population (profane) astray, keeping the publics minds numb in order to maintain their rule. Instead of sharing, teaching, and perpetuating the truth of fasting, light assimilation, and the regeneration of the body, the masses were deceived into "celebrating" death, darkness, and the debilitation of body, mind, soul, and spirit.

In certain groups, the concept of Saturnalia has further degraded over time, today it is associated with debauchery, feasting, and role reversals. One nickname for Saturnalia is "Topsy Turvy Day," a name derived from the ritualistic practise of "role reversal." One popular tradition was a reverse role-play "game" between masters and their slaves -- the masters would be put to work and survive on limited food rations (thus secretly being in a state of fasting and regeneration), while the slave was encouraged to laze around and binge (thus unwittingly being in a state of degeneration). On the surface, slaves saw this ritual as a welcome treat, but really this was yet another way of governing powers keeping the knowledge of sacred sciences to themselves and denying the public the opportunity for cosmic renewal. Ironically "Topsy Turvy Day" was also known as the "Feast of Fools," and it literally was a day made to fool innocent minds -- a feast of fools, for fools.

During Saturnalia, formal behaviours were cast aside, and people engaged in behaviour that would normally be frowned upon or restricted. This included gambling, drinking in excess, and public disorder, often in stark contrast to the normally strict Roman societal rules. The social boundaries between the classes were blurred, and the festivities encouraged everyone to partake in merriment on an equal footing. **This all equates to a mass distortion of the significance of Saturn's role in the solstice cycle.** The misrepresentation of Saturnalia as a festival of excess, similar to modern Christmas traditions reflects humanity's fall into materialism and moral degradation. The wide-spread deception is that Christmas is a time for degenerating conducts, such as getting excessively drunk. **This is not the true Saturnalia reserved for the masters, it's the opposite.** The Hebrew word for Saturn is "Shabbatai," which is derived from the word "Sabbath" meaning rest. The true concept of Sabbath is about invoking the healing parasympathetic nervous system and activating cellular autophagy (cell renewal) --"resting" in detoxification, in meditation, in reflection, and in discipline for the benefit of your entire being and priming your vessel to receive cosmic influences.

It is my belief that the original Saturnalia marked the darkest or shortest day of the year, a day when the initiate would savour one last meal or "supper" (feast) before entering into a period of fasting, retention, and reflection. This "practise time" would have then lasted approximately 3.5 days, coinciding with the duration of solstice. And break-fast on Christmas morning would have been both a celebration of the macrocosmic Sun and the microcosmic Light within.

> *"Verily I say unto you, except ye be converted, and become as little children (pure in body, mind, soul, and spirit), ye shall not enter the Kingdom of heaven."*
> **Matthew 18:3 (KJV)**

Saturn, Santa and Satan

Over the years, both Saturn and the Sun have been associated with the character of "Santa." Elsewhere in this book, we've unpacked the notion of Santa as a personification of the expansive Sun and infinite Creative Light, so how can Santa also correlate with "Satan" the "adversity" and Saturn the planet of time, materiality and contraction? Let's take a look.

Mystics and astrologers believe that Saturn and the Sun alternate their labour in the government of this world. This notion illustrates the interplay between the Sun and Saturn as cosmic forces that govern different aspects of life and the world. This idea is rooted in ancient alchemy, where celestial bodies are believed to have influence over the physical and metaphysical aspects of existence. In this view, reality is governed by both creation and limitation; by the influence of **infinity and generation (the Sun)** and **time and decay (Saturn).**

> "Upon the esoteric planisphere, **the Sun becomes the great archangel, who defeats Satan (Saturn)** and tramples upon the head of the serpent of matter; and thenceforward, guards the way of life and immortality, with the flaming swords of solar power."
> Page 258, The Light of Egypt by Thomas H. Burgoyne

Santa and the Sun

The sun is often seen as a source of life, light, and energy. It represents the divine spark in the microcosm and the infinite, timeless, creative force in the universe. The sun is associated with qualities like power, authority, will, and the conscious self.

- In the body, the Sun (Santa) is assigned to the **crown chakra** (North Pole) at the top of the energetic system.

- The geometrical **"dodecahedron"** is usually assigned to "spiritual energy" in the third eye chakra, that further morphs into the "sphere" associated with the crown chakra.

- The Sun, and indeed the crown chakra are associated with the colour white, a colour that also features in Santa's attire.

- The Sun (Santa) is also akin with the alchemist's "gold" and spiritual enlightenment.

- The Sun (Santa) parallels photon-light (electromagnetic energy), and consequently electrons, and atoms such as nitrogen, "the fire of life" and phosphorus, "the light of life."

Santa and Saturn

Conversely, Saturn is associated with structure (materiality), discipline, time, and limitations. It's depicted as a stern teacher or the "Great Malefic." It represents the constraint of time, which is a restriction in the material world but non-existent in the light realm. Time is a necessary factor in the experience of "reality," thus Saturn can be deemed fundamental for the cycles of nature, and the seemingly linear development of spiritual awareness.

- In the body, Saturn (Satan) is assigned to the **root chakra** at the bottom of the energetic system.

- The geometrical **"cube"** or **"Kaaba"** is usually assigned to "base energy" and the root chakra.

- Saturn, and indeed the root chakra are associated with the colour red, a colour featured in Santa's attire and traditionally assigned to "Satan."

- Saturn (Satan) is also akin with the alchemist's "lead" and spiritual ignorance.

- Saturn (Satan) parallels the carbon-12 atom (666) -- the element of rigidity and materiality.

Remember, in the analogy where the sun signifies spirit, Saturn represents matter. With the illustration of this interplay between Saturn in the root chakra at the base of the spine, and the Sun in the crown chakra at the apex of the body, it's easy to see how **Satan and Santa** demonstrate the extreme ends of a polarity, similar to Judas (base energy) and Judah (crown energy) in the bible. The alternating exertions of these energies symbolises the alchemical process of transmutation, where <u>**base-saturn-satan** energy is raised, and refined into **crown-sun-santa energy.**</u> When Santa is flying in his sleigh, he's in **spirit from** and when he's in the fireplace at the base of the chimney he takes **material form.**

> *"The secret of the philosophers stone is to make the fixed volatile and to spiritualize the materialistic Saturn in the fire of pure Spirit."*
> Page 35, Alchemical Treatises of Solomon Trismosin, by J.K

More imagery helping us to visualise the ascending force is seen with the geometric shapes assigned to these chakras and cosmic bodies:

- Starting at the root chakra, Saturn's Cube (lead) turns, elevates, and transforms into the third eye dodecahedron, which eventually perfects itself to become the sphere (gold) of the crown chakra.

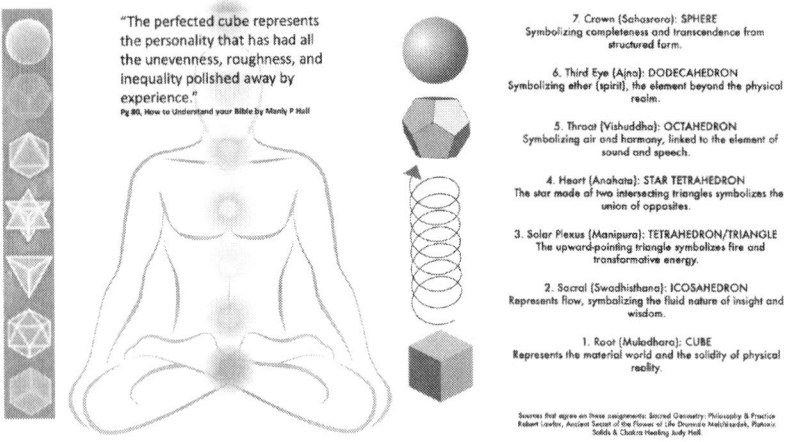

The 2D perimeter of a cube forms a hexagon. The origin of the terminology used when cursing someone i.e., "to place a hex on them" is reminiscent of the 2D hexagon/3D cube assigned to the root chakra and its so-called "Saturnic" or "Satanic" energy.

The phrase, "think outside the box" also appears to find its origin with the cube of materiality and the innate desire to transcend limited views. Along with the "Cube of Saturn," there is also what's known as the "Cube of Space," a form described in the Sefer Yetzirah as *"the cube from which all matter emerges"* which is parallel to "Metatron's cube," the geometrical shape that embodies every possible material format witnessed in "reality" -- a literal blueprint for reality. The cube of space is intricately tied to Saturn, representing the matrix of matter, structure, and earthly foundations. In the realm of Platonic solids, the cube specifically corresponds to the "earth" element, embodying stability and material manifestation. In this way, it highlights the interconnectedness of the divine world and the material world.

In addition to these perspectives, Saturn is the 6th planet from the sun and the 6th chakra from the crown, the number 6 is tied to the atomic value of carbon (the base substance and cube to be transformed) -- **Saturn is bound by its ring and spirit is bound by matter.** No true freedom or liberation can come from material idolatry.

Another visual display of these polar energies comes with the fact that the name "Santa" is an "anagram" for Satan. Writing these two words in vertical formation shows the "N," which is the Hebrew "nun" meaning "seed," moving upwards from the bottom position to the mid position.

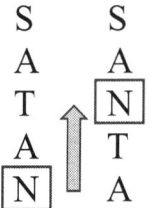

This also highlights the connection between "Saturnic" forces, the carnal mind, and procreative energy or essences (seed). The seed must be preserved and raised, in order to experience the full expression of enlightenment in the crown.

> *"The seed germs of life, take on human form as they enter the stomach and the spleen. Then, at the second stage, **these human cells are taken down (fall) by Saturn into Tartarus (hell).** This means that in the organs of procreation they are conjoined with "animal germs."*
> **Page 285, The Zodiac and the Salts of Salvation by G W Carey**

Mystics say that the sexual contraction that follows the spilling of procreative essences gathers billions of "satanic atoms" which are transmitted into the body via the root chakra. These "Saturnic" atoms fuel carnal desire (lower instincts) by replacing the lost "solar atoms" which are transmitted into the body mainly via the breath, through the pneumogastric nerve into the solar plexus. They suggest that by lessening solar energy and heightening saturn energy, "evil" or the (d)evil is formed within the organism due to the imbalance of energy caused by ejaculation. The terminology used here is pretty archaic, but the moral of "save-seed" and the scientific benefits of retention stand.

> *"If you want to destroy any nation without war, make adultery or nudity common in the young generation."*
> **Saladin**

In an astrological chart, the relationship between the Sun and Saturn (such as through aspects like conjunctions, oppositions, etc.) can indicate how an individual balances creative (Sun) and restrictive (Saturn) forces. For example, the alternation of their influence symbolises the need to balance creativity (Sun) with responsibility (Saturn), or ambition (Sun) with caution (Saturn). **The Sun and Saturn as a polarity don't just**

represent light and darkness, but also expansion and contraction. This duality is necessary for the world to function harmoniously. Although Saturn is often demonised, these forces work together in a cyclical process to maintain balance and order in the universe, guiding both physical and spiritual evolution in the world. Without the "time and space" aspects associated with Saturn they'd be no means for us light beings to have an earthly, "material" experience.

The Santa/Satan polarity can also be seen in the macrocosm with theories about the North and South Poles of the Earth. The North Pole (where Santa comes from) is often viewed as an entry point for creative, positive energy, symbolizing higher consciousness, enlightenment, and life force. It is seen as a gateway for spiritual energy entering the Earth. The North Pole vortex can be seen as a planetary equivalent to the crown chakra in humans, where divine energy flows into the body from above. This energy is believed to enter the Earth at the North Pole, infusing the planet with life and higher purpose. The North Pole is sometimes perceived as the "axis mundi" or world axis, a central point connecting the Earth with the heavens. This makes it an important conduit for creative light and pure energy, shaping existence itself.

In contrast, the South Pole is thought to release or funnel out destructive, dissolving, or purging forces. These energies represent decay, or purification, associated with death and the removal of old forms. The South Pole vortex symbolizes a natural counterbalance to the creative energy of the North Pole. While the North brings in creation, the South Pole is seen as an exit point for spent or negative energies, reinforcing the idea of cyclical processes—birth and death, growth and decay.

Some esoteric systems link the South Pole vortex with the root chakra, which deals with grounding and survival. Just as the root chakra can deal with primal fear and physical needs, the South Pole is seen as a vortex handling lower, more adverse forces like entropy or chaotic energy. In mythology, the South Pole is thought to connect to the underworld or the unseen realms of transformation and shadow. In these analogies or illustrations, the "adverse" energy isn't necessarily evil, but is related to the "essential" force of destruction that paves the way for renewal.

The interaction between the North and South Poles reflects cosmic duality -- creation and destruction, light and darkness, "positive and negative forces." Both poles are essential for maintaining the balance of energies on Earth. The South Pole's "adverse" energy can be seen as a necessary force for transformation. Just as destruction makes room for new creation, the energy funnelled out through the South Pole allows for the renewal process initiated by the creative forces entering through the North Pole. The "two houses becoming one" allegory that echoes throughout art, history, and literature (Romeo and Juliet for example), really pertains to the acceptance and merging of extreme poles. Those sensitive to polar energies may feel the creative surge of light and inspiration linked with the North Pole, while simultaneously grappling with the challenges of survival, fear, or primal instincts tied to the South Pole.

Mystic teachings promote the idea that humanity must learn to integrate both polar energies -- using the Creative Light funnelled by the North Pole to rise in consciousness, while also embracing the purging and transformative forces of the South Pole to cleanse the self of erroneous or debilitating energies and substances. In essence, these vortices reflect the complementary forces that govern existence -- **light and dark, creation and destruction, Santa and Satan, evil and live (reverse anagram), ease and adversity, Judas and Judah, etc. etc.**

"Playing into" the negative aspect of the cube can lead to "imprisoned" or limited consciousness, where one is chained to the "cult of the black cube." This type of "Saturnic" possession can manifest as an unwitting bondage to a system of materialism, where the individual or society becomes seemingly separated from the divine. In this scenario, the person may feel as though their wings have been clipped as they find themselves stuck in the rat-race of mundane life, forgetting to find time for freedom, creativity, adventure, and even simple things such as ample rest.

As ruler of matter, Saturn also governs the ego, the identity that we perceive as self, --programmed and conditioned by our experiences, circumstances, and external influences. Many people claw and clammer to serve this "ego" version of themselves, tirelessly seeking to glorify their "identity" and persona. Saturn worship (Satanism) is the ruthless exaltation of the "egoic self." The hideous lengths some people go to, just to preserve their image is inconceivable. Any grievous or harmful thoughts or acts held or performed by the individual are always driven by the Saturn/Satan principle.

In truth, most of what we perceive as "self" is an illusion, so it's okay to surrender and allow ourselves to be led back to the true higher self (divine spark within). Any circumstance that skews the harmonious state within can simply be addressed in prayer, *"True Source Love, I give all my troubles to you, please resolve this situation for the best good of all. I accept that my perspective is limited and that you are all-knowing, therefore I trust your hand over this situation. And it is so. Amen."*

Many have noticed the echoes of the "Saturnic Cube" throughout the material world. For example, there are black cube monuments placed around major cities, Muslims have their black cube in Mecca, and televisions resemble the idea of a black box. It's important to remember, that while televisions can encourage material and self-obsession, they can also teach and inform. There's no matter without spirit. It's up to the individual to shepherd their own exposure to the Saturnic influence. We must all wise up and recognise that we should not allow "screens" to dictate our thoughts, attitudes, or emotions (or our fashions and diets for that matter).

When dramatized and misinterpreted the figure of Saturn seems very fearful, and all kinds of naïve or degenerate minds do terrible things in the name of "Saturn" or "Satan." This is all part of a grave delusion, perversion and demonisation of a cosmic principle. Clouding the minds of innocent people has been a control tactic used for millennia. The friendly Saint with his "naughty and nice" list wasn't enough to control really "bad" kids, so "Krampus" was introduced -- a very "satanic" looking monster, with horns (of course), who takes children into slavery and tortures them if they are naughty. Of course, children were traumatised by such threats, and the alchemical states of their bodies seriously altered as a consequence. Mimicking unthinkably cruel scenes is human error, "free-will" gone truly awry. The performance of harmful rituals cannot be blamed on "Saturn," only on the deceptive allure of the carnal mind left to run rampant.

> "*Currents penetrate the innermost recesses of the human mind, and possess the soul to such an extent, that deep down in the heart of man; no matter how pure and disinterested he may appear; there lurks the slimy reptile of selfishness, even when he least expects it.* **It is this grim monster, SELF that each aspirant to truth seeks to conquer.**"
> Page 154, The Light of Egypt by Thomas H. Burgoyne

Thankfully, we live in a time when people are awakening to spiritual truth and are removing their blinkers so-to-speak. The cube is dissolving, people are realising their power, and the veil of Saturn (material dominance) is tearing, just as it did in the Biblical, Holy of Holies.

Saturn Eats the Children and Herod Kills the Children

The allegories of, 1) Herod calling for all babies under the age of 2 years to be killed in an attempt to eradicate Jesus and 2) Saturn abhorrently "eating" children are both metaphorical examples of the same cosmic principal.

Both Herod and Saturn are associated with the carnal mind, lower instincts and the "base substance" of the root chakra. These instincts include lust, hatred, envy, sloth, gluttony, deception etc. all of which are devitalizing states of consciousness, that impede the flow of Creative Light in the body, mind, soul, and spirit. In an alchemical sense, these harmful frequencies can retard cellular regeneration (mitosis), thus "killing" or "eating" the "Jesus Seed" or "chi" (children) within us. *"Jesus is a germ/seed of life,"* **G W Carey**. The "Jesus Seed" born in the solar plexus every 29.5 days coinciding with the moons cycle is an allegory for stem cell production (birth) and proliferation, stem cells are the "infant" or "baby" cells within us subject to "Herod's" or "Saturn's" attack.

The fact that artworks and texts depicting the "Massacre of the Innocents" may have been taken in a literal sense by ignorant fools, operating purely from their base instincts is a very tragic affair indeed. Such practises are a massive perversion of cosmic principals and divine law. Unfortunately, arcane texts have been wildly misinterpreted, ultimately leading to unfathomably destructive and abhorrent consequences in "real world affairs."

In the "Secret Doctrine of Anahuac," a set of coded teachings from ancient Mesoamerican cultures, that serve as parables for cosmic cycles and the spiritual evolution of humanity, it states the following,

> *"The Saturnian serpent does not eat anything filthy; no initiate, nor even those which have reached the level of 'Adeptus Exemptus' could enjoy the powers of the snake without having been previously devoured by it. It is not enough to achieve the ascent of the igneous serpent of our magical powers along the spinal column, from chakra to chakra; it is urgent, undelayable, to be devoured by the snake... only then will we become something distinct, different."*
>
> **Pages Unnumbered, The Secret Doctrine of Anahuac by Anon.**

This passage depicts the Anahuac belief that the initiate on the path to ascension had to be **eaten by the Saturnian serpent.** When taken literally this idea sounds horrendous and unscrupulous and the creators of these codes have a lot to answer for. Truly though, being eaten by a saturnian serpent is an inner alchemical process. The ancient Mesoamerican civilizations believed in cycles of creation and destruction, they understood the universe as being subject to various cosmic forces, which impacted their body's and the Earth.

The true symbolic meaning of the Secret Doctrine of Anahuac emphasized the transformation of human consciousness. Through specific rituals, ceremonies, and inner work, individuals could rise to higher spiritual levels, often associated with the gods and celestial beings. Anahuac civilizations incorporated sacred symbols, such as the serpent, the sun, and other natural elements, into their religious and esoteric traditions. These symbols had multiple meanings related to spiritual evolution, the balance of cosmic forces, and the cycles of life and death. Their gods were seen as embodiments of natural forces (i.e., Tlaloc as the god of rain, and Quetzalcoatl as the feathered serpent representing higher wisdom), they believed human beings could attune to these forces through rituals and spiritual practice.

It might seem confusing to understand, but **the Anahuac's believed the 'Holy Spirit' to be the one who gave 'her' children away to Saturn ready for him to swallow.** This is an illustration, an allegory for Creative Light descending into the root chakra, where it is effectively 'swallowed by the beast' (Saturn/Satan). Remember, traditional "beast" imagery is usually reminiscent of the "goat" shape formed by the glands and organs of the procreative region in the body and the planet Saturn is assigned to the root chakra. The Anahuac doctrine says that after Saturn (the root chakra) swallows the initiate (procreative essences), it then vomits them out or regurgitates them (processes the essences so they can be reabsorbed by the lymphatic system). On the earth plane, the reemergence of the "vomited" initiate or "child" symbolised their rebirth, or baptism by fire. Such vulgar allegories were designed to keep the profane (general population) from understanding the science of ascension.

The Doctrine states that through this process the initiate became a "feathered serpent" or a "god." This imagery aligns with the caduceus and its feathered mount, again this symbolises the preservation of procreative energies and essences and has nothing to do with cannibalism. **Anyone who thinks it does or justifies wicked behaviour due to their own ignorance is sorely mistaken!** Preservation of vital fluids allows for a raising and refining effect toward super consciousness awakening. The Anahuac Doctrine explains that the initiate can only be "swallowed" when they become pure or "childlike" in body (chaste), mind (thought), soul (detoxified), and spirit (essence). Then and only then could the initiate be transformed into the winged serpent. As mentioned elsewhere in this book, the Bible also calls for its followers to become childlike,

> *"Verily I say unto you, except ye be converted, and become as little children, ye shall not enter into the Kingdom of heaven."*
> Matthew 18:3 (KJV)

Again, any obscure, outward practises that do not serve the good of all mankind are abhorrent perversions of sacred truths. It's devastating to consider the fact that the misinterpretation of coded stories, such as this, has led to sorrowful devastation.

In the macrocosm, Saturn is implicated in the whole solstice process. As the keeper of time, Saturn is responsible for the Sun being "devoured" and reemerging a few days later. As the extreme opposite of "Santa," Saturn/Satan is often represented with a long white beard highlighting its polarised connection with Santa. Saturn is also seen holding a scythe and a clock. Of course, the clock illustrates the concept of time and Saturn's alleged governance over it. The month of December is said to be astrologically ruled by Capricorn "the goat," ruler of planet Saturn, which further implicates Saturn in the "disappearance of the sun," -- Saturn/Satan takes his metaphorical scythe and "kills the sun/son." A grotesque image invented to create a wall of fear around the alchemical (physiological) and astrological (cosmic) meaning. As the keeper or manifester of the time principal, and therefore the ruler over materiality, Saturn must first "conquer" the sun, thus allowing for the rebirth of a new cycle. The material world operates in cycles -- generation, operation, decay, generation, operation etc.

Whether identified as "Kronos" in Greek mythology (who also symbolically ate his offspring), Shani in Hinduism, Yama, or another deity in a different cultural context, Saturn's influence as a universal archetype suggests its rule or influence over the material dimension of time and space, whereas the Sun presides over the metaphysical dimension of no-time and no-space i.e., infinite possibility.

Sea of Galilee

After Jesus's "circumcision" on the 8th day (See Circumcision), and the death of King Herod (See King Herod), Mary and Joseph take their "baby" (germ or cell) to Nazareth in Galilee, thus fulfilling the prophecy that Jesus would become a Nasarean (See Nasarean).

"Galilee" means circuit, -- the systems of the body are circuits for performing various functions. Energy constantly flows through the circuits of the nervous, circulatory, lymphatic, and respiratory systems of the body. These interlinked circuits support life, health and vibrancy. The circulatory system is responsible for pumping blood throughout the body via the heart, arteries, veins, and capillaries. It delivers oxygen and nutrients to tissues and removes waste products. The lymphatic system works alongside the circulatory system, collecting excess fluid (lymph) from tissues, filtering it through lymph nodes, and returning it to the bloodstream. The nervous system regulates the circulatory system by controlling heart rate and blood vessel contraction, **every electrical pulse supplies power for the continuous circuitry of the body.** In turn, the circulatory system supplies oxygen-rich blood to the brain and nerves, supporting their function. Thus, vital energy cycles through the body via a continuous circuit of interconnected systems.

Man has a dual nervous system:

- **The voluntary nervous system,** centred in the cerebrum is governed by the <u>conscious mind.</u>

- **The involuntary nervous system,** centred in the cerebellum is governed by the <u>subconscious mind.</u>

The nervous system carries all sorts of messages to and from the mind. In the Metaphysical Bible Dictionary, Charles Fillmore asserts that *"the nervous sea of vitality is designated in the history of Jesus as the Sea of Galilee."*

The <u>**involuntary system**</u> **of the body is a silent, automatic, caregiver for the human temple.** The **involuntary** actions of the body are controlled by the **subconscious mind.** Involuntary actions include the vital processes that we don't have to knowingly think about, such as cell generation and regeneration (mitosis), temperature regulation, heart rhythm and health, the circulation of the blood, the crucial impulse to breathe, digestion, fuel assimilation, and the elimination of waste. The **subconscious mind** cannot take initiative, i.e., "think for itself," but it automatically carries out the optimal health care plan available to every cell of the body at every given moment.

When the **conscious mind** i.e., our thoughts, fears, weaknesses etc. interfere with the normal involuntary functioning of the body, then the subconscious must compensate in an instinctive way and this inner conflict can result in disease or illness. But when the conscious mind aligns with truthful ideas of health, healing and abundance it gives the right directions to the subconscious allowing the involuntary functions to carry on their normal work of optimising and maintaining life and health in the body.

Charles Fillmore says that "Jesus" returning to "Nazareth" symbolises the "Christ Seed" <u>crossing</u> from the **voluntary nervous system (conscious** mind – "life") into the **involuntary nervous system (subconscious mind – "death") and back again -- resurrection!**

<u>When the seed makes this transition, it initiates deep healing transformations via the subconscious mind which positively alter the temple body on a deep astral and cellular level. This is a key aspect in spiritual rebirth.</u>

> *"But after I am risen again, I will go before you into Galilee."*
> Matthew 26:32 (KJV)

In the body, the crossover point is between the corpora quadrigemina (mount of olives), and the cerebellum (tomb). The "olivary bodies" (corpora quadrigemina) are a relay station for "I am" impulses between the cerebrum and cerebellum. To say "I am" is to be in the knowing mind, -- the conscious mind.

As the resting place between death and resurrection, the tomb (cerebellum) is the region of the brain implicated in processing energy between the subconscious and conscious mind (and vice versa). As the process of inner alchemy unfolds the conscious mind is reprogrammed to align with the secret knowledge of the subconscious mind. As the conscious mind "sacrifices itself" it then lays "dead" in the tomb for a few days, but ultimately allows for subconscious powers to be "resurrected."

> *"The cerebellum clearly demonstrates the proper functioning of the intellect as it begins to move into Christ consciousness. As we become aware of the underlying activity that coordinates, balances, and harmonizes every action in creation, the cerebellum begins to receive this picture. Then we have available to us the information that represents*

> *the total body of creation, and we can become co-creators with the primary Creator."*
> **Revelation the book of Unity by J. Sig Paulson and Ric Dickerson – Unity Magazine May 1975, Vol 155. No 5, Page 9**

Contrary to what is taught, esotericists believe that the subconscious mind functions through the lower brain or cerebellum. The Latin term "sub" means under, and the cerebellum (subconscious mind) is situated "under" the conscious brain (cerebrum). When the "Christ Seed" is crucified, it remains in the cerebellum (tomb) which essentially switches, diffuses, or "resurrects" its energy from "involuntary power" to the central intelligence, "voluntary power". *"The cerebellum, a negative (lunar) organ or <u>switchboard,</u> switches the magnetic aura from the ganglionic to the cerebral and spinal nerves, as dictated by cerebral thought.* **Each brain has its nervous system.***"* Unity Magazine August 1903, Vol XIX. No 2, Page 67, The Three Brains by Mrs. G. A. Bartholomew, B.D

Shepherds and Fields

Luke 2:8 (KJV) speaks of the "shepherds" who were visited by the "Angel of the Lord" (see Angel of the Lord) while they were sat in a "field" watching their flock.

Fields are vortexes of energy, every organism from tiny blood cells to human beings, and even enormous planets are surrounded by their own electromagnetic (light) field. Even our universe is encapsulated within its own energy field (donut shaped, torus or toroidal field), also known as the "unified field" and the "divine matrix."

> *"The field is the world."*
> **Matthew 13:38 (KJV)**

The natural law of cause and effect, lovingly dubbed "karma" operates via energy fields. Whatever energy we release into our own toroidal field via our thoughts, emotions, and actions can't help but return to us because energy constantly circulates out and in, causing ripples in the unified field which are then echoed back to the cause. This is the scientific truth behind the notion *"what you sow (into your field) you shall surely reap."* And why Matthew 13:37 states, *"He that soweth the good seed is the Son of Man."* Meaning, he that purifies himself physically, mentally, and emotionally is untouchable or invincible.

A shepherd is someone who watches over their sheep, cares for them, and guides them. They can be seen as parallel to our wise and protective thoughts which assist the development of the Creative Light body. The fact that the Angel of the Lord visits the shepherd's field, illustrates how Divine Mind communicates via electromagnetism (light).

Unity teacher Charles Fillmore puts it like this,

> *"The attention of the protective thoughts (shepherds) causes a spiritual quickening."*
> **Metaphysical Bible Dictionary by Charles Fillmore.**

In other words, sheep are the animalistic urges and tendencies that need transformation, and the shepherd is the higher self, leading this process. When the carnal mind is guided and refined, we become what we truly are in our core -- beings of light. You are the shepherd of your mind. Allow the truth to be born within you, and shepherd it with divine love, protect it from sense consciousness (Herod) and elevate yourself into a being of light.

On the physiological plane, the original meaning of "animal sacrifice" has to do with retention and preserving the "animal seed" (seminal fluids). On the emotional and mental planes, "animal sacrifice" has to do with "offering up" the lower carnal/ego nature including any aspects of lust, selfishness, anger, greed, violence, self-indulgence etc. To truly release or surrender these lower influences is the path to true, felt, anointing. It's very unfortunate that the gross misinterpretation of this sacred science led to the corrupt, mimicking, "Saturnic" ritual of physical animal slaughter which is believed to "appease the adversary."

The true shepherd symbolizes the awakened individual, one who has mastered the lower mind and become a true human (light being).

Sleigh

Santa's sleigh can be viewed as a literary representation of the "chariot" or "vehicle" of ascension, akin to the mystical "Mer**kaab**ah."

Chariots and ascension vehicles of all kinds, such as Cinderella's carriage (which takes her to the "ball" -- sphere of the crown chakra), or the Vimana of Vedic lore relate to DNA, -- the master of transformation! (See Reindeer for other examples of sleighs).

In the light world, or unmanifest realm of life, the sacred, geometrical "scaffolding" of DNA is the ratcheting or twisting dodecahedron.

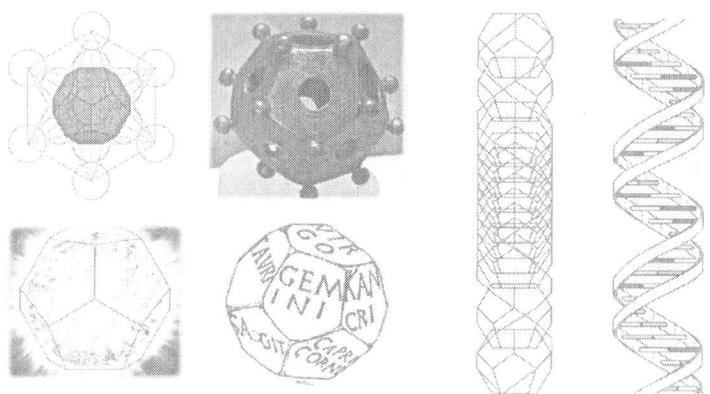

Many sacred texts, such as the Bible, and artworks, such as Salvador Dali's "Last Supper" depict the dodecahedron as the ascension vehicle. This subject was covered in depth in Elevation: The Divine Power of the Human Body. The DNA double helix resembles two intwined serPENTs emerging from "pure water" (See Mary), each one of the 12 sides of the dodecahedral structure is a PENTagon. The sides of DNA are comprised of carbon (See Coal, Lead and Carbon) and phosphorus, the carbon element of this molecule presents itself as a PENTose sugar known as deoxyribose.

In the same way that "Santa rides his Sleigh," Light rides the DNA ascension vehicle; DNA is essentially a *"crystal that transports electrons and emits photon light (electromagnetic energy)."* Jeremy Narby, The Cosmic Serpent. The cells of all living beings emit photons (light) and DNA is the source of that light.

DNA light emissions are stimulated by DMT secretions, DMT is one of the biochemicals of enlightenment produced more abundantly through right living. DNA light emissions may account for the many "mythological" reports about saints and sages glowing or wearing the "robe of light/perfection."

DNA is the molecule of life! DNA is the same for all species -- it's the genetic information of roses, bacterium and humans and is continually being coded and produced in cells. Most of the cells in the different species around the world, and in the human body contain DNA which gives instructions for how to grow, function, and reproduce.

The concept of "ascension vehicles" appears in many esoteric, spiritual, and mythological traditions. These vehicles often serve as metaphors for the soul's journey to higher dimensions, the divine, or enlightenment and the alteration of DNA to programme an evolved body and existence is at the heart of these teachings. Below are examples:

In Kabbalistic tradition, the Merkabah (meaning "chariot") is a vehicle that mystics use to ascend to the divine realms. Within the etymology of the word "Merkabah" we find the root word "Kaaba." This is very significant because "Kaaba" means "cube."

The "Kaaba," or "cube" equates with the root chakra (as do Saturn and carbon/coal/lead).

This cube in the root of the body evolves through many forms as it ascends, eventually morphing into the dodecahedron of spirit at the third eye, and the sphere of the crown chakra (See Saturn, Santa and Satan). The Merkabah is mentioned in the Book of Ezekiel, where the prophet has a vision of a divine chariot composed of wheels within wheels and living beings. It's seen as a vehicle for the soul's ascension through the spheres of existence to reach union with God.

Although not illustrating the form of a dodecahedron, **Cinderella's pumpkin carriage,** which magically transforms for her journey to the "ball," represents the theme of transformation and elevation from mundane existence to a higher state of being (symbolized by the royal ball). Cinderella's pumpkin carriage resembles the shape of an electromagnetic torus field, another divine structure relative to alchemical transformation. Just as Cinderella's form changes when her carriage takes her to the ball (sphere), DNA reflects an encoded potential for transformation and the realization of higher consciousness.

In Indian texts, **Vimanas** are vehicles used by gods and kings for travel between realms.

Vimanas serve as metaphors for spiritual vehicles that help the soul ascend from the earthly realm to higher planes of existence.

In Islamic mythology, the **Buraq** is a celestial creature that transported the Prophet Muhammad from Mecca (where the Kaaba/Cube is situated) to Jerusalem during the "Night Journey" to the heavens. The Buraq, often depicted as having both human and animal features, symbolizes the blending of different realms (physical and spiritual), much like how the geometry of DNA bridges the material and energetic aspects of life.

In both Hinduism and Buddhism, the **lotus** is a symbol of purity and spiritual enlightenment. It is often described as a "seat" for deities and divine beings, such as Lakshmi. The lotus represents the soul's journey from the depths of material existence (muddy waters) to the heights of spiritual purity (blossoming into the light). The unfolding pattern of the lotus flower is often compared to the spiralling nature of DNA, representing growth, transformation, and the ascension from base materiality to spiritual perfection.

The concept of ascension vehicles, whether mythological, esoteric, or symbolic reflects a universal idea of transformation, spiritual growth, and the journey toward higher consciousness. Each culture's version of this vehicle aligns with the principles of spiritual evolution, and concepts that resonate with DNA. The dodecahedral aspect of DNA represents cosmic order and the boundless possibilities of human and spiritual development.

Sleigh Bells and Christmas Bells

Bells are a symbol of the true Christmas Spirit or divine spark that resides in the heart. Other esoteric names for the divine spark, which directly connects to "Christ consciousness" are the "master atom," "the master builder," "the atom nous" or "the nous atom." "Christ Mind" 1 Corinthians 2:15-16 (KJV), centred in the heart is the divine principle of unconditional love, compassion, and spiritual wisdom, the direct path to transcendence and the "bliss state" -- "the peace of God, which passeth all understanding." Philippians 4:7 (KJV) Practising Bhakti, a disposition of unconditional love is the foundation for assembling light in the body.

Both sound and light are at the heart of all creation, *"In the beginning was the word (sound/vibration/tone)"* John 1:1 (KJV). This isn't simply a mystical saying, the sciences of cymatics and sonoluminescence support this Scripture entirely -- matter is born from light and sound. Every sound has a parallel colour that resonates with it (or by it). In the Bible "stones" sometimes signify "tones," i.e., different sound frequencies, or keys. "Precious Stones" like on Aaron's breastplate, are also precious tones. Not only does every frequency of sound correspond with a colour (ray of light), but they also coincide with their own mineral cell-salt. As the formers and repairers of cells, mineral cell-salts are crucial to generating, healing, and regenerating the temple-body at a deep cellular level. The alchemy of ascension (sacred secretion practise) works via this programmed mechanism. As we raise our vibratory frequency the physical alchemy of our body elevates and transforms also:

1. Our health promoting thoughts and words (sound frequencies) induce an inner rainbow vortex, featuring the colours that coincide with each positive sound/tone/vibration.

2. The rainbow vortex compels the manifestation of the mineral cell-salts assigned to each colours/sound.

3. Mineral cell-salts rearrange the chemical (alchemical) essence of the body on a deep astral and cellular level.

This process is also known as "remineralising the body," and is akin to "building the solar/mineral body."

Most philosophical, religious, and spiritual teachings from around the world honour the mode of sound in their buildings and practises. In ancient Egypt, bells were used to rouse or wake crops in order to help them grow, boats carrying bells sailed the Nile to mark planting and fertilization seasons. Around 433 BC in China, the Marquis Yi of Zeng was buried with 64 (8x8) bells. The temples of Muslims and Christians alike include bells in their towers that are traditionally used for the "call to prayer." London's famous clock tower, is actually named after the huge 13 tonne bell that resides inside it, "Big Ben." At the time when Big Ben first "rang out" a reporter for the Times famously said, *"the vibration penetrates every vein in the body"* and this is exactly how resonant sound healing works, and why church bells were originally installed. Buddhist Pagodas feature dozens of little gold bells in their décor that were said to, "echo the divine voice," and of course, Tibetan singing bowls and Chinese gongs are also forms of healing bells. Bells have long been used for healing, meditation, communication, making music, and keeping time.

In the alchemy of ascension, bells are synergistic with the heart and cardiac plexus which act as a catalyst for biochemical upgrades in the body. The transmutation of lower energies into higher, spiritual energies results in a purification of the heart. Heart purifications and the expansion of love, acceptance, and surrender (serenity) send out (sound/vibration) waves into the body causing the pituitary gland to secrete enhanced amounts of oxytocin. In turn, oxytocin stimulates pineal metabolism i.e., the transformation of serotonin and melatonin into DMT and the other biochemicals of enlightenment that have been explained in depth in previous books like The God Design: Secrets of the Mind, Body and Soul.

This mechanism emphasizes the importance of the heart as not just a physical organ but a spiritual centre that connects individuals to the divine.

The Geometric Structure of the Heart is a Bell-Shaped chestahedron. The chestahedron is a seven-faced geometric form that Rudolf Steiner and Frank Chester proposed as the underlying shape of the human heart. Many years prior to this discovery, Leonard Da Vinci drew illustrations showing the heart as a dynamic energy vortex. Unlike the traditional idea, of the heart as a simple pump, the chestahedron model emphasizes its dynamic, spiral structure. The heart's geometry is related to how it creates energy vortices, which drive blood circulation through vortex motion rather than sheer mechanical pumping. This flow aligns with sacred geometry, where the heart functions as both a physical organ and an energetic centre, radiating frequencies (inaudible sounds) outward.

Da Vinci's depiction of the heart vortex.

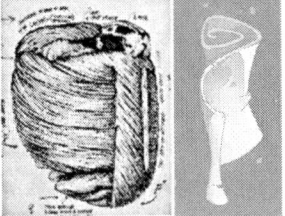

The "rolled" or spiraled organ of the heart and the "scroll of love" emblem used in many religious writings such as Sufi and Cathar.

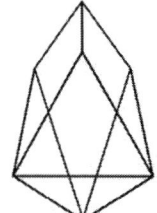
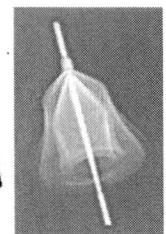

The sacred geometrical "chestahedron" form of the heart and the bell formed by its rotation, illustrating the bell of the heart.

The surface area of each of the seven-sides of a chestahedron are all equal. When a chestahedron is placed in a box, it sits on an angle 36 degrees off centre, notably this is the same angle on which the heart sits in the chest. Placing a chestahedron in water creates a bell-shaped vortex, similar to the heart vortex spiral. Your heart is actually one muscle rolled or "wrapped like a present" into a spiral or "scroll." This imagery aligns with what the Cathars and Sufis call the "book of love," which is said to bring immortality to its keeper. The heart is an energy generator. Blood enters the heart and creates a spiralling vortex that turns the water in blood into plasma (the fourth state of water).

Plasma makes up about 55% of blood and acts as a conductor of electromagnetic energy generated by the heart. This energy powers the body by delivering electrical charges to cells, aiding in communication, metabolism, and oxygenation. Plasma carries nutrients and hormones, ensuring the body functions optimally. In a more spiritual sense, plasma serves as a bridge between the physical and energetic bodies, transforming "water into plasma" to distribute life force energy throughout the body.

The heart's electromagnetic field is the strongest in the body, surpassing even that of the brain. This field is shaped by the toroidal movement of energy around the heart, acting like a vortex that generates and interacts with vibrations, including sound waves. When understood as an energy vortex, the heart resonates with frequencies that are pivotal in practices like sound healing.

In sound healing, different tones and frequencies are used to influence the body's energy fields, particularly the heart's vortex energy. The heart, as an energetic centre, responds profoundly to sound vibrations, which can balance, harmonize, and heal. Certain frequencies resonate specifically with the heart chakra, fostering emotional healing, calmness, and equilibrium. Sound vibrations like "bell chimes," gongs, and singing bowls can sync with the heart's electromagnetic waves, promoting coherence in its rhythm, which reflects in the body's overall well-being, and promotes heart/brain coherence which in turn stimulates pineal metabolism.

The Destruction of Bells in the 1900s

Bells have historically been used in spiritual and communal settings for their healing resonance and ability to clear negative energies. The "destruction of bells" in the 1900s, especially during wartime periods, is symbolically linked to the disruption of higher knowledge and the suppression of holistic healing modalities. For example, in Belgium, the historic St. Michael's Bell in Ghent was removed. Then there's the famous crack in the "Liberty Bell" of Philadelphia, a bell that was originally instated to proclaim freedom and liberty throughout the land. Furthermore, the 200 tonne Tsar Bell of Moscow, considered to be the largest bell in the world, has an enormous "chip" in its otherwise beautifully preserved form.

The public were told that bells had to be melted down to create ammunition to use in the wars, but more likely, it was to hide the importance of acoustic resonance. In esoteric thought, the removal of bells from public spaces represents the silencing of powerful vibrational tools that kept both communities and individuals in better health and harmony. The energetic disruption from this loss may be viewed as contributing to spiritual and emotional imbalance on a larger scale. Over 170,000 bells were destroyed in the 1900s, before this, and before the perversion of sacred sciences, churches and cathedrals were centres for healing, and ascension. The stain-glass windows radiated different light frequencies, while the spires channelled cosmic energy into the building, all while the bells were ringing out their healing choruses.

Bells, with their powerful resonating frequencies, are closely linked to the heart's energy. Just as bells produce sound waves that radiate outwards in concentric circles, the heart's electromagnetic field emits energy in a toroidal shape, akin to a continuous bell-like vibration. When bells were silenced in the 1900s, the energetic and symbolic disruption of this connection between sound and the heart's energy vortex diminished the flow of positive healing vibrations. Sound healing practices, often using bells, gongs, or other instruments, can restore and amplify the resonance between the heart's vortex and the healing frequencies once broadcast by bells.

These connections demonstrate how the geometry and energetics of the heart, specifically as a chestahedron and vortex, align with sound frequencies, creating profound effects on both physical and spiritual health. The loss of bells' vibrational resonance in the 1900s underscores a possible secret agenda to promote "death culture" and spiritual ignorance, whilst underscoring the importance of sound healing in maintaining the vitality of the heart.

Stable

Traditionally, stables are places where compost and fertile soil are created from hay and other organic substances. Usually, these structures had no walls as they had to be kept well-ventilated so that the air could pass through easily. The circulation of air through stables facilitates the transformation of hay into fertile soil.

The Bibles Christmas stable was said to be in Bethlehem (Solar plexus – see Bethlehem). Similar to a traditional stable, the solar plexus is an airy place. The breath nerve, known as the pneumogastric nerve (CNX) allows air to fill and circulate the organs and glands innervated by the solar plexus so that they can digest the food and drink that we consume and create "fertile soils" or fuel for the body.

The stomach, spleen and other organs vitalised by the nerves of the solar plexus play a vital role in the great regeneration or assimilation of Creative Light in the body. Everything we consume has to be processed in this life forming hub. Drug, alcohol, and food addictions, largely caused by food manufacturers deceptive marketing strategies are difficult to overcome making it increasingly challenging for us "initiates" to fully purify and prime our temple bodies to properly receive and assimilate the Creative Light within us. *"There's no room at the Inn"* means, there's no room *in you* i.e., there's no space for light to come in and transform you, *"if your body is full of darkness, light cannot dwell there."* **Paraphrase Matthew 6:23 (KJV).**

The stomach and intestines are vessels in which the sustaining minerals for life are prepared. These minerals support the birth of the "seed" or cells in the spleen (See Manger). Without the process of digestion, the inner alchemy of ascension would not be possible. Like the transformation of hay into fertile soil in stables, digestion in the body sets the vital mineral cell-salts contained in food free, creating a mineral base for the body. This mineral base is carried into circulation throughout the rest of the body via absorption into blood and lymph at the small intestines. Speaking on digestion, Doctor Carey warned in "God Man: the word Made Flesh" that the seed can be ruined by, *"alcoholic drinks, or gluttony that causes ferment-acid and even alcohol in the intestinal tract, thus 'No drunkard can inherit the Kingdom of Heaven.'"*

Historically, the essence produced by digestion in the small intestine was known as "First Matter," "Lac Virginis" or "Prima Materia". It is described as an "oily water", or "fatty lymph" and it supplies the blood with energy derived from food. First Matter is comprised of the common elements - Carbon, Hydrogen, Nitrogen, Oxygen, and Phosphorus (CHNOP); all the constituents of DNA.

The animals present in the stable narrative can be seen to represent the carnal mind, or animal instincts of the body such as lust, anger, greed, laziness etc. To reach the final degree of enlightenment all of these elements have to be "sacrificed" i.e., given up, 'put to death' or overcome. The terrestrial man has to die in order for the heavenly man to be born.

Star of David, 6-Pointed Star

Traditionally, the star of David is illustrated as a 6-pointed star. It is a symbol for the way energies converge in the body, and throughout many other aspects of the macro and microcosms of life.

> "*The Star or David is the perfect symbol of our quest in life. We need to **raise** the vibration of the lower triangle and **pull down** the inherent qualities of the Divine to reside at the heart, to be the full potential of a human being.*"
>
> Page 84, Open Your Heart with Kundalini Yoga by Siri Datta 2008

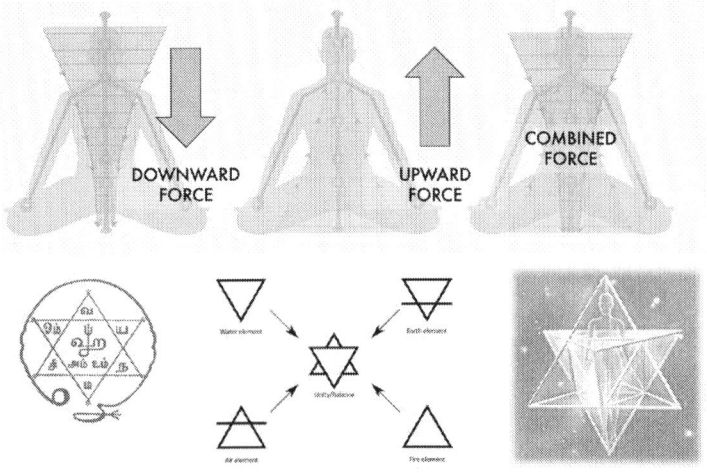

The 6-pointed star is also known as the "hexagram," this is because a hexagon can be traced around its perimeter, which is similar to the flat 2D perspective of a cube. "The seal of Solomon," "Shatkona (Hinduism)," and the "star of the Great Work (Alchemy)," is formed from two interlocking triangles representing **the upward force of electricity and the downward pull of magnetism.** Together these two forces create our electro-magnetic torus fields or "auras." The interlocking triangles of this sacred symbol also highlight the importance of union and balance between polarities of all kinds (See Dual Life Force). For example, harmony between the Male-solar secretions produced by the Pineal Gland and female-lunar secretions produced by the Pituitary Gland create the "felt" experience of enlightenment, and when hydrogen and water unite water (the mother of life) forms.

Traditionally the star of David corresponds with the heart plexus, the middle chakra where "Christ Consciousness" and unconditional love overcomes illusion and suffering.

> *"Jerusalem is the "city of David," which **is the great nerve centre at the back of the heart.** From this point Spirit sends its radiance to all parts of the body."*
> Page 496, The Metaphysical Dictionary by Charles Fillmore

The birthplace of "Christ consciousness" is the heart, where the divine spark resides. *"Christ **comes from** the descendants of David"* John 7:42 (KJV). The expansion of love from this point is a catalyst for the alchemical upgrades that happen in the body which signal the release of the biochemicals of enlightenment. In Revelation 3:7 (KJV), the *"key of David"* also symbolises the path to unlocking and understanding the "I am" stemming from heart coherence and allowing the "feeling" body to be heard and not supressed. The divine principal allows health and vitality to flow throughout the body, mind, soul, and spirit -- not just at Christmas, but always. In the book of Samuel,

David (Divine love) collects five stones, one to kill each material sense and thus triumphs over the giant Goliath.

Like all sacred geometrical shapes, the star of David is embedded in the "cube of space," a shape that holds all forms and is also known as "Metatron's cube." The cube of space is a means for illustrating the integrated nature of creation and the universe, all shapes are folded or nested within it, highlighting how all forms rise from the unified field, from the Oneness. The illusion of a cube also appears in the 2D hexagonal centre of the 6-pointed star, again illustrating the transformation of spirit into matter and vice versa. Without matter, spirit has no expression, so both elements are integral to reality as we perceive it.

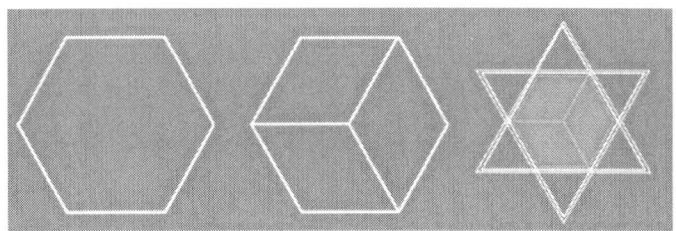

Stars in General

Stars are cosmic expressions of alchemy, they majestically weave together mass, energy, and radiation in ways that profoundly benefit Earth and its inhabitants. Esoterically, stars embody principles of enlightenment, personal transformation, and spiritual ascension. Their different geometrical forms carry deep symbolic meanings that correspond to the alchemical journey of the soul and the structure of reality itself.

> *"The Olympic spirits are those which inhabit the firmament and the stars of the firmament, deciding and dispensing fate as far as it pleases God and as far as he permits."*
> **The Arbatel of Magic III/15**

Each type of star, with its distinct geometrical patterns, mirrors the natural laws of the universe and the alchemical processes of transformation within the body. Just as stars themselves are "born" from the fusion of matter and energy in the cosmos, so too do human beings undergo their own "alchemical birth," moving from a state of base matter to spiritual illumination. Stars are linked to the inner light of the soul, the Divine Spark within every person that seeks to return to its source. *"God made the two great lights -- the greater light to govern the day and the lesser light to govern the night. He also made the stars."* **Genesis 1:16 (KJV)** This verse highlights the symbiotic relationship between the stars and life on Earth. From an esoteric perspective, it implies that stars govern not only physical light but also spiritual illumination, serving as cosmic guides toward enlightenment.

Tridecagram (13-pointed star):

The tridecagram, a lesser-known esoteric shape, represents the synthesis of opposites, such as the union of masculine and feminine energies, often symbolizing transformation on a cosmic scale. Thirteen is often seen as a "divine number" and associated with cycles of the Moon and the feminine (there are 13 moon cycles in each solar year, not 12). In alchemical terms, this star reflects the completion of cycles, the unity of spirit and matter, and the return to cosmic oneness.

Dodecagram (12-pointed star):

The dodecagram corresponds with cosmic order, the 12 zodiac signs, and the 12 disciples of Christ. Esoterically, this star represents the divine manifestation of the universe as a sacred order, reflecting the symphony of life and creation. Alchemically, it corresponds to the 12 stages of transformation, from base matter (lead) to spiritual enlightenment (gold). The dodecahedron, a 12-sided polyhedron, also relates to the ether, the fifth element in alchemy, symbolizing spirit and the final stage of integration. The dodecahedron is a nest of 12 vortices of spiralling energy all converging at its centre (the 13th point). Refer back to the entry for "Sleigh" with regards to DNA and the Dodecahedron.

Octogram (8-pointed star):

The octogram represents regeneration and rebirth. In esoteric traditions, eight is often associated with the cycles of life, death, and resurrection (See Circumcision and Reindeer). In alchemy, the number eight reflects balance and harmony between the material and spiritual realms. It is the symbol of a new beginning after a transformative process. The octogram also corresponds with the Star of Venus, the phosphorescent planet, symbolizing divine love, beauty, and the unfolding of higher consciousness, echoing the Biblical idea that *"God is love"* 1 John 4:8 (KJV). The Essenes also revered the 8-pointed star over other forms and saw it as a symbol of the merging of solar and lunar essences (Xxenogenesis) within.

> *"The Solar-Seed has one opportunity per month to impregnate or fructify the Christ-Lunar-Germ-Seed. When, the Moon (x) plus the Sun (+) come together they equal the eight-pointed star of the Essenes (*) overcoming the enmity that was between them. Accomplishing this at the specific time laid out by the creator's calendar is the immaculate conception of the Christ spirit into the mortal physical being."*
> Page 36, The God Design: Secrets of the Mind, Body, and Soul by Kelly-Marie Kerr

Heptagram (7-pointed star):

Seven is a sacred number in many esoteric systems, representing spiritual perfection and completion. In alchemy, the seven stages of transformation reflect the seven classical planets (Sun, Moon, Mercury, Venus, Mars, Jupiter, Saturn), each corresponding to different metals and processes. In human anatomy, the seven chakras (seals) or energy centres in the body mirror this sacred structure, aligning with the "seven rays of light" in esoteric spiritual traditions. The Bible references "seven" as the number of divine completion, such as the seven days of creation (Genesis 2:2).

Hexagram (6-pointed star):

The hexagram, also known as the Star of David or Seal of Solomon, represents the harmonious balance of opposites: the upward-pointing triangle (spirit) and the downward-pointing triangle (matter). In esoteric traditions, it reflects the balance of masculine and feminine energies and is associated with the heart chakra, the centre of love and compassion. The hexagram also resonates with the electromagnetic field of the heart, the torus, which radiates energy from the core of one's being (See Star of David, 6-Pointed Star).

Pentagram (5-pointed star):

The pentagram is one of the most ancient and widely used symbols in esotericism. Representing the five elements (earth/carbon, water/hydrogen, air/oxygen, fire/nitrogen, and spirit/phosphorus) -- all the elements of DNA. It is a symbol of harmony between human beings and nature. Alchemically, the pentagram embodies the completion of the Great Work, the union of spirit and matter, and the attainment of enlightenment. The five points also correlate with the human body, the four limbs, and the head, symbolizing the microcosm of the human form mirroring the macrocosm of the universe. See the entry for "Coal, Lead and Carbon" regarding the upright and inverted versions of this star symbol.

These geometrical stars, each with their symbolic meanings and connections to alchemical processes, serve as metaphors for the journey of the soul. As stars emit energy that sustains life, they also symbolically represent the forces that guide human beings through spiritual growth and enlightenment, much like the alchemical path toward the union of the material and the divine.

Swaddling Clothes, Wrapping Paper, Veil

In the Gospel of Luke, Mary wraps the baby Jesus in "swaddling clothes," a deeply symbolic act that can be seen through an esoteric lens.

Metaphorically, we as spiritual beings are wrapped in "flesh suits" -- our physical bodies. The true Christmas presents, or "presence," are spiritual gifts, symbolizing the **Creative Light** within us. This Creative Light awakens us to our limitless potential and releases us from limited states of consciousness.

The concept of *swaddling clothes* and wrapping paper can be understood as the material world enveloping the spiritual world. Spirit -- represented by energy, electromagnetism, and light is the core essence of life, while matter provides the structure and medium for experiencing life. In this way, **imagination** (spirit) and **manifestation** (matter) are the two poles of a unified whole, constantly interacting to bring spiritual experience into material form.

In the physiology of the body, Doctor Carey assigns the "swaddling clothes" metaphor to the mineral salts and gossamer or "silk" capsule that protect the pineal and pituitary potencies or "Christ Seed" on its journey through the body.

Carey explains that on the ASCENT of the "seed," the "swaddling cloth" or cell-casing (gossamer capsule) is removed at the "cross" at the base of the skull (Golgotha) as part of the biochemical crucifixion or inner alchemy that happens within the temple body.

> *"The oil in the seed, when born, is covered by a crust of mineral salts, which, when baptized in Jordan by John, is loosened in order that the shell may fall apart when the seed, goes over the cross, in order that the precious material may ascend into the pineal gland."*
> Page 62, God Man: The Word Made Flesh by G W Carey

The **ritual of the bride removing her veil at the altar** reflects this same esoteric truth. It's a profound symbol in the Rosicrucian "alchemical wedding." Here is an elaboration of the key points:

Bride and Groom as Pituitary and Pineal Glands:

The bride represents the pituitary gland, the seat of intuition and nurturing energies, and the groom represents the pineal gland, the spiritual centre responsible for vision and higher states of consciousness. In this symbolic marriage, the union (kiss, X) of the pituitary and pineal glands is the moment of spiritual awakening. When the bride and groom meet at the altar it reflects the union of these two potent forces within the body, leading to enlightenment.

This union is crucial in the process of spiritual ascension, climaxing with the release of the biochemicals of enlightenment, where these two glands harmonize to awaken the latent spiritual faculties within an individual. The "altar," therefore, becomes a metaphor for the place of divine union within the human brain, where spiritual knowledge and power are unleashed.

The Veil as the Christ Seeds "Gossamer Capsule" or "Swaddling Clothes":

The veil that the bride wears corresponds to what Doctor Carey called the "gossamer capsule" -- a protective covering that surrounds the Christ seed or spiritual essence as it moves through the body. This can be likened to the "swaddling clothes" mentioned in alchemical writings, which symbolize the material form that encases the divine light. In the context of the body's physiology, this protective layer represents the state of unawakened spiritual potential, shielded by the limitations of matter.

When the bride removes her veil, it symbolizes the unveiling of spiritual truth and the release of the "Christ seed" from its protective casing. The removal of the veil at the altar mirrors the alchemical process in which the swaddling clothes (the material or mineral salts) fall away, allowing the seed to complete its sacred journey and rise to higher consciousness.

The Aisle as the Spine:

The aisle that the bride walks down parallels the spine in the human body, specifically the kundalini channel, through which the spiritual energy must rise. Just as the bride moves toward the groom, the energies of the **pituitary gland** rise upward through the spine to meet the **pineal gland** at the altar of consciousness. The bride's journey mirrors the ascent of the Christ seed and its energetic counterpart as it travels from the base of the spine (root chakra) upward toward the pineal gland, culminating in the union of spiritual forces at the crown of the head.

The "crossing of the seed" or "crucifixion" at the base of the skull -- also known as "Golgotha", the "place of the skull"—is a pivotal moment in the spiritual journey. Here, the spiritual essence crosses from the **involuntary nervous system (subconscious)** to the **voluntary nervous system (conscious mind),** symbolizing the movement from unconscious spiritual potential to conscious spiritual awareness (See Galilee).

Crossing from the Involuntary to the Voluntary Nervous System:

This crossing is essential in the alchemical process, as it marks the moment when the Christ seed moves from the subconscious mind (involuntary nervous system), which controls the body automatically, into the conscious mind (voluntary nervous system), where spiritual forces can be awakened through conscious effort and intention.

This is akin to Charles Fillmore's teaching that "Jesus" returning to Nazareth symbolizes the Christ seed making the transition between the voluntary nervous system (conscious life) and involuntary nervous system (subconscious death), allowing for the resurrection and renewal of the individual. When the seed crosses this threshold, it initiates a powerful healing process, reprogramming the mind and body on both a conscious and subconscious level.

The Cross at Golgotha:

Again, Doctor Carey explains that the "gossamer capsule" surrounding the Christ seed is dissolved at the "cross" -- a symbolic location at the base of the skull. This is the moment of spiritual crucifixion, where the material layers are peeled away, and the divine light within is released.

The Christ seed then rises, making its way toward the pineal gland, where it undergoes resurrection.

Carey's explanation that *"the oil in the seed, when born, is covered by a crust of mineral salts,"* mirrors the idea that the "bride's veil" is the final layer of material protection that must be removed for spiritual awakening. The "oil" in the seed is "loosened" as the "veil" is lifted, allowing the precious spiritual essence to ascend into the pineal gland.

The Symbol of Marriage as Inner Alchemy:

The entire marriage ceremony, still well preserved and revered in these modern times can be understood as a metaphor for the process of inner alchemy -- the sacred union of the masculine and feminine energies within the body. When these two forces (represented by the pituitary and pineal glands) are harmonized, they spark the enlightenment process, leading to the transmutation of material consciousness into divine wisdom.

The "lifting of the veil" symbolizes the unveiling of divine truth and spiritual reality, just as the Christ seed's protective layer is removed at the cross. The union of bride and groom at the altar is the moment of the sacred marriage, where the individual's spiritual forces are brought into balance, allowing for the full realization of divine potential.

This process is echoed in Matthew 26:32 (KJV): *"But after I am risen again, I will go before you into Galilee."* Here, Jesus's resurrection signifies the Christ seed completing its journey from the subconscious realm (death) back to the conscious realm (life), leading to spiritual rebirth.

The alchemical wedding is a powerful symbol of the internal transformation that takes place within the human body and consciousness. The ritual of a bride removing her veil at the altar reflects the unveiling of spiritual truth and the ascent of the Christ seed, as it crosses from the involuntary to the voluntary nervous system and makes its way toward higher consciousness. Through this sacred union of masculine and feminine forces, represented by the groom (pineal) and bride (pituitary), the individual is awakened to their divine nature and attains spiritual rebirth.

This journey from subconscious to conscious awareness, the crossing at Golgotha, and the ultimate union at the altar all mirror the profound spiritual processes that lead toward enlightenment and the resurrection of the divine essence within each person.

Three Wise Men

There is a much deeper meaning for the "three kings" and their gifts than the literal interpretation, as will be explored. In order to build the picture clearly, it's helpful to begin with the more obvious points.

The "three kings" who visited Jesus (Matthew 2:11) were Chaldeans, "wise ones" or "magi" known as men who studied the stars. With their calculations the wise men could foresee the birth of Jesus i.e., the arrival of winter solstice and the rebirth of the Sun that mirrors the process within the human body.

Vedic astrologers observed that the rising of Sirius signalled the arrival of summer solstice, and the rising of Orion announced the arrival of winter solstice. The Egyptian Kemet's (Chemists) knew Orion as Sahu the "God of Resurrection." In Christian astro-mythology, the three prominent belt stars of the Orion constellation were dubbed "The Three Kings." Those three stars, now known as Alnitak, Alnilam and Mintaka are often viewed as the three wise men: Caspar, Melchior, and Balthasar in the macrocosm. These "belt stars" also line up with Sirius (the bright star) and the Sun on the 25th of December.

In the microcosm, the three wise men coincide with the pineal gland, pituitary gland, and the thalamus. This notion becomes particularly clear when investigating the meaning of the gifts that the three kings brought for baby Jesus.

Gold, Frankincense, and Myrrh

The three wise men were said to bring gifts to the baby Jesus of Gold, Frankincense, and Myrrh.

Frankincense is PINE-resin (oil), associated with the PINEal gland, PINgala nadi and Christmas pine trees. **A symbol of the positive, male, electric potency in the body.** Frankincense is known for its purifying and sanctifying properties. When burned in a censer it produces a fragrant smoke that was historically used to enhance endogenous DMT synthesis and heighten meditative states and spiritual awareness. *"And the temple was filled with smoke from the glory of God, and from his power"* Rev 15:8 KJV.

Myrrh is Commiphora tree resin (oil), which has long been used to heighten spiritual connectivity and is associated with the pituitary gland and the Ida nadi. **A symbol of the negative, female, magnetic potency in the body.** Myrrh contains a sesquiterpene compound which is said to complement pituitary activity and has long been used to heighten spiritual connectivity. The pituitary is the moon of the microcosm, and its oxytocin and vasopressin secretions stimulate pineal activity i.e., melatonin "upgrades."

Myrrh and Frankincense are also parallel to the Biblical "milk and honey," another symbol for the mother substance of the pituitary (milk/myrrh) and the father substance of the pineal (honey/frankincense).

Gold symbolises the divine substance created by the union, or harmonising of pineal and pituitary energy and essences, blended in the 3rd ventricle of the thalamus.

Three Wise Men (Part 2)

In some ancient depictions the three wise men are symbolically dressed in **black, white, and red.** A good example of this is seen in "Three Kings March," a third century slab painting at the Church of England in Saddleworth UK.

These colours are also worn by Santa Claus -- his read coat with white trim, and black boots, and they appear in many other stories and fables too. For example: Snow white has "hair as black as ebony," "skin as white as snow" and "lips as red as a rose;" the Sanderson Sisters in Hocus Pocus are clearly shown with red, white, and black hair; in the Wizard of Oz Dorothy has her red slippers, the good witch wears white and the wicked witch wears black, and even Mickey Mouse embodies these three colours. So, what's the relevance of these colours?

They signify three phases on the alchemical path known as "The Great Work." The Great Work is akin to Angelo Morphism, building the Soma Heliakon (Solar Body) or assembling Creative Light within. All of which are historical terms used for the process which is parallel to what's known as the preserving and raising of the sacred secretion in modern times.

The three phases of the alchemists Great Work are as follows:

The Black Phase = Negredo.

White Phase = Albedo.

The Red Phase = Rubedo.

Negredo (blackness) is the "lesser work."

The Great Work begins with Negredo "the blackness phase," which is parallel with the "lead" of the transmutation-of-lead-into gold allegory, and with the "coal" given to "naughty" children by Santa.

Lead and Coal are symbols for the base substance or "first matter" that has to be transmuted into the biochemicals of enlightenment (gold) during spiritual awakening. According to sages and mystics, "first matter" is protoplasm (cytoplasm/soma) which is the foundational substance that all the billions of cells of the body emerge out of.

"First matter" is viewed as the most subtle substance in the body and is influenced by thought, emotion, and action.

Entering Negredo initiates the purification process, eliminating energies and toxins that prevent spiritual growth and cellular regeneration. Negredo can be seen as the rock bottom turning point, the "aha moment," the repentance point and the "dark night" suffering point that ultimately lights a fire of urgency and inspiration for change within.

Albedo (Whiteness)

After the initial phase, comes the second aspect called "Albedo" – the whiteness.

This phase involves the mineral body. As first matter is purified to become virginal (see Mary – the Virgin Mother), more electromagnetic energy (light) in its various aspects and potencies can be absorbed by the body, thus the cellular terrain can be remineralised, meaning optimised by the presence of mineral cell salts. I recommend the work of George Carey and William Schussler for further research regarding mineral salts and their correlation with light.

In the progression from Negredo to Albedo, the "lead," "prima Materia" or "base substance," begins its journey towards becoming "silver." This symbolizes the emergence of light and purity from the darkness and chaos of the previous stage.

The "calcination" process initiated in Negredo continues into Albedo, eliminating residual energies and toxins, allowing for cellular regeneration and spiritual awakening.

The physical process of calcination derives its name from its most common application, the decomposition of calcium carbonate (limestone) to calcium oxide (lime). The term "calcination" also refers to a process that can be used to process phosphate ores and improve their phosphorus content, also removing impurities like organic matter, carbonate, and fluoride. These processes were/are said to provide the basis for the secret alchemical code.

Rubedo (Redness)

Rubedo represents the final integration and perfection of the soul and spirit, where the base substance, having been purified and remineralised, reaches its ultimate state of enlightenment and wholeness. You could also say that the soul (fluid body) has become crystal (CHRISTal) clear.

In the progression from Albedo to Rubedo, the "silver" of the purified substance transforms into "gold," symbolizing the attainment of the highest spiritual state. This phase signifies the realization of the true self and the manifestation of spiritual perfection.

The redness of Rubedo is often associated with the "Red Elixir" or "Elixir of Life," which symbolizes the rejuvenation and eternal vitality of the soul. In Rubedo, the seeker wears the "crown of enlightenment," symbolizing the attainment of wisdom and spiritual power by the Kundalini (Creative Light) rising to the crown chakra. *"Wisdom creates the most beautiful atoms of energy that we call Christ (Solar Light)."*
Audio Course. The Path of the Bodhisattva, Anonymous

In the story of Snow White this can be seen in her attainment of the "crown" at the "royal castle" situated at the head of the kingdom which is an allegory for the temple body. In Sikh Dharma, the "10th gate" located at the crown chakra is literally referred to as "the castle of the beloved." The finale sees Snow White literally being awakened and receiving her "happily ever after" which is parallel to the yogi's "Nirbikalpa" meaning immortal bliss.

Rubedo is often described as the "Divine Marriage" or "Mystical Union," where the masculine and feminine aspects of the self are united in perfect harmony. On a chemical level this marriage is the harmonising of the pineal and pituitary glands which causes the release of the biochemicals of enlightenment.

Further research into the significance of the colours black, white, and red in ancient alchemy shows a fascinating correlation with the element known as phosphorus.

The name phosphorus means "light" or "gold" (phos) and "bearing" (phorus) or "luminous!"

Elemental phosphorus exists in three forms:

- **Black phosphorus** (a reddish black crystal)

- **White phosphorus** (a waxy solid)

- **Red phosphorus** (a red powder)

Perhaps this is where the tri-coloured imagery truly stems from. Black phosphorus is found as reddish black crystals (rocks) that resemble "lumps of coal," and red phosphorus is the form that produces "golden" flames, so it's very possible that the lead into gold imagery originates with the transmutation of phosphorus.

Phosphorus is the element that naturally forms triangles and pyramids, PO43 is the triangular phosphate that makes up the backbone of DNA, and Plato said that the world is made out of triangles, a notion echoed in the many parallel "trinities" (triangles) of different teachings and religions around the world. According to Plato, phosphorus is the main active principle within the unseen fabric of the universe i.e., the invisible light realm and its geometric shapes that provide the "scaffolding" for manifest life.

Phosphorus, known simply as "light", by ancient alchemists and esotericists, binds with air (mostly nitrogen and oxygen), water (hydrogen and oxygen) and earth (mostly carbon) to create more complex atoms and molecules for the emergence of various life forms. Due to this action, phosphorus was/is known as "the former of salts" (as in "mineral-salts" or "cell salts," -- the molecules that build cells).

After calcium, phosphorus is the most abundant mineral in the body and is a key constituent in the procreative energies and essences (seminal fluids) that we are advised to preserve on the path of enLIGHTenment. In Ancient and Modern Initiation, Max Heindel states, *"the degree of consciousness and intelligence is in proportion to the amount of phosphorus (light) contained in the brain."* All the body's energy production and storage systems depend on varying forms of phosphorus such as ATP (adenosine tri**phosphate**), and in addition to this, phosphorus/light "forms" and strengthens our bones and teeth, powers our nervous system (thought impulses), helps form the membrane of our cells, helps maintain a normal pH (acid/alkali) level in the body, helps oxygen delivery in the body, and helps form our genetic material (DNA).

DNA is the blueprint or coding for the continuation of life. Every cell in every living organism in all creation contains DNA. Along with carbon, phosphorus intelligently forms the sides of the DNA double helix ladder; the sides of the microcosmic DNA ladder are the spiralling serpents that emerge from "pure water" (see Mary – The Virgin Mother). All life on earth shares the elemental energy source of phosphorus – the light bearer!

Phosphorus and Ho'oponopono

According to George Washington Carey in his book, "The Zodiac and the Salts of Salvation," **"Natrium Phosphate" is the "Christ" of mineral cell salts.** Natrium Phosphate, now known as Sodium Phosphate, is an alkaline mineral cell salt that helps to neutralise acid in the body. Carey also postulates that **"acid" is Satan, the adversary, in the body.** These assignments emphasise "Christs" triumph over "Satan" or -- Natrium Phosphates triumph over acid in the chemistry of our bodies.

Not only does Natrium Phosphate (Sodium Phosphate) help to neutralise acids in the body, but it also supports digestion and assists with the elimination of waste. Its neutralising effect is crucial for maintaining a healthy pH balance, which can prevent conditions caused by excessive acidity. It ensures that body fluids are neither too acidic nor too alkaline. Sodium Phosphate is crucial in helping to eliminate waste from the body, particularly uric acid, a byproduct of protein metabolism. This prevents the buildup of toxins that can cause joint pain or kidney stones. As an alkalizer, it also helps the skin by preventing conditions like acne, which can be aggravated by excess acidity. Proper acid balance ensures that the skin remains healthy and clear. Natrium Phosphate is important in cell respiration and the transformation of glucose into energy. This process is vital for sustaining energy levels and preventing fatigue. Natrium Phosphate is one of Schussler's "alkaline trio," the other two are calcium phosphate, and magnesium phosphate. These salts are widely used in **Schussler cell salt therapy** as they are considered gentle, natural remedies for promoting health at the cellular level.

What's really interesting about the "Christ" cell-salt is its relation to the Hawaiian Ho'oponopono prayer. The following Hawaiian dictionary definition of Ho'oponopono resonates with the nature and energy of Christ:

"(a) "To put to rights; to put in order or shape, correct, revise, adjust, amend, regulate, arrange, rectify, tidy up make orderly or neat,

administer, superintend, supervise, manage, edit, work carefully or neatly; to make ready, as canoe men preparing to catch a wave."

(b) *"Mental cleansing: family conferences in which relationships were set right (Ho'oponopono) through prayer, discussion, confession, repentance, and mutual restitution and forgiveness."*

*Literally, "ho'o" is a particle used to make an actualizing verb from the following noun. Here, it creates a verb from the noun pono, which is defined as: "...**goodness, uprightness, morality, moral qualities, correct or proper procedure, excellence, well-being, prosperity, welfare, benefit, true condition or nature, duty; moral, fitting, proper, righteous, right, upright, just, virtuous, fair, beneficial, successful, in perfect order, accurate, correct, eased, relieved; should, ought, must, necessary."[13]"***

This is a compelling link to the harmonizing role of Natrium Phosphate in the body, but what makes the correlation virtually undeniable is the chemical structure of this health promoting cell-salt, which is a visible anagram for the word "Ho'oponopono."

NATRIUM PHOSPHATE, The "Christ" Cell Salt

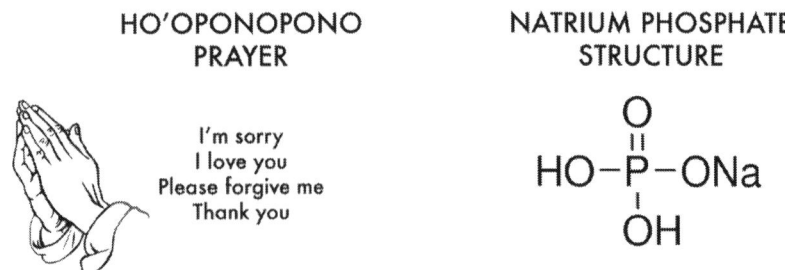

It's possible that this prayer actually evokes the positive effects of natrium phosphate in the body, such as its role in switching on the body's parasympathetic nervous system (healing and restoration mode). This insinuates an even deeper connection between the prayer and the cell-salt, demonstrating the link between sounds and their ability to affect matter.

If you haven't used this prayer before, it has a profound effect on the human temple -- body, mind, soul, and spirit. All words carry an energetic signature, which is why the Bible advises us that *"Death and life are in the power of the tongue"* Proverbs 18:21 (KJV). Every single sound we make and the words we speak resonate into the unified-field and have their effects. The wording of the Ho'oponopono prayer is said to be extremely potent for vitalising the body from the inside out.

To utilise this incredible prayer, you simply need to repeat the words over and over for a set duration of time, three minutes is a great place to start. You need to be in an authentic, honest and sincere state when doing this i.e., feeling into the meaning of each word as you say it.

The prayer's repetition encourages the body to shift from the fight-or-flight mode (sympathetic nervous system) into a calm and restorative state (parasympathetic nervous system). This state facilitates healing by lowering heart rate, improving digestion, and releasing tension, which helps to relieve stress and trauma stored in the body. Ho'oponopono centres on forgiveness and letting go (surrendering). Saying "I'm sorry" and "Please forgive me" invites the release of guilt, shame, or past traumas. Many individuals hold unresolved emotional pain in their cells, which can lead to chronic stress or disease. This prayer helps to clear emotional blockages by addressing the subconscious mind, where trauma is often stored. Emotions like guilt, fear, anger, and resentment hold lower vibrational energy, while love, gratitude, and forgiveness raise the body's vibration. The phrases "Thank you" and "I love you" elevate the energy of the person reciting them, replacing negative emotional patterns with positive ones. Since emotions have a physiological impact on the body, releasing negative emotions through this prayer can facilitate cellular regeneration. Studies in psychoneuroimmunology suggest that **emotional healing strengthens the immune system,** allowing the body to heal faster from injuries and illnesses. The "Thank you" and "I love you" phrases work to align the body with a higher state of healing and vitality.

On a spiritual level, this prayer fosters a deeper connection with the divine and the unified field of energy that surrounds all living things. Repeating these phrases sets an intention for healing, forgiveness, and love to permeate yourself (your cells) and your environment. In short, the Ho'oponopono prayer affirmations act as a powerful tool for self-transformation and healing.

One final point about Natrium Phosphate is that under a microscope it resembles a rose. Roses are a central Rosicrucian and Essene symbol, representing the soul and its potential to blossom. In the context of Christmas, roses often symbolize the unfolding of divine love and wisdom, particularly through the birth of Christ (who has also been referred to as a rose).

Harnessing Phosphorus (Light)

> "...the moral of this gospel of the flesh, is to produce plenty of phosphorus by means of good eating and drinking. Those who say, "Let

> *us eat and drink, for tomorrow we die" are diametrically opposed to the Holy Scriptures."*
> Page 147, Modern Doubt and Christian Belief, A Series of Apologetic Lectures Addressed to Earnest Seekers by T Christlieb

With all this in mind, its apparent that phosphorus is both literally and symbolically associated with "light", inner "illumination", and spiritual "enLIGHTenment" in alchemical and esoteric traditions. It's indisputable that phosphorus is a crucial element in the human body, especially in processes involving energy and the nervous system. The masters of old believed that increasing phosphorus levels and utilizing it efficiently could enhance both physical and mental well-being, possibly leading to greater insight or spiritual clarity.

Below are five ways to assist phosphorus levels in the body:

1. Dietary Intake of Phosphorus-Rich Foods

Phosphorus is naturally present in many foods, particularly in protein-rich sources. Consuming **natural, organic foods, (not processed junk foods)** that are rich in phosphorus can directly support healthy phosphorus levels in the body. Lentils, chickpeas, avocados, seeds and nuts are excellent sources of phosphorus.

2. Optimize Calcium and Vitamin D Levels

Phosphorus works closely with calcium in the body to maintain bone health and proper cellular function. Vitamin D is necessary for the proper absorption of phosphorus in the intestines. Ensuring adequate levels of both calcium and vitamin D will help the body efficiently use the phosphorus it receives. You can increase vitamin D intake through increased exposure to natural daylight (it doesn't have to be sunny), and by consuming vitamin D-rich foods like healthy oils such as olive oil, avocado oil, flaxseed oil etc. Calcium can easily be obtained from leafy greens such as spinach, rocket, kale etc.

3. Reduce Consumption of Processed Foods and Additives

Many processed foods contain high levels of harmful phosphorus additives, which can cause an imbalance and disrupt the natural phosphorus-calcium balance in the body. Phosphorus additives are often poorly absorbed by the body and can lead to kidney issues or other health concerns if over-consumed. By reducing processed foods, the body can regulate natural phosphorus levels more efficiently. You should consider avoiding soft drinks like soda, processed meats, and packaged snacks that often contain phosphorus-based preservatives.

4. Support Kidney Health

The kidneys play a vital role in maintaining proper phosphorus balance in the body. If the kidneys are not functioning optimally, phosphorus can accumulate to unhealthy levels, potentially leading to complications like bone disease or calcification. Kidney function can be supported through proper hydration, eating a balanced diet rich in fruits and vegetables, and avoiding highly processed foods.

In conclusion, optimising phosphorus levels in the body, when done properly, can help support both physical and cognitive function. For alchemists and esotericists who believed that phosphorus was linked to spiritual light, maintaining healthy phosphorus levels could be seen as contributing to overall vitality and enlightenment. However, achieving a balance between phosphorus and other minerals like calcium and ensuring kidney health is essential for maintaining this vital element's beneficial effects. **I am obliged to say, I am not a qualified medical doctor and cannot give specific healthcare advise. This book is written to shed light on esoteric perspectives, always do your own research.**

Wreath

The Christmas wreath can be viewed as a symbol of the sphere or circle of life, and of the universal emblem of the **"Circle with a Dot in the Centre"** which is a gateway to spiritual Understanding.

The "Circle with a Dot in the Centre" is one of the most profound esoteric images in spiritual tradition. Found across many different cultures, this symbol represents the core of existence and the process of spiritual awakening. It highlights the form of the "emergence of life" -- from the atomic structure to the vastness of the solar system, and from the individual to the universe, this symbol holds deep significance regarding the cyclical nature of life, and the circular pattern of different forms, thus illustrating the interconnectedness of all things.

Synergistic terms for the "circle with a dot in the middle" include:

Circumpunct, Monad, Sun Symbol (Solar Symbol), Gold (Alchemy), Point Within a Circle (Freemasonry -- part and parcel with their compass emblem), Bindu (Hinduism), Ra or Re (Ancient Egyptian Symbol), Anima Mundi (Alchemy and Mysticism), Circled Dot (Astronomical Symbol) and the Symbol of Consciousness (Spiritual and Philosophical).

At its core, this universal structure serves as a reminder of the relationship between matter, spirit, and the journey of life. It is also linked to the law of cause and effect, echoing back the energy we emit, and serves as a powerful tool for inner alchemy and the awakening of kundalini energy.

Imagine standing in a valley surrounded by mountains. When you shout, your voice bounces off the rocky surfaces and echoes back to you. If you shout, "I love you," the mountains will return that phrase to you: "I love you, love you, love you." But if you shout something negative like "I hate you," the echo will return the same energy: "I hate you, hate you, hate you." This is not just a physical law but a spiritual one as well. Every action, thought, or word we emit sends out waves of energy into the universe, which eventually return to us. These waves are shaped by our intent and frequency. No one and no-thing can escape from the effect of their past actions which are bound to echo and reflect back.

It may come as no surprise that sometimes the return effect takes many lives to return to us as the distance it has to travel may be very far away. It is the matter that reflects the echo, not the spirit. The spirit acts and matter reacts. Matter responds to an impulse. Its role is to stand up to the Spirit to oppose and to limit it. Humans are constantly emitting waves of energy, whether beneficial or harmful, through their thoughts, feelings, and actions. These waves travel through the space-time dimension until they reach their limits and return to their source, manifesting as rewards or consequences.

This law is part of the sacred secretion practise, those who understand this law are careful to only send out waves of purity, love, kindness, and tolerance. Thus, the energy they receive assists them on their path, and allows energy to rise freely through the body. In this way, the circle with the dot in the centre acts as a metaphor for the cyclical nature of energy and karma—again, the spirit acts, and matter reacts, creating an unending loop of reflection and return.

At the heart of the symbol, the dot represents the spirit or the divine spark within us, while the surrounding circle symbolizes the space-time boundary in which material existence unfolds. This pattern can be found throughout the universe. For example, the structure of a cell follows this model: the nucleus is the spirit, endless zero-point creative energy at the centre, and the surrounding cytoplasm is the soul. Similarly, the solar system has a sun at its centre, and the planets revolve around it within a defined space (or so they say, there's also a theory that puts Earth at the epicentre of the universe). Even fruits and seeds reflect this pattern: the seed (spirit) is encased in flesh (the soul), and the outer skin (or body) protects it.

An atom and the solar system are identical in their basic structural design, a circle with a dot in the centre.

This recurring structure demonstrates the principle that without spirit, matter cannot exist, but that spirit remains unaffected by the limits of space. Spirit, represented by the dot, is timeless and spaceless, while matter, represented by the circle, functions within the constraints of time and space.

In kundalini yoga, the circle with a dot is a powerful symbol for understanding the flow of energy through the human body. The dot in the centre represents kundalini energy, the latent spiritual force resting at the base of the spine (Muladhara or root chakra). As the kundalini awakens, this energy begins to rise, traveling through the body's chakras, removing toxic blockages and refining the individual's spiritual frequency. As the energy rises it moves into the sphere of energy above the Muladhara (the sacral), and then into the solar plexus sphere and so on and so forth because the chakras are spheres within our main bodily sphere. Thus, the circle and dot act as symbols of the alchemy of ascension akin to the sacred secretion transmutation. The spirit, or the divine spark, seeks to free itself from the boundaries of matter, represented by the circle.

By cultivating good thoughts, words, and deeds, one clears the toxic energies and residues within the body, allowing the kundalini to flow more freely. This process raises one's vibrational frequency, facilitating the spiritual ascent beyond the limits of matter into the realms of spirit. Every negative action or hateful word has an autonomous (automatic) response in the biochemistry or alchemy of our bodies. On some level we innately know the consequence of our actions because we're all familiar with shame, and remorse on some level. Even Shame and remorse have chemical substance, so it's up to us to exit old cycles and change the mechanics of our psyche toward love, healing, and enlightenment.

The circle with a dot in the centre also represents the fundamental law that the universe operates within the framework of space and time (Saturn's alleged jurisdiction -- see Saturn, Santa and Satan), and everything within it—matter, life, and energy—circulates in this finite dimension. The serpent of matter holds the spirit within its coils, limiting its full expression. These limits are essential for experiencing duality, suffering, and joy, which are the conditions necessary for the soul's evolution in the material world.

The return journey to the divine, or enlightenment, happens when the spirit breaks free from the limitations of matter, returning to its source. This process is mirrored in the life cycles of all living things. For example, an egg requires a protective shell to incubate life. Once it hatches, the shell is discarded. Similarly, the physical body serves as a protective layer for the spirit. When the body dies, the spirit is released to return to the higher dimensions.

In conclusion, the symbol of the circle with a dot in the centre is a powerful representation of the relationship between spirit and matter, time and space. It encapsulates the cosmic design of the universe as well as the inner structure of every living being. By understanding this symbol, we come to realize that all actions, thoughts, and words we send out into the universe are reflected back to us. As we journey through life, our goal is to purify these energies, allowing us to raise our frequency and free the spirit from the coils of matter.

Through the awakening of kundalini energy and the practice of inner alchemy, we align ourselves with the true centre of existence—our divine spark. Although we exist within the boundaries of time and space, our true essence is timeless and spaceless, capable of transcending the material world and returning to the infinite source. As we refine our thoughts, words, and deeds, we move ever closer to this realization, inching toward enlightenment and the harmonious balance between spirit and matter.

ASSEMBLING LIGHT AT SOLSTICE

In this time of regeneration and transformation, we draw from the spiritual forces of both the solar (Christ) and lunar (Mas) cycles. This balance helps to harmonize the spiritual and material aspects of life, guiding us toward deeper inner peace. As James Lovelock said in "Gaia Theory," winter solstice is the moment when the energy of the Earth, just like our bodies, contracts inward to rest. Through "right" living, this sacred pause allows the regeneration of cells, tissues, and mental clarity, aligning us with nature's cycle of renewal. With the heightened cosmic influences of solstice, especially in the Northern Hemisphere, we are presented with a powerful opportunity to elevate our spiritual journey.

Throughout this book, we have explored a wide range of Christmas symbols, traditions, and practises emphasising the opportunity that winter solstice offers for spiritual advancement. We've looked at the way in which Christmas traditions have slowly "degraded" over the years and sadly become less about the promotion of life, health and vitality as they once were. Journeying through these age-old teachings, we've discovered or "rediscovered" many spiritual practices that were originally designed to support the mind, body, soul, and spirit at Christmas (Solstice) time, rather than demoting them. These teachings have provided insights into the sacred sciences of nature, such as fasting, celestial prophecy, star mapping, plant medicine, energy healing, and sound healing.

When seeking to assemble light within and align oneself with higher spiritual frequencies, it is essential to recognize the practices and habits that hinder this process. One of the most significant barriers is overindulgence in sugary foods. **Excess sugar consumption** can lead to inflammation, insulin resistance, and disruptions in metabolic function. This not only impacts physical health but also clouds mental clarity, making it more challenging to maintain a meditative and reflective state. The rollercoaster of energy highs and crashes that come with sugar intake can disrupt the balance needed for deep spiritual work, pulling one away from the inner stillness that supports connection to divine energy.

Similarly, consuming **alcohol can obstruct the path to assembling light.** Alcohol is a depressant, which can impair the body's ability to regenerate on a cellular level, especially during times like the solstice when the body is naturally inclined toward repair and renewal. It also affects the clarity of mind and distorts perception, making it difficult to maintain a clear channel for higher vibrations. The spiritual impurities associated with alcohol use can create an energetic "fog," hindering one's ability to tune into subtle realms and access higher states of consciousness. True spiritual alignment, particularly during the Christmas season, benefits from abstinence from such substances, allowing for a purer, more unclouded journey inward.

In the unpublished letters between Carl Jung and Sabina Spielrein (available on research gate), Spielrein says, *"the analogue (etymology) of the term "alcohol" is "an emission of seed, i.e., soma."* This clearly refers to the "seed" or "cell" of life, highlighting the debilitating affect that alcohol has on the body and the sacred secretion process. If we take the Bibles turning of water into wine at the wedding of Cana parable literally it appears that Jesus encouraged drunkenness. But, since "Jesus" represents the "I am" or spiritual body within us, and "wine" represents the biochemicals of enlightenment produced by the alchemy of ascension, this is obviously not the case. *"And be not drunk with wine, wherein is excess; but be filled with the Spirit"* Ephesians 5:18 (KJV).

Esoteric (hidden) teachings warn that alcohol disrupts the vibrational frequency of the body, and acts as a hindrance to the smooth flow of kundalini or life force energy. How alcohol is legal, when it's one of the most addictive and harmful substances known to man is in inexplicable. On a scientific level alone, alcohol is known to adversely affect vital organs, including the liver and kidneys. These organs are crucial for the filtration and purification of bodily fluids, including the subtle energies associated with kundalini which is synergistic with nitric oxide. Alcoholism interferes with nitric oxide synthase (NOS), the enzyme responsible for synthesizing nitric oxide in the body. Nitric oxide plays a crucial role in regulating blood flow, immune response, AND even neurotransmission.

Smoking and vaping introduce toxins directly into the lungs and bloodstream, leading to oxidative stress and cellular damage. These habits hinder the flow of life-force energy, known in many traditions as "prana" or "chi," which is crucial for sustaining the body's vitality and spiritual ascension. The harmful chemicals in tobacco or vape products create blockages in the subtle energy channels, making it difficult to maintain a harmonious state of being. For those seeking to elevate their spiritual practice, breathing exercises and pure, deep breathing are key tools, and these practices are undermined by the damage caused by smoking or vaping.

In addition, **consuming violent or overly sexual content** through television or other devices can have a detrimental impact on the mind, soul, and spirit. Such content often triggers lower vibrational emotions such as anger, fear, or desire, which can lead to energetic imbalances. These states of mind disturb inner peace and create dissonance in the mind, making it more difficult to enter a state of meditation or spiritual receptivity. **They can also** cause the mind to become fixated on worldly distractions, rather than turning inward to explore deeper spiritual truths. Engaging in these types of media during times like the winter solstice -- a time meant for reflection, purification, and rejuvenation -- can derail one's progress, keeping them anchored in lower vibrations.

> *"Envy, hatred, ambition, and covetousness will destroy the capsule that contains the seed (cell of life) and thus corrupt the blood, as surely as sexual contact.* **Alcohol in all its deceptive forms is the arch enemy to this life-seed and seeks by every means known to destroy it.** *"No drunkard shall inherit the Kingdom of Heaven" because alcohol destroys the redeeming substance that enables man to understand or think in his heart the thoughts of the Spirit. Alcohol cuts the capsule that holds the Esse born every month in Bethlehem. Alcohol eats the fruit of the tree of life. Gluttony is another enemy to regeneration. All excess of food that is not burnt up in the furnace —the stomach and intestinal tract, all that is not properly digested,* ***ferments and produces acid which develops alcohol.***
> Page 91, The Wonders of the Human Body by G W Carey.

True preparation for spiritual enlightenment, particularly during sacred times like Christmas or the winter solstice, requires a conscious effort to avoid these habits. By refraining from substances and activities that lower one's vibrational state, the mind and body remain clear, the soul becomes more receptive, and the spirit aligns more readily with the subtle energies of renewal and transformation. **This is the season to purify the body and mind, allowing space for cellular regeneration and the infusion of divine light, promoting a deeper connection to the sacred cycles of nature and the self.**

Remember, Scripture advises that anointing involves *"baptism by water and fire."* This means that assembling light in the body is a two-fold process honouring both the "water body" (reborn of water), and the "solar body" (reborn of fire). Therefore, cleansing on a physical level (body and soul -- water) and cleansing on a spiritual level (mind and spirit) is essential.

- **Cleansing the soul and body (water)** is mostly about diet and emotional clearance which clears the lymphatic and endocrine systems.

- **Cleansing the mind and spirit (fire)** is mainly about mental clearance and vibrational/energetic upgrade.

These purifications are necessary to prepare ourselves (our cells) to properly receive spiritual light. This dual aspect cleansing procedure expands our consciousness making it possible to align with divine principles and adjusts our internal energy and even each cell through DNA and epigenetic changes. **This alignment with our higher self allows us to recognize our innate abundance and further primes us for spiritual illumination.**

As we approach Christmas, it is time to get drunk on the holy spirit rather than toxic alcohol, it is time to celebrate with meditation and songs of gratitude, complemented by a lifestyle of purity and fasting. Although practical insights have been offered throughout this book, I thought it would be useful to summarise each practical point, reiterating their roles in guiding us toward spiritual transformation and ascension. Therefore, this final chapter is a guide to integrating those teachings into daily life, fostering a deeper connection with the divine and aligning with the rhythms of nature. From fasting to sound healing, these practices help us harmonize with universal energies, guiding us toward transformation and ascension.

Summary of Key Practices:

- **Fasting** is an essential tool for cleansing the body, mind, soul, and spirit. By purifying the body of impurities, you prepare yourself receive and assemble more light within. Fasting also helps to decalcify the pineal gland, receiver and distributor of solar light through the body. Clearing calcium carbonate buildup in bodily channels and glands allows for clearer perception and heightened intuition. Different methods like the **Daniel Fast, a juice fast, or a kitchari fast** can assist in this purification.

- **Proper Hydration** supports all body cells and systems, including restoring the flow of soma (Christ oil). Staying properly hydrated is crucial for mental clarity, physical vitality, and overall well-being. Hydration supports the body's natural detoxification processes by flushing out toxins and impurities. This is especially beneficial during fasting or cleansing practices, as it helps to purify the body and prepare it for deeper spiritual work. Due to the structured water and minerals inside fruit and veg, juice fasts are fantastic for ensuring proper hydration.

- **Visualization exercises** are a powerful tool for transformation. Picturing yourself enveloped in divine light or as a radiant being, influences your subconscious mind. Through consistent visualization, you can break limiting mental patterns and create space for new possibilities. Visualization exercises also facilitate healing, imagery of light and divine figures can aid in releasing stored trauma and emotional blockages, opening pathways for greater spiritual clarity.

- **Breath** connects us to life itself, serving as a bridge between the physical and spiritual realms. **Pranayama breathing exercises** -- such as alternate nostril breathing, or deep diaphragmatic breathing helps balance the body's energies. Proper breathing practices reduce excess CO_2, allowing for an alkaline state that promotes endogenous DMT production, which is linked to heightened states of awareness and spiritual insight. Breathing exercises energises the spinal cord. This stimulates the flow of cerebrospinal fluid, enhancing the body's connection to higher consciousness.

- **Sound healing** through listening to Tibetan bowls or similar, or through chanting and reading sacred texts can dissolve the egoic identity and uplift the spirit. Mantras, hymns, and carols resonate deeply within the cells of the body, promoting inner harmony. The repetition of sacred phrases tunes the mind to higher frequencies, actually recalibrating body systems and facilitating a state of inner peace and divine connection. Vibrations from chanting can heal emotional wounds, reducing stress and anxiety, while fostering a sense of unity with the universe.

- **Daily exposure to daylight** plays a crucial role in spiritual and physical well-being. Sunlight supports vitamin D production, crucial for regulating calcium and decalcifying the pineal gland. Natural light realigns our internal clocks, promoting mental clarity and overall vitality. Sunlight also helps to activate alchemical processes: Just as plants convert sunlight into energy, the human body metabolizes light, assisting in the transformation of dense energies into higher vibrations.

- **Physical practices like Kundalini Yoga** and the use of energy locks (bandhas) help to channel energy through the chakras, promoting spiritual awakening. These practices emphasize the alignment of body and spirit, asana (posture) practices support the flow of energy through the chakras, removing blockages and preparing the body for deeper meditation. As well as cooling the watery/lunar (mas) aspect within, yoga stokes the inner fire (Christ) also. Through movement and breathwork, yoga awakens the "fire" within, increasing the body's ability to process and transform both physical and spiritual energies.

- At the heart of all spiritual progress lies **love -- compassion for oneself and others.** The path of **Bhakti** emphasizes love as a transformative force that leads to spiritual liberation. It encourages heart centre activation because unconditional love and acceptance elevates the body's vibrational frequency, releasing oxytocin and facilitating the release of DMT from the pineal gland. Bhakti allows us to transcend and dissolve negative emotions. Emotions like anger and resentment bind us to lower frequencies. Letting go through love enables us to break these chains, freeing ourselves for higher spiritual experiences.

- **Meditation (listening) and prayer (speaking)** are key in shifting from a reactive state to one of peace and openness. Practices like Ho'oponopono, a prayer of forgiveness, help release deep-seated traumas and encourages cellular healing Meditation allows the body to transition into repair mode, akin to nature's regenerative processes during the winter solstice. As our thoughts become more aligned with divine principles, the mind reflects this by turning inward for self-reflection and renewal, like the Earth during winter.

- **Self-inquiry (interoception)** or the practice of tuning into the sensations within the body, helps cultivate a deeper connection with one's physical and emotional states. This heightened awareness can lead to better emotional regulation and a more balanced mind. By focusing on internal bodily signals, like how you really feel about things, rather than just what you think of them (interoception) can help you recognize the early signs of stress and tension, and or situations or behaviours that aren't consistent with your highest good. This allows for intuitive progress along your true path, or the path most aligned with your authentic self.

- **Julbastu,** the traditional sauna practice during the Christmas season, facilitates physical detoxification by promoting sweating, which helps eliminate toxins from the body. It also supports emotional and spiritual cleansing, creating a sense of renewal. The heat from the sauna improves blood circulation, which can aid in muscle relaxation and recovery. It also fosters a deep sense of relaxation, providing a peaceful space for spiritual reflection and inward focus.

- **Energy/essence conservation and focus (retention)** involves conserving physical and mental energy, allowing you to redirect that energy towards higher spiritual goals and creative pursuits. This focus can enhance mental clarity and deepen meditation. Practicing retention can lead to a greater sense of empowerment (will-power) and alignment with your higher self, not to mention vitalising the temple on all levels (physical, mental, emotional, spiritual).

By integrating these practices or other similar exercises into your life, you can harmonize the secretions of the endocrine system, promoting energy flow and balance through the chakras, nurturing a sense of lightness and inner clarity. Through devotion and consistent practice, you will feel the benefits multiply. Remember, self-care is an extension of divine love: *"A new commandment I give you, love one (self) and other"* (John 13:34, KJV). Through these practices, we begin to resonate with the light, just as nature prepares for renewal in the darkest of times. Let your journey be one of self-discovery, a path towards the ever-growing light that resides within. As you embrace the cycles of nature and the depths of your own spirit, you assemble the light within yourself, becoming a beacon for others.

Bibliography

BIBLES:

The King James Bible Version (KJV)
The Besorah of Yahusha Natsarim Bible Version (BYNV)
The New International Bible Version (NIV)
The Message Bible Version (MSG)
The New Living Translation (NLT)
The Holy Megillah (Nazarene Version)
The Tree of Life Version (TLV)
Strongs Biblical Concordance

BOOKS (Alphabetised by surname):

Physical Spirituality: Changing the paradigm by Michael Abramowitz
Audio Course. The Path of the Bodhisattva, Anonymous
Pages Unnumbered, The Secret Doctrine of Anahuac by Anon
Science Discovers the Physiological Value of Continence" By Doctor Raymond Bernard
The Secret History of The World Jonathan Black
The Theosophical Glossary Madame Helena P. Blavatsky
The Secret Doctrine Vol 1. Madame Helena P. Blavatsky
Isis Unveiled: The Secret of The Ancient Wisdom Tradition Madame P. Blavatsky
The Perfect Way Anna Bonus Kingsford
The Chemistry of Consciousness Doctor Barker and Doctor Borjigin
The Essene Gospel of Peace: Book 1 - Gospel of Peace Edmund Bordeaux Szekely
The Essene Gospel of Peace: Book 2 - The Unknown Books of the Essenes" Edmund Bordeaux Szekely
The Essene Gospel of Peace: Book 3 - Lost Scrolls of the Essene Brotherhood Edmund Bordeaux Szekely
The Essene Gospel of Peace: Book 4 - The Teachings of the Elect by Edmund Bordeaux Szekely
The Essene Gospel of Revelations Edmund Bordeaux Szekely
The Science of The Soul and The Stars by Thomas H. Burgoyne
Unity Magazine August 1903, Vol XIX, The Three Brains by Mrs. G. A. Bartholomew, B.D
The Essene Jesus by Edmond Bordeaux Szekely
The Divine Economy, Unity Metaphysics 2 Eric Butterworth
The Light of Egypt by Thomas H. Burgoyne
God Man: The Word Made Flesh by G.W Carey and I.E Perry
The Tree of Life by George W. Carey
The Zodiac and The Salts of Salvation (Extended Version) by George W. Carey and Ines Eudora Perry
Eternal Drama of Souls, Matter and God Jagdish Chander
Dark Retreat Mantak Chia
Modern Doubt and Christian Belief, A Series of Apologetic Lectures Addressed to Earnest Seekers by T Christlieb
A Visit from St. Nicholas by Clement Clarke Moore
The Key to the Universe by Harriette Augusta Curtiss
Alchemy of The Mind by Vanita Dahia
The Thesaurus of English Word Roots by Horace Gerald Danner
Open Your Heart with Kundalini Yoga by Siri Datta
The Biology of Kundalini by Jana Dixon
Darkness and Light by Meister Eckhart
Patterns in Comparative Religions by Mircea Eliade
The Secret Initiation of Jesus at Qumran: The Essene Mysteries of John the Baptist by Robert Feather
There is a Santa, by William J. Federer
The Twelve Powers of Man John Fillmore
Metaphysical Bible Dictionary by Charles Fillmore
Christian Healing: The Science of Being" by Charles Fillmore

All the Glory of Adam by C.H.T. Fletcher-Louis
The World's Sixteen Crucified Saviours: Christianity Before Christ by Kersey Graves
The practice of Hesychasm in Eastern Orthodox Christianity, focusing on achieving divine union by G.I. Gurdjieff
God, The Bible, The Planets and Your Body by Kedar Griffo
Romans and Ancient Greeks in a Mans Brain by R. Goulimari
The Secret Teachings of All Ages by Manly P Hall
The Lost Keys of Free Masonry by Manly P. Hall
The Occult Anatomy of Man by Manly P. Hall
Ancient and Modern Initiation by Max Heindel
Rays from the Rose Cross Magazine, Cosmic Christmas Article by M. Heindel
Who Was Jesus by Dr Hilton Hotema
More Pious Fraud by Dr Hilton Hotema
Awaken the World Within by Hilton Hotema
The Secret of Regeneration by Hilton Hotema
The Mystery of Man by Hilton Hotema
Psyches Palace by David Aaron Holmes
The Temple Body by Duane and Nancy McEndree
The God Design: Secrets of the Mind, Body and soul by Kelly-Marie Kerr
The Cell of Life: Awakening and Regenerating by Kelly-Marie Kerr
Alchemical Treatises of Solomon Trismosin, by J.K
The Harmonies of the World by Johannes Kepler
The Perfect Way by Anna Kingsford
Centring: A Guide to Inner Growth by S Laurie and M Tucker
Posthuman Transformation in Ancient Mediterranean Thought by M. David Litwa
The Gospel of Thomas: The Gnostic Wisdom of Jesus by Jean-Yves Leloup
A Metaphysical and Symbolical Interpretation of the Bible by Mildred Mann
Iscador: Mistletoe and Cancer Therapy by Christine Murphy
Yoga of The Holy Bible by Martin Myrick
The Cosmic Serpent by Jeremy Narby
How God Changes Your Brain by Andrew Newberg and Mark Robert Waldman
Thinking and Destiny by Harold W Percival
The Living Message by Eugene H. Peterson
The Initiation of Ioannes by James Pryse
Rig-Veda, Book 8, Hymn XLVIII. Soma.
A Beginners Guide to Creating Reality by Ramtha
The Apocalypse: A Series of Special Lectures on the Revelation of Jesus Christ by J M Roberts
Religion, Spirituality and Healthcare by P. Roche de Coppens
Introduction to Submolecular Biology by Szent-Gyorgyi
Spirit - To Be by Chez As Sabur
Endogenous Light Nexus Theory of Consciousness by Karl Simanonok
The Harlot and The Beast by Larry Sparks
The Hope of God's Light by President Dieter F. Uchtdorf
The Essenes, the Scrolls, and the Dead Sea by Joan E. Taylor
Kaya Kalpa: The Ancient Art of Rejuvenation by Doctor Chandrasekhar Thakkur
The Path of Initiation in the Sacred Arcana by S. A. Weor
The National Geographic: How 40,000 Tons of Cosmic Dust Affects You and Me by S Worral
Autobiography of a Yogi by Paramahansa Yogananda
The Second Coming of Christ by Paramahansa Yogananda

ONLINE SOURCES:

The Metaphysical Dictionary at www.truthunity.com
www.archive.org
www.ncbi.nlm.nih.gov
Strong's concordance at www.biblehub.com
www.collinsdictionary.com
www.neuroquantology.com
www.researchgate.net
www.biblegateway.com

Books and platforms created by the author Kelly-Marie Kerr

BOOKS:

- **Christmas Magic, The Cosmic Story**
  An illustrated designed to introduce the true meaning of Christmas to children.

- **Christmas Alchemy, Harnessing Cosmic Energy**
  An exploration of the deeper meaning of Christmas, both in the cosmos and in the body. Including an A-Z of secret Christmas symbols.

- **The Sacred Secretion, Your Complete Guide to Kundalini Energy, Christ Oil, Alchemy, and the Monthly Seed.**
  Kelly-Marie's latest book is a compendium of all the most important Sacred Secretion information. Including a full anatomical breakdown of the alchemical process and practical instructions to complete your own practice.

- **The God Design, Secrets of the Body, Mind and Soul**
  A thorough study and explanation of both the spiritual and physical elements that form the phenomena known as the sacred secretion. **Including the full details of the biochemicals of enlightenment.**

- **Elevation, The Divine Power of the Human Body (A Study of the Bible Book of Revelation)**
  The Bible book of Revelation explains the true science of enlightenment: body, mind, and soul in a dramatic, fantastical, and epic parable only 22 chapters. Elevation debunks the symbols and myths providing truth and clarity to its reader.

- **The Cell of Life, Awakening and Regenerating**
  A full disclosure of the *3-Fold Enlightenment* or *Great Regeneration*, revealing the scientific parallel of the "Jesus" seed born in the body every lunar month. The "seed" is our opportunity for TOTAL renewal and regeneration.
  "Every 29.5 days a seed is born in, or out of the solar plexus – the oil unites with the mineral salts and thus produces the monthly seed which goes into the vagus."
  Page 90, GOD MAN: The Word Made Flesh by G W Carey

- **ReGENEration Calendar, Your Super Consciousness Awakening or Sacred Secretion Times**
  A full year calendar providing the sidereal and tropical dates for the moon entering each star sign (zodiac), plus guidelines and meditation techniques to help you on your journey.

PLATFORMS:

- YouTube channel, "Kelly-Marie Kerr"
- Website, www.seekvision.co.uk / www.thesacredsecretion.com
- TikTok, @seekvision
- Instagram, @seekvision
- Facebook, @seekvision33
- Patreon, Seek Vision (Kelly-Marie Kerr) - Patreon membership includes 1 to 1 session

FREEDOM YOGA:

- Paid membership to the "Kelly-Marie Kerr" YouTube channel gives you access to 33 Essene based yoga videos that you can use to create your own playlists of any length and focus. You can then use your playlist as a custom yoga practice.

COURSE:

- **Super consciousness Awakening**
  Available on Teachable

Printed in Great Britain
by Amazon